Rethinking the Social

Studies in Critical Social Sciences Book Series

Haymarket Books is proud to be working with Brill Academic Publishers (www.brill.nl) to republish the *Studies in Critical Social Sciences* book series in paperback editions. This peer-reviewed book series offers insights into our current reality by exploring the content and consequences of power relationships under capitalism, and by considering the spaces of opposition and resistance to these changes that have been defining our new age. Our full catalog of *SCSS* volumes can be viewed at https://www.haymarketbooks.org/series_collections/4-studies-in-critical-social-sciences.

Series Editor
David Fasenfest (York University, Canada)

Editorial Board
Eduardo Bonilla-Silva (Duke University)
Chris Chase-Dunn (University of California–Riverside)
William Carroll (University of Victoria)
Raewyn Connell (University of Sydney)
Kimberlé W. Crenshaw (University of California–LA and Columbia University)
Raju Das (York University, Canada)
Heidi Gottfried (Wayne State University)
Alfredo Saad-Filho (Queen's University Belfast)
Chizuko Ueno (University of Tokyo)
Sylvia Walby (Royal Holloway, University of London)

Rethinking the Social

Sociology of Crisis Experience in
Central and Eastern Europe

Edited by
Kaja Gadowska
Anna Giza

Haymarket Books
Chicago, IL

First published in 2024 by Brill Academic Publishers, The Netherlands
© 2024 Koninklijke Brill NV, Leiden, The Netherlands

Published in paperback in 2025 by
Haymarket Books
P.O. Box 180165
Chicago, IL 60618
773-583-7884
www.haymarketbooks.org

ISBN: 979-8-88890-554-8

Distributed to the trade in the US through Consortium Book Sales and Distribution (www.cbsd.com) and internationally through Ingram Publisher Services International (www.ingramcontent.com).

This book was published with the generous support of Lannan Foundation, Wallace Action Fund, and the Marguerite Casey Foundation.

Special discounts are available for bulk purchases by organizations and institutions. Please call 773-583-7884 or email info@haymarketbooks.org for more information.

Cover design by Jamie Kerry and Ragina Johnson.

Printed in the United States.

Library of Congress Cataloging-in-Publication data is available.

Contents

List of Figures VII
Notes on Contributors VIII

1 Postpandemic Futures: Sociology of Crisis Experience in Central and Eastern Europe 1
   Anna Giza and Kaja Gadowska

PART 1
The Social Crisis as a Crisis of Social Sciences

2 Sociology and the Alienation of Knowledge 15
   Anna Giza

3 Sociology and Social Change: Polish Researchers and the Transformation 37
   Izabella Bukraba-Rylska

4 Postcolonial Parallels, Global Entanglements, and Practices of Decolonization: Varieties of Postcolonial Discourses on Poland 65
   Joanna Wawrzyniak and Małgorzata Głowacka-Grajper

5 The Absent Bourgeoisie: Implications of the Relative Weakness of the Polish Economic Elite in the Long Twentieth Century 91
   Tomasz Zarycki

PART 2
Staying Close to Social Experience

6 Industry 4.0 as a Sociotechnical Imaginary Experienced from Below: the Case of Small and Medium Industrial Enterprises in Poland 113
   Renata Włoch

7 Multiculturalism and Multilingualism in Smaller 'Cities of Immigration and Emigration': Płock, Kalisz and Piła, 2019–2022 133
   Anne White

8   The COVID-19 Pandemic as a Source of Workplace Innovation: the Worker Perspective   151
    Adam Mrozowicki and Jacek Burski

9   Social Life in an Era of Growing Uncertainty   172
    Mirosława Marody

PART 3
In Search of a New Perspective

10   Law in the Anthropocene Era   185
    Marek Zirk-Sadowski

11   Knowledge in the Face of Populism   201
    Michał Kaczmarczyk

12   Democracy and Authoritarianism in the Twenty-First Century   217
    Grzegorz Ekiert

13   On the Influence of Sociology on Society and on the Sociologist   239
    Krzysztof T. Konecki

    Index   259

Figures

12.1 Democratic decline since 2005 222
12.2 Global share of autocratizing and democratizing countries 224
12.3 Consolidated and semi-consolidated democracy scores 225
12.4 Regional averages in political rights and civil liberties 226
12.5 Hybrid to fully authoritarian democracy scores 231
12.6 *Nations in Transit* national democratic governance ratings 232

Notes on Contributors

Izabella Bukraba-Rylska
is Professor of Sociology, worked at the Polish Academy of Sciences and at the University of Warsaw, and currently works at Collegium Civitas in Warsaw. Her scientific specializations include rural sociology – models of economic migration of the rural population, studied using the monographic method; sociology of culture – cultural transformation of the rural population; and metasociology and posthumanities – neomaterialism, neonaturalism, sensory anthropology, and somatic sociology. She has authored over 300 publications, for example, *Socjologia wsi polskiej* (The Sociology of Polish Village; PWN, 2008); *W stronę socjologii ucieleśnionej* (Toward Embodied Sociology; Wydawnictwa Uniwersytetu Warszawskiego, 2013); and the handbook *Socjologia. Pytania podstawowe* (Sociology: Fundamental Questions; PWN, 2021). bukryl@gmail.com; ORCID: https://orcid.org/0000-0001-9178-9171.

Jacek Burski
is Assistant Professor at the Division of Sociology of Work and Economic Sociology at the Institute of Sociology, University of Wroclaw. He is also a postdoctoral researcher in the COV-WORK project on the pandemic crisis and labor (www.covwork.uwr.edu.pl), funded by the National Science Center (NCN), and runs the NCN's Miniatura project on the biographical experiences of young doctors in Polish health care system. His main interests include sociology of work and biographical sociology. jacek.burski@uwr.edu.pl; ORCID: https://orcid.org/0000-0001-9987-2420.

Grzegorz Ekiert
is Laurence A. Tisch Professor of Government at Harvard University and Senior Scholar at the Harvard Academy for International and Area Studies. He was Director of the Minda de Gunzburg Center for European Studies (2012–2024) and Chair of Social Studies undergraduate concentration (2000–2006). At CES, he co-chairs the Seminar on Democracy – Past, Present, and Future. His research and teaching interests focus on comparative politics, regime change and democratization, civil society and social movements, and East European politics and societies. His books include: *The State Against Society: Political Crises and Their Aftermath in East Central Europe* (Princeton University Press, 1996); *Rebellious Civil Society: Popular Protest and Democratic Consolidation in Poland* (co-author J. Kubik; University of Michigan Press, 1999); *Capitalism and Democracy in Central and Eastern Europe: Assessing the Legacy of Communist*

Rule (co-editor S. Hanson; Cambridge University Press, 2003); *Ruling by Other Means: State-Mobilized Movements* (co-editors E. J. Perry and Y. Xiaojun; Cambridge University Press, 2020). His papers have been published in numerous social science journals and edited volumes in the USA, Europe, and Asia. ekiert@fas.harvard.edu; ORCID: none.

Kaja Gadowska

is Associate Professor of Sociology at the Jagiellonian University in Krakow, Director of the Institute of Sociology at the Jagiellonian University (2020–2022), and Vice President of the European Sociological Association and Head of its Policy Committee (2019–2021, 2021–2023). Her research interests concentrate on dysfunctions of the public sphere and the relations between the politics, economy, and administration in postcommunist countries. Author or co-author of numerous texts published in Poland and abroad. Her recent works include the books *Dysfunkcje administracji. Służba cywilna w perspektywie neoinstytucjonalnej* (Administration Dysfunctions: Civil Service From a Neoinstitutional Perspective; Jagiellonian University Press, 2015); *Legal Change in Post-Communist States: Progress, Reversions, Explanations* (co-editor P. Solomon, Jr.; Ibidem Verlag, 2019); *Sfera publiczna w Polsce i jej współczesne konteksty* (Public Sphere in Poland and Its Contemporary Contexts; co-editor J. Arcimowicz; Institute of Public Affairs, 2020); and *A Sociological Agora: Master Lectures from Poland* (editor; Jagiellonian University Press, 2021). kaja.gadowska@uj.edu.pl; ORCID: https://orcid.org/0000-0002-4985-6331.

Anna Giza

is Professor of Sociology, associated with the Faculty of Sociology at the University of Warsaw since the 1980s. She has served two terms as Vice-Rector for the Financial Policy and Development, and currently serves as the Dean of the Faculty of Sociology. In the years 1994–2005 she worked for an international corporation (Unilever), first as the market research manager, then as the manager for regional innovations centers in CEE, and finally as the communication advisor of the Board. Thanks to her work for Unilever, she was able to observe closely the process of economic and social changes taking place in Poland and in the whole region of Central and Eastern Europe. She has also cooperated closely with nongovernmental organizations in Poland and CEE, observing their formation and growth. Her scientific interests include theoretical sociology, methodology of social research, and the theories of social change. Main publications: *Rodzina a system społeczny. Reprodukcja i kooperacja w perspektywie interdyscyplinarnej* (Family and the Social System: Reproduction and Cooperation From an Interdisciplinary Perspective; Wydawnictwa

Uniwersytetu Warszawskiego, 2005); *Gabinet luster. Kształtowanie samowiedzy Polaków w dyskursie publicznym* (The Mirrors' Cabinet: On the Shaping of Poles' Social Self-Knowledge in Public Discourse; Wydawnictwo Naukowe Scholar, 2013); *Uczeń czarnoksiężnika, czyli społeczna historia marketingu* (The Sorcerer's Apprentice, or the Social History of Marketing; Wydawnictwa Uniwersytetu Warszawskiego, 2017); *Transformations of Social Bonds: The Outline of the Theory of Social Change* (co-author M. Marody; Peter Lang, 2018). agiza@uw.edu.pl; ORCID: https://orcid.org/0000-0002-8667-262X.

Małgorzata Głowacka-Grajper
is a sociologist and social anthropologist. She is Associate Professor at the Faculty of Sociology at the University of Warsaw, where she also serves as Head of the Division of Social Anthropology and Ethnic and Migration Studies. Her main research interests include the issues of contemporary national and ethnic identity, social memory, and research on the relationship between the local and national dimensions of memory. Currently, she is working on a project on the postcolonial perspective on imperial Russian heritage in Poland. glowackam@is.uw.edu.pl; ORCID: https://orcid.org/0000-0002-8992-8117.

Michał Kaczmarczyk
is Associate Professor at the University of Gdańsk, Doctor of Science at the Jagiellonian University in Krakow (2013), and lecturer at the State University of New York at Buffalo (2010–2012) and at the Jagiellonian University in Krakow (2022–2023). He has received numerous scholarships, including fellowships at the Swedish Collegium for Advanced Study in Uppsala (2015–2016), Max-Weber-Kolleg in Erfurt (2019–2020), and iCourts at the University of Copenhagen (2018). For his recent book, *The Aporia of Freedom* (Brill, 2023), he received the Jan Długosz Award. His research interests focus on the sociology of law and sociological theory, with numerous articles on both topics published in scientific journals, including *European Journal of Sociology*, *Historical Social Research*, *Transnational Legal Theory*, and *Studia Socjologiczne*. michal.kaczmarczyk@ug.edu.pl; ORCID: https://orcid.org/0000-0003-0828-7272.

Krzysztof T. Konecki
is Professor of Sociology at the Institute of Sociology, Faculty of Economics and Sociology, University of Lodz. He is the editor-in-chief of *Qualitative Sociology Review*, a Board Member of the Polish Sociological Association, a member of the Committee of Sociology of the Polish Academy of Sciences, and a former member of the Executive Committee of the European Sociological Association. His research interests include qualitative sociology, the sociology of interaction,

symbolic interactionism, sociology of the body, the methodology of social sciences, visual sociology, communication and intercultural management, organizational culture and management, and contemplative sociology. He has recently published a book: *The Meaning of Contemplation for Social Qualitative Research: Applications and Examples* (Routledge, 2022). krzysztof.konecki@gmail.com; ORCID: https://orcid.org/0000-0002-7370-3490.

Mirosława Marody

is Professor Emeritus of the University of Warsaw, full member of the Polish Academy of Sciences. Her main area of interest is changes in the functioning of individuals in modern society, summarized in the book *The Individual After Modernity* (2021, Routledge). Author and co-author of many studies and analyses of Polish society. In 2019, together with her team, she published the book *Społeczeństwo na zakręcie* (Society at the Crossroads; Wydawnictwo Naukowe Scholar) about the changes that have occurred in the attitudes and values of Poles over the last thirty years. In 2021, the book *Wartości w działaniu* (Values in Action; Wydawnictwo Naukowe Scholar) was published under her editorship. marodymi@is.uw.edu.pl; ORCID: https://orcid.org/0000-0002-8448-9522.

Adam Mrozowicki

is Associate Professor at the Institute of Sociology, University of Wroclaw, where he heads the Division of the Sociology of Work and Economic Sociology. He also leads the COV-WORK project on the pandemic crisis and labor (www.covwork.uwr.edu.pl), funded by the National Science Center (NCN), and the University of Wroclaw's team in Horizon Europe's INCA project on democracy and digital platforms (https://inca-project.eu/). His academic interests include the sociology of work, comparative employment relations, precarity, workers' agency and subjectivity, critical social realism, and biographical methods. adam.mrozowicki@uwr.edu.pl; ORCID: https://orcid.org/0000-0002-5809-5036.

Joanna Wawrzyniak

is Associate Professor of Sociology and Director of the Center for Research on Social Memory at the Faculty of Sociology, University of Warsaw. She is also President-Elect of the Memory Studies Association and Vice-Chair of the COST Action "Slow Memory: Transformative Practices for Times of Uneven and Accelerating Change" (2021–2025). Her most recent publications include co-edited volumes *Remembering the Neoliberal Turn: Economic Change and Collective Memory in Eastern Europe after 1989* (Routledge, 2023) and *Regions of Memory: Transnational Formations* (Palgrave, 2022). wawrzyniakj@is.uw.edu.pl; ORCID: https://orcid.org/0000-0001-9836-5638.

Anne White
is Professor of Polish Studies and Social and Political Science, University College London School of Slavonic and East European Studies (SSEES). She is a sociologist and social anthropologist, conducting her research mostly in Poland, but also in the UK. She runs a Polish Migration website at SSEES and has published three books as well as numerous scholarly articles about migration from and to Poland. anne.white@ucl.ac.uk; ORCID: https://orcid.org/0000-0002-4431-6707.

Renata Włoch
is a sociologist and Associate Professor affiliated with the Faculty of Sociology at the University of Warsaw. She leads the Division of Digital Sociology and has played a key role in the establishment of the DELab UW, a research center focusing on the impacts of digitalization on economy and society. With a background in qualitative research, she has provided expertise for public institutions and produced research reports for both businesses and non-governmental organizations. Her research interests are diverse, covering topics from migration and international security to global social issues. Since 2014, her primary focus has been on digital transformation, leading to her co-authorship of *The Economics of Digital Transformation* (co-author K. Śledziewska; Routledge, 2021), which examines its effects on the labor market and business operations. r.wloch@uw.edu.pl; ORCID: https://orcid.org/0000-0003-4502-4738.

Tomasz Zarycki
is a sociologist and social geographer, Assistant Professor at the University of Warsaw, and deputy director of the Robert Zajonc Institute for Social Studies (ISS UW). His publications include *Ideologies of Eastness in Central and Eastern Europe* (Routledge, 2014) and *The Polish Elite and Language Sciences: A Perspective of Global Historical Sociology* (Palgrave, 2022). t.zarycki@uw.edu.pl; ORCID: https://orcid.org/0000-0003-2330-4499.

Marek Zirk-Sadowski
is Professor of Law and Former Head of the Division of Theory and Philosophy of Law at the Faculty of Law and Administration of the University of Lodz. He has served as the Faculty's Dean (two terms) and Vice-Rector of the University

of Lodz. He was also Vice-President and President (2006–2007) of the International Association for the Philosophy of Law and Social Philosophy (IVR). A judge of the Supreme Administrative Court since 1994 and its President in the years 2016–2022, he has published over 200 scientific works. zirksadowski@gmail.com; ORCID: https://orcid.org/0000-0003-1740-0863.

CHAPTER 1

Postpandemic Futures: Sociology of Crisis Experience in Central and Eastern Europe

Anna Giza and Kaja Gadowska

Sociology has been in an intimate relationship with crisis from the very beginning of its career as a positive science taken out from the corpus of philosophy, and more generally, humanities. First, both Henri de Saint-Simon and Auguste Comte saw the establishment of sociology as a cognitive remedy for the multidimensional crisis spreading in nineteenth-century Western Europe, accompanying the emergence of what has since been called "modern industrial society": a specific formation linking mass society, free market, and liberal democracy within the framework of the nation state. Second, the establishment of sociology as a positive science immediately caused an epistemological crisis and a schism that continues to this day. It can even be said that sociology is in a permanent crisis, expressed both in the inability to establish a common paradigm and in constant uncertainty as to its own status as a science. Third, subsequent theorists problematized the relationship between sociology and the social crises it diagnoses and researches. In its radical version, the question concerns the responsibility of sociology for social crises and problems as well as "tearing protective secrets from the people" in the service of power. In the epistemological version, the question is whether what sociology identifies as a crisis is actually a crisis or rather seems to be a crisis from the perspective of the normative model of society adopted in sociology. This is where we come to the most important, fourth aspect of the relationship between sociology and crisis: the colonizing potential of social theories, in particular the theory of modernization and the model of modern society. This potential results from recognizing what was specific and local for Western Europe, the process of changes that took place there over the sixteenth–nineteenth centuries, and the resulting social formation as universal models of the "modernization transition" and "modern society," respectively. It was from this normative models' perspective that the level of social development was diagnosed, and social changes were programmed in "emerging" countries, with the intention of "modernizing" them. From this point of view, Central and Eastern Europe (CEE) is an exceptionally valuable laboratory revealing its cognitive and critical volume.

The crisis we are currently experiencing is, like the previous ones, a long-term process of the breakdown of "normality," in the shadow of which new practices and new ideas are germinating; they can become the beginning of a new world. Any crisis can, of course, end in a disaster regardless of the accuracy of the actions taken, but the disaster becomes inevitable if we do not notice emerging alternatives in time. This is an enormous intellectual challenge. It is difficult to distance oneself from one's own cognitive framework, and within it only the passing world has meaning and significance. Therefore, we see only – or primarily – its agony, failing to recognize what emerges from the apparent chaos. This means that every crisis is chiefly a crisis of thinking, the inadequacy of which translates into practice. The old model of the social world not only leads to a kind of blindness, but also determines actions that are essentially counter-productive.

This book aims to introduce a fresh and innovative perspective in sociology, forged through a clash of its well-established theoretical framework with vibrant empirical research focused on case studies from CEE, a clash which ultimately compels the former to reformulate its own assumptions. Indeed, the southernizing and decolonizing movements within the field of social science hold the promise of a significant transformation in the long-standing, universally recognized mainstream sociological paradigm (cf. Boatcă and Costa 2016). This transformation not only results from amplifying the voices from colonized regions but also stems from a heightened recognition that these regions serve as a valuable social laboratory: an *experimentum crucis* for sociological theories. Strikingly, the decolonizing movement has overlooked CEE, the countries of which have so far been left out of postcolonial analyses. This omission results from the central role of race in postcolonial theory (Wiese 2010). In addition, the region became subject to a dual exclusion as the concept of Global North and Global South, which gained popularity with the end of the Cold World, left out societies that do not fit easily into the categories of oppressors and the oppressed (Piacentini and Slade 2024; Müller 2020).

As noted by a number of authors, the perspective that conceptualizes Europe as a dichotomy comprising the West and the East – with the latter intrinsically semi-Oriental, semi-peripherial, backward, and thus "not fully European"– has obscured the experiences of Eastern European societies within the postcolonial framework (cf. Głowacka-Grajper and Wawrzyniak in this volume; Cavanagh 2004; Boatcă 2012; Wolff 1994). Despite scholars acknowledging the issue of internal European colonization, notably in the context of Ireland's history, the visibility of Eastern European societies remains limited.

In this book, we argue that CEE offers a particularly valuable case study for social sciences. First of all, its colonial experience is significantly more complex. After all, countries in this region were colonized not only by Western Europe but also Russia or the Ottoman Empire (e.g. Bulgaria), and this resulted in a distinctive "self-colonizing culture." Poland, for instance, identified itself with the West in resistance to Russia, while Bulgaria, in distancing itself from the Ottomans, looked toward Russia. Russia itself played a dual role as both a colonizer and a subject to the colonial influence of Western Europe. In fact, the October Revolution was an endeavor to break free from Western domination, and the subsequent colonization of the neighboring countries by the Soviet Union served as a means for empire-building. The fall of the Berlin Wall symbolized liberation from the Soviet domination and a return to Western influence.

Therefore, CEE presents a complex tapestry of historical dynamics, making it a crucial subject for social scientific exploration. In fact, the dynamics of this region can be characterized as a triple natural social experiment: postcolonial, postsocialist, and self-colonizing. Such a confluence creates a distinctive testing ground for sociological theories, particularly those stemming from the modernization paradigm. However, we have not quite exhausted this opportunity so far.

In our book, we aim to bridge this gap by:

(1) making the experiences of Eastern European societies *visible and meaningful within the postcolonial discourse*;
(2) problematizing what social scientists, entrenched in the assumptions of the modernization theory, have *overlooked in the experiences of postsocialist transformation* – a clear case of self-colonizing culture;
(3) showing what can be seen by departing from the preconceived notions of "normal" and "modern" and, instead, *remaining mindful to the lived social experience of real people*;
(4) proving that *sociological knowledge has become alienated from the social production of knowledge* and irrelevant to people or has even become a source of social crisis;
(5) experimenting with *new approaches to theorizing and researching society*.

Ultimately, we seek to correct the dearth of CEE in the southernizing approaches to social studies, challenge the domination of universal Western knowledge, and renegotiate the CEE position within the discipline by expanding and promoting robust conceptual developments and empirical insights from the region.

This volume showcases emerging and cutting-edge sociological analyses that make sense of the rapid social transformations we are currently witnessing. The book consists of three parts, each including four chapters.

Part 1, titled "The Social Crisis as a Crisis of Social Sciences," features texts on the intellectual project of "modern society" and the consequences of its domination. Here we put forward the problem of the adequacy of mainstream sociology for understanding the currently experienced crisis. If the cognitive paradigm of modern science and the technical civilization founded on it lie at the root of the planetary crisis, then the same paradigm transferred to social sciences most probably contributed to the societal crisis. This is what this part of the book is about: showing why and how the mainstream sociological model causes crisis phenomena. Three broad dimensions of impact are discussed. First, the model of society adopted by mainstream sociology – and economy as well – refers to the specific social formation that emerged in Western Europe in the mid nineteenth century, but it claims universality. For Central and Eastern European societies, especially during the transformation period, the "modern society" model served as the tool of colonization and self-colonization. Second, as far as the model is believed universal, it blinds sociologists: they can only monitor the "progress of modernization" based on preconceived notions. It is striking that the most insightful books on the Polish transformation were written by foreigners: Elisabeth Dunn (2004), Janine Wedel (2001), or David Ost (2005). Third, there is an exploitative mindset inherent in the modern cognitive paradigm (Heidegger 1970), accompanied by the wish to intervene in the game of power (Sloterdijk 1987). Monopolizing the cognitive and narrative competences resulted in the alienation of sociological knowledge – which in the most direct way leads to societal crisis. In Poland's case, the process of alienation was strengthened by the distinguished position of the intellectual elites in the transformation, due to the lack of bourgeoisie.

In the opening chapter "Sociology and the Alienation of Knowledge," Anna Giza analyzes the key features of this project and the resulting social consequences, probing into the problem of the disruption of the relation between society as experienced and reproduced by people and society as constructed and researched by the science of sociology. Since the nineteenth century, social sciences have gradually taken over the monopoly on the production of legitimate knowledge about society that was scientifically modeled as quasi-nature, that is, a macro-entity beyond individual control and governed by its own laws. The credibility of common self-knowledge was negated, and the acting subjects were denied agency in favor of objective forces, which resulted in two different "societies" emerging: one given in participants' experience, and one given by science. The severance of the connection between the two meets all the characteristics of "alienation," understood as the subjects' loss of control over their own products and elements of their own subjectivity. The author argues that this is what underlies the social crisis.

In the chapter entitled "Sociology and Social Change: Polish Researchers and the Transformation," Izabella Bukraba-Rylska discusses some of the dimensions of the sociological discourse concerning the transformation in Poland. Polish sociologists took the categories of "modernization" and "progress" for granted, and used them uncritically to monitor social changes and promote a copycat model of transformation. The rhetoric of "catching up" and closing the gap between Poland and Western countries prevailed, which fueled, among others, firm anti-ruralism. The characteristics of rural residents were in line with the rhetoric of "orientalization" of that part of society and were a manifestation of "racial neoliberalism" and even hate speech. At the same time, Polish sociologists manifested a selectively critical attitude toward their discipline, frequently disregarding local, often pioneering, achievements, while failing to notice the weaknesses of Western social thought.

The third chapter, "Postcolonial Parallels, Global Entanglements, and Practices of Decolonization: Varieties of Postcolonial Discourses on Poland" by Joanna Wawrzyniak and Małgorzata Głowacka-Grajper, delineates recent trends within the expanding body of multidisciplinary literature that either characterizes CEE as a (post)colonial space or situates this region within the broader context of global empires and colonialism. First, the chapter categorizes the diverse range of existing approaches into three primary clusters: (post)colonial parallels, global entanglements, and decolonial options. Second, it explores potential empirical applications of these approaches to the CEE region. Finally, it draws attention to how postcolonial theory has been instrumentalized by national essentialist elements in Polish public discourse.

In his chapter "The Absent Bourgeoisie: Implications of the Relative Weakness of the Polish Economic Elite in the Long Twentieth Century," Tomasz Zarycki explores the history of Poland in the so-called long twentieth century from a sociological-historical perspective, focusing on the bourgeoisie as a critical social stratum. Beginning with the late nineteenth century, the chapter examines the rapid economic ascent of the bourgeoisie and its increasing conflicts with other elite factions, especially the intelligentsia. Across subsequent periods, notably during and after the World Wars, the bourgeoisie lost not only its economic resources but also its political and symbolic standing, which contributes to the continued dominance of the intelligentsia in the Polish power structure. The central argument of the chapter posits that the historical and contemporary weakness of the Polish bourgeoisie, coupled with the eroded memory of its past, is a significant factor in the specificity of Polish society, shedding light on its various social and political structures.

All chapters in Part 1 deal with the consequences of imposing the model of "modernity" on the Polish society. The transformation project – implemented and promoted by the intelligentsia, including academic elites[1] – did not take into account the realities or the specificity of the country and the region, constituting a great example of self-colonization.

What would happen if sociologists stayed closer to social experience? This is what Part 2, titled "Staying Close to Social Experience," is about, trying to look at the current social crisis without normative presuppositions.

The mainstream social sciences have often aspired to emulate the model of "true science" by building models, quantifying, generalizing, and discovering the laws and rules governing reality. However, this approach tends to render scientific knowledge distant, general, and irrelevant to people. To maintain an open-minded and mindful perspective, it is essential to stay close to living social experiences. It may well be that what is perceived as a "crisis" is, in fact, a sign of new social forms emerging or a rupture in "normality" opening the way for novel phenomena. Nonetheless, observing these changes requires moving away from the old "scopic system" (Knorr-Cetina 2000) and refraining from looking down through the lenses of broad impersonal processes like "digital transformation," "migration flows," or "urbanization." The truth is that these processes do not unfold on their own; they result from silent, cumulative pressure exerted by real actions undertaken by real people. For these reasons, it is worthwhile stepping down and closely observing the social practices beyond digitalization or migration taking place in real social settings. This is the focus of Part 2.

The aim of the chapter "Industry 4.0 as a Sociotechnical Imaginary Experienced from Below" by Renata Włoch is to explore the concept of digital transformation as a significant sociotechnical imaginary influencing societal expectations regarding economic development. Sociotechnical imaginaries, as defined by Jasanoff and Kim (2015), encompass collectively held and institutionally stabilized visions of desirable futures. These visions are driven by shared understandings of achievable social life and order through advancements in science and technology. A common thread in these claims is the assertion that digitalization will disrupt markets, leading to the elimination of companies that fail to adopt digital systems for optimizing their operations. Drawing on data from thirteen case studies of Polish manufacturing companies and seventeen interviews with representatives of Polish digital system providers, the analysis examines how the imaginary of digital transformation influences the functioning of these companies. The study's conclusions aim to

---

1   There were nine academics in the first government, not mentioning the advisors and advocates gathered around liberal media.

position the logic of digital transformation within the broader framework of digital capitalism.

In the following chapter "Multiculturalism and Multilingualism in Smaller 'Cities of Immigration and Emigration': Płock, Kalisz and Piła, 2019–2022," Anne White observes that Poland is undergoing a "migration transition," becoming a "country of immigration." The wave of labor migration from Ukraine since about 2014, initially mostly short-term and circular, is increasingly turning into migration for settlement, and migrants of other nationalities are also becoming more numerous. As more non- or half-Polish families settle and bring up their children in Poland, Polish society is becoming more diverse. In some respects, this can be conceptualized as multiculturalism, in the sense of ethno-cultural diversity, including linguistic diversity. The chapter looks at how the migration transition is experienced at grassroots level in three smaller Polish cities which are recent destinations for migrants from Ukraine, Belarus, and Georgia, but also Venezuela, Mexico, Nepal, Indonesia, and other non-European countries. It focuses on Ukrainian and Polish linguistic beliefs and practices, and on the process of mutual accommodation which is the hallmark of successful migrant integration. White argues that this apparently successful linguistic collaboration helps speed the migration transition in the three cities, making Ukrainians feel more at home and ready to settle, although the state also needs to play a greater role in providing formal language instruction, both Polish for Ukrainians and Ukrainian for Poles. Still, the fact that Polish residents of the cities had already begun to adapt linguistically to the presence of Ukrainians helps explain their generally welcoming reception of refugees after the 2022 full-scale invasion.

In their chapter on "The COVID-19 Pandemic as a Source of Workplace Innovation," Adam Mrozowicki and Jacek Burski discuss the role the COVID-19 pandemic played as a driver for workplace innovation. The analysis focuses on the ways the employees of public services necessary for the functioning of society, that is, education, health care, and social care, dealt with the challenges of the first months of the pandemic. Unlike the majority of studies that concentrate on anti-crisis activities undertaken by the management, this chapter examines grassroots actions of the employees consisting in self-organization and mutual help in a state of organizational crisis. The analysis was based on focus interviews and biographical interviews conducted with the employees of the three examined sectors. Focusing on workplace innovations in online teaching in primary schools, creation of COVID wards in hospitals, and reorganization of work of nursing homes during lockdowns, the authors conclude that in the first phases of the pandemic, grassroots innovations made it possible to maintain the continuity of the provided educational, health, and social care, which adds a new dimension to the discussion on "essential work" in the pandemic. Furthermore, they point to the occurrence of innovative forms of resistance in the form of grassroots organization of trade unions in the examined workplaces.

In her chapter on "Social Life in an Era of Growing Uncertainty," Mirosława Marody argues that the prevailing sense of uncertainty is not solely tied to the future, where we struggle to anticipate the outcomes of the negative events we witness and are engaged in. Rather, it is intricately linked to the present, where the challenge lies in preserving our sense of agency, testifying to our autonomy and ability to shape our lives. The conventional means of achieving this, often centered around consumption, are now faltering in the face of the recent crises. The methods proposed by contemporary culture for mastering uncertainty clash with the ongoing battle between individual demands for greater autonomy and the increasing supervisory, manipulative, and controlling capabilities of the techno-state. The resolution of this conflict necessitates the establishment of a new axionormative order and a corresponding reality. Therefore, the mounting sense of uncertainty is less about the speed, depth, or extent of the changes in our surroundings than about our incapacity to interpret them through shared terms that guide daily actions. This shortfall in shared interpretation has led to a significant deficit of meaning, now being filled by a multitude of competing values emerging from social practices. These values give rise to more or less recognizable "communities of meaning" as individuals seek to navigate the complex landscape of uncertainty.

The closing part of the book, entitled "In Search of a New Perspective," is a self-reflection of sociologists, who attempt to respond to the challenges addressed to the "old" paradigm. This is even more important because science – including sociology – is both the creator and victim of this paradigm, that is, "modernization" and "efficiency." Globalization, marketization and managerialism have triggered unplanned processes of a "game with the system," in which the values constitutive of science have become instrumentalized. This makes it extremely difficult to experiment with new ideas, methodologies, and curricula.

However, the complexity of the situation has escalated with the advancements in the processes of globalization. This section embarks on a search for new perspectives, aiming to develop a fresh theory of knowledge, reinterpret the crisis in democratic governance, and propose a novel approach to the law that grants rights to nature. This endeavor is essential at this critical moment to navigate the intricacies of our present challenges.

In his chapter on "Law in the Anthropocene Era," Marek Zirk-Sadowski indicates that although in Poland knowledge about the Anthropocene is commonly associated with ecology, the Anthropocene should rather be considered as a dynamic category that touches the very ontology of our world. The exploration of the Anthropocene began with a scientific examination of the effects of changes in the natural environment surrounding humans. The recognition of the crisis in the relationship between civilization and nature has spurred various cultural phenomena. A specific dimension of the reaction to the Anthropocene involves changes in the law, which has shown promise in empowering nature, albeit solely in a legal sense. However, local legal discourses are insufficient to address the problems revealed by the Anthropocene, requiring international collaboration. The central challenge lies in establishing an international framework for the so-called rights of nature (RoN). This entails autonomously constructing rights granted to nature, modeled after the concept of human rights, and developing institutional forms to support them.

The second chapter in this part, entitled "Knowledge in the Face of Populism," by Michał Kaczmarczyk, examines the rising ressentiment toward professional expertise, a phenomenon that seems counterintuitive given the increased emphasis on education and the growing value of knowledge in contemporary societies. The prevalence of this sentiment is noticeable not just in social research but also in the rhetoric of political parties, journalistic narratives, and scholarly discussions that challenge the "tyranny of experts" or intellectual elitism (Easterly 2015). The research hypothesis presented argues that this contradiction may be attributed to changes in the nature of social knowledge, which is becoming more diverse and widely shared, thereby diluting the traditional dominance of professionals. Populist ideologies capitalize on this expansion of inclusivity to devalue professional authority. The author concludes by highlighting the urgent need to reconceptualize traditional notions of professionalism in light of these changing conditions.

In the following chapter "Democracy and Authoritarianism in the Twenty-First Century," Grzegorz Ekiert notes that in recent years significant academic attention has been devoted to the phenomenon of democratic backsliding characterized by an assault on the rule of law, attempts to steal elections, and efforts to subjugate the judicial system and control free media. Still, the parallel political developments affecting hybrid and authoritarian regimes have by and large been neglected. This related process can be described as dictatorial drift and implies the transition from "soft" forms of authoritarian rule to "hardcore" authoritarian policies characterized by the concentration of executive power, the destruction of political institutions such as fair elections, independent judiciary, free media, and autonomous civil society organizations, and worsening political repressions. This chapter describes both democratic backsliding and dictatorial drift and argues that both are, to a significant degree, demand-side phenomena: in countries undergoing such transformations, considerable parts of the electorates support anti-liberal and authoritarian policies. These two processes are illustrated by political developments in formerly communist countries in CEE and in Central Asia.

The closing chapter "On the Influence of Sociology on Society and on the Sociologist" by Krzysztof Konecki describes one of the motives for practicing sociology, namely the debunking motif. Its importance is reconstructed not only for the society, but also for the sociologist who implements it. Still, it is most often overlooked in epistemological and methodological considerations regarding the practice of sociology. In such situation, sociology appears as a form of social action, entangled in interactions not only with other social actors, but also in the sociologist's dialogue with themself: the researcher and theorist thrown by fate into a given social reality.

This book invites sociologists and a wide range of interested readers to reflect on the relevance of emergent analyses to interpret the wide-scale changes in the world.

We have to ask ourselves: What if the scientific portrayal of "society" is an artificial construct? Latour's proposition in 1993 (2011) that "we have never been modern" prompts us to reconsider the entire model of modernization, challenging the assumption of the decline of communities and their "traditional values." Could it be that the concept of intervening in the power dynamics of "modernity" is a tool for global colonization and the exploitation of social resources, such as selflessness, sympathy, gratitude, and care for the well-being of others? These questions and alternative cognitive proposals have been integral to the social sciences since their inception, and now, more than ever, they demand serious consideration as a means of attaining a different perspective on the crisis we currently face.

References

Boatcă, M. (2012). The Quasi-Europes: World Regions in Light of the Imperial Difference. In: Tom Reifer (ed.) *Global crises and the challenges of the 21st century: Antisystemic movements and the transformation of the world-system* (pp. 132–153). Paradigm Publisher.

Boatcă, M., & Costa, S. (2016). Postcolonial sociology: A research agenda. In E. Gutierrez Rodriguez, M. Boatcă, & S. Costa (Eds.), *Decolonizing European sociology: Transdisciplinary approaches* (pp. 13–31). Routledge.

Cavanagh, C. (2004). Postcolonial Poland: An empty space on the map of current theory. *Common Knowledge*, 10(1), 82–92.

Dunn, E. (2004). *Privatizing Poland: Baby food, big business, and the remaking of labor.* Cornell University Press.

Easterly, W. (2015). *The tyranny of experts: Economists, dictators, and the forgotten rights of the poor.* Basic Books.

Heidegger, M. (1970). *Budować, mieszkać, myśleć* (K. Michalski, Trans.). Czytelnik.

Jasanoff, S., & Kim, S.-H. (Eds.). (2015). *Dreamscapes of modernity: Sociotechnical imaginaries and the fabrication of power.* The University of Chicago Press.

Knorr-Cetina, K. (2000). *Epistemic cultures: How the science makes knowledge.* Harvard University Press.

Latour, B. (2011). *We have never been modern* (C. Porter, Trans.). Harvard University Press.

Müller, M. (2020). In search of the global East: Thinking between North and South. *Geopolitics 25*, 734–55.

Ost, D. (2005). *The defeat of solidarity: Anger and politics in postcommunist Europe.* Cornell University Press.

Piacentini, L., & Slade, G. (2024). East is East? Beyond the global North and global South in criminology. *The British Journal of Criminology, 64*(3), 521–537.

Sloterdijk, P. (1987). *Critique of the cynical reason* (M. Eldred, Trans.). University of Minnesota Press.

Wedel, J. R. (2001). *Collision and collusion: The strange case of Western aid to Eastern Europe.* Palgrave.

Wise, A. K. (2010). Postcolonial anxiety in Polish nationalist rhetoric. *The Polish Review, 55*(3), 285–304.

Wolff, L. (1994). *Inventing Eastern Europe: The map of civilization on the mind of the Enlightenment.* Stanford University Press.

PART 1

The Social Crisis as a Crisis of Social Sciences

CHAPTER 2

Sociology and the Alienation of Knowledge

Anna Giza

1   Introduction

Sociology has been established in a specific context, both social and intellectual. In the middle of the nineteenth century, when Henri de Saint-Simon and Auguste Comte were laying the foundations for a new science, an entirely new form of social life emerged in Western Europe. Elias writes about this pivotal period in the following manner:

> At the point of utmost feudal disintegration in the West … certain dynamics of social intertwining come into play which tend to integrate larger and larger units. Out of the competition of small dominions, the territories, themselves formed in the struggles of even smaller survival units, a few, and finally a single unit slowly emerges victorious.
> ELIAS 1982: 319

The intertwining mechanisms Elias mentions are, on the one hand, the market, and on the other hand, the nation state, which, with the use of effective monopolization of force and the centralization of the rational bureaucracy model-based administrative apparatus, integrated the mosaic of different territorial communities into a higher-level collective. As a result, Western Europe sees the formation of a new type of social entities, the epiphenomena of the state, habitually referred to as "modern societies." Gradually, this specific social–economic–political formation becomes synonymous with "modern society" as such, and the historical process that led to its creation and expansion[1] becomes the universal model of social development narrowly understood as "modernization." The multidimensional crisis that accompanied the profound changes taking place in Western Europe was a direct impulse to establish a science of society, which was to provide reliable knowledge due to

---

1   Occupying eight percent of the globe's surface, Western Europe managed to conquer eighty-four percent of the globe between 1492 and 1914, physically, economically, and culturally (Hoffman 2017).

being based on the model of the triumphant modern sciences, identified at the time with Newtonian mechanics.

Thus, both the social and intellectual context of the establishment of sociology was local and specific. Today, almost two hundred years after the publication of Auguste Comte's six-volume work *Course of Positive Philosophy* (1830–1842), we are becoming more and more aware of how much the specificity of the time and place influenced the development of sociology and the founding project of "society" as its research domain. Considering a specific Western European socio-economic formation as a universal model of "modern society", and recognizing the historical process through which this formation emerged as a universal paradigm of "modernization," is increasingly viewed as illegitimate. Moreover, its imposition as a compulsory framework for theorizing on – and governing – society is regarded as a form of colonization. The positivist model of "science" based on Newtonian mechanics turned out to be similarly local and "ideological" (Siemek 1983). The development of natural sciences has moved far away from the deterministic model of nature which prevailed in the nineteenth century (Prigogine and Stengers 1984). However, positivist trends in the social sciences do not seem to notice this. The old masters – Edmund Husserl (1989), Martin Heidegger (1970), and Alfred Whitehead (1925) – warned against the consequences of the modern concept of nature as the *res extensa* deprived both of values and freedom, highlighting its implicit legitimization of the exploitation of nature. Today's planetary crisis[2] proves the validity of their criticism. The transfer of the modern cognitive perspective to the domain of social sciences could, by analogy, lead to the exploitation of social resources[3] and, as a result, a social crisis. The idea of Corporate Social Responsibility, and today of sustainable development, comes from the realization that market exploits these resources, and therefore companies should either re-invest in their restoration or strive to minimize the damage caused. Numerous representatives of humanities and social sciences have written about the risks inherent in viewing society as quasi-nature (Mokrzycki 1984). The famous metaphor of the iron cage (Weber 1930) refers to capitalism from which religious values have "evaporated": a purely mechanical, meaningless reality. Walter Benjamin

---

2   I use the term "planetary crisis" and not "climate crisis" because it allows us to include various dimensions of the crisis, e.g., that of biodiversity, and emphasize its scale (cf. Malinowski 2023: 75).
3   By "social resources" I mean goods that stay under control of families, groups, and local communities, and are crucial for well-being. These are goods such as privacy, free time, attention, energy, income, and social values that determine cohesion, solidarity, and social bonds such as trust, empathy, or reciprocity.

(1982), in turn, wondered about the status of "disenchantment," not ruling out that the "impersonal forces" of the market only *seem* impersonal, but in fact constitute a new incarnation of old gods.

By viewing society as a domain of objective laws, the positivist project of social science leads to double disruption of the relation between the social practices performed by individuals in everyday life and "society" conceived and researched scientifically. First, active social knowledge, which constitutes the basis of all actions, whether by defining situations (Thomas and Thomas 1928) or by conferring subjective meaning to the actions of others (Weber 1978), is considered defective because it is produced contrary to scientific methodology and by non-professionals. In this view, people produce and reproduce "society" in their everyday practices, but at the same time they cannot get to know it because they lack appropriate, which means scientific, cognitive competences; their actions are governed by regularities beyond their knowledge or control. Second, the relation between the world of everyday social practices and the macro (collective) reality they underpin is broken. Based on the Cartesian dualism, intentionality and objectivity cannot be reconciled. Thus, society as given in the living experience of people and society as a whole of activities aggregated in the mechanism of collective life are different entities: the basis of the former are ideas and meanings, and the latter are based on cause-effect relationships and statistical dependencies. This double disruption is the main problem of this chapter. The emergence of social sciences that gradually monopolized the production of valid knowledge about society triggered a process of "alienation," that is, subjects losing control over the final product of their activity, which appears to them as external and alien. In this chapter, I would like to argue that the *alienation of knowledge* is the main cause of the contemporary social crisis manifesting itself in the decline in support for democracy, the increase in the popularity of right-wing movements and anti-scientific sentiments, and the growth of populism.

I will begin with an analysis of a specific social formation, commonly referred to as "modern industrial society," recalling the classical sociological categories commonly used to describe it. The return to the original theories is important because it allows one to identify these elements of the concepts of "modernization" and "modern society" that have been misunderstood or simplified over time. In the next step, I will discuss the positivist (mechanistic) project of the object domain of sociology and the reasons why it has dominated – at least in the domain of institutional sociology as defined by Burawoy (2005) – the alternative project of interpretative sociology. I will argue that these are the preconceptions inherent in the positivist project that inevitably led to breaking the relation between common knowledge and scientific knowledge and, consequently, to alienation. In the summary, I will discuss the concept of the *alienation of knowledge*, arguing for its importance and the new insight it provides us with.

2   Modern Industrial Society of Western Europe

The first and most important challenge for the newly established sociology was theorization of the changes taking place in Western Europe, usually collectively referred to as the "modernization transition." Although the cultural, economic, social, and political elements that ultimately constituted modern capitalist industrial society had been overwhelmingly present earlier, they were combined and integrated in the nineteenth century. The resulting "survival unit," to refer to Elias's (1982) extremely accurate term, was characterized by a number of *powerful competitive advantages*, ranging from military advantage (Hoffman 2017) through economic to cultural one, most fully represented by science. Modern nation states in Western Europe have also proven to be exceptionally effective in permanently tying together a colorful mosaic of territorial communities and feudal aristocratic families. Scholars generally agree that the nation state owes this integrative ability to three main factors: monopolization of violence, centralized administration capable of uniform action, and the gradual liberation of individuals from the power of groups and communities. The most important factor is the last one: the emancipation of individuals from the control of families and local communities. It was carried out through two parallel processes: strengthening individuals and limiting the control of families and communities over various types of resources. The first process, which can be described as a positive aspect of emancipation, took place by expanding the scope of individual rights guaranteed by the state, such as the right of all children to an equal share in inheritance or the right to vote. The second process is more ambivalent. It involves the gradual expropriation – to use Marx's vocabulary – of families and communities from resources and means of production. This freed individuals from their economic control, but at the same time made them dependent on the labor market and the capricious economic situation. In a similar vein, Christopher Lasch (1977) describes the process of "expropriation" of families and communities of various social competences, which were taken over by the state and transformed into centralized systems of "public services." As a result, most of the processes that previously took place within communities, such as the transmission of knowledge, supporting those in need, or raising children, came under the control of middle-class professionals: teachers, educators, and social workers. Individuals freed from the control of groups and communities did not actually become "free." It would rather be said that they became subject to a different type of control: the control of impersonal market mechanisms, public policies, and public systems. The dependence of individuals on the market and the state in fulfilling their most vital needs is, in my opinion, the main reason why integration within the nation state turned out to be so durable and effective. Feudal monarchies, of course, assumed authority over various territories, collected taxes, and exploited various resources, but never created central mechanisms and structures that conditioned the very possibility of conducting any economic activities and the key social ones. In a modern industrial society, it is impossible to earn income outside the market, avoid the registration system, or acquire the skills outside the formal education system. This means that in the frame of the nation state *a new level of collective life appeared, above the level of families and territorial communities*: the one created by the mechanisms of the market and the state and remaining under their control. Individuals are somehow "connected" to them, becoming market entrepreneurs, employees and citizens, customers, voters, or activists of the third sector. While still belonging to the "traditional," as they are often called, communities, they additionally function in the new spaces, "feeding" and powering new types of social entities: workplaces, administrative units, public sectors, as well as the entire spectrum of social and political organizations.

Since individuals function on both levels of this new type of society, circulating between them, "up" and "down," I propose to call them *modes of social life*, thus emphasizing the fact that they are not separate collectivities. In classical sociology, this new mode of social life is usually called the associative mode (*Gesellschaft*), which differs from the community mode (*Gemeinschaft*) in the mechanism of affiliation. Community is entered by birth, while association by choice. *Gesellschaft* thus emerges as an "arbitrary" entity, and its functioning is based on the law – which is perfectly expressed by the Latin maxim "ubi societas, ibi ius." However, *both modes are always present in social life*, although in different proportions. In a "traditional" society, the community mode dominates, while in a "modern" one – the associative mode dominates. It is also worth recalling that both modes are implemented (reproduced) *by the same set of individuals*, who "circulate" between them in various cycles and rhythms. The difference between the two requires the acquisition of special skills and competences, starting from self-control (Elias 1982) through "blasphemy" (Simmel 1975), that is, the ability to distance oneself from excess stimuli, up to mastering an "elaborated linguistic code" that enables decontextualization of the message (Bernstein 1971).

The "modernization transition" means – and all the classics of sociology agree on this – a *sudden increase in complexity*, taking place by building over families and local communities a *new type of social space*, dependent on the market and the state. If *Gemeinschaft* and *Gesellschaft* always coexist, composing the social whole together, it is crucial to theorize their cooperation and/or mutual relations. According to Nicolai Hartmann's (2012) social ontology, the community level should be considered existential (basic) because it is within it that the processes of material – including biological – reproduction of society take place. That is why *Gesellschaft* cannot exist without *Gemeinschaft*, while the latter can exist on its own, as evidenced by most of human history. For the same reason, the power or resilience of levels is inversely proportional to their location in the system – the higher, the weaker – with lower levels characterized by much greater flexibility and adaptability. This means that the *community mode of existence of society is basic*, the associative mode is nested in it through individuals "delegated" to it, and the highest level – the state – is only *a set of rules organizing relations and processes within the entire social system*. From this point of view, modern society has the features of a *hierarchically nested system*, which is not a collection of individuals, but an organized system of groups and connections between them. The metaphor of a "society of individuals" used by Elias (2010) does not mean that it is reduced to an aggregate of individuals: it only expresses an idea analogous to the concept of a "self-directed individual" introduced by Riesman (1950), that is, a self-regulating and self-controlled participant in social life.

As McLaren (2015: 9) writes, "the key to living systems is their ability to impose constraints on a multitude of diverse, more quickly adapting subsystems that induce them to act in the interests of the whole. [Weakening this ability] opens room for subsystems to parasitize on others." At the same time, however, excessive constraints and their excessive rigidity cause the system as a whole to lose its adaptive capacity, succumbing to stagnation and entropy. If not "invisible hands," these are the regulatory activities of the state that determine the condition of the complex social whole.

Coming back to distortions and trivialization of the classic theories of "modern society," it seems there is the tendency to tacitly *reduce it to the associative mode*, and subsequently to oppose it to the "traditional society," which in turn is tacitly identified with the community mode. As a consequence, *modernization is understood as the gradual displacement of traditional communities alongside with the traditional values* that founded them, and replacing them with associations founded on individualistic, modern values, as the team that has been conducting the European Values Survey seems to assume:

> A continuous increase in economic prosperity promotes both secularization and self-expression values. … Thus, in the long run *both dimensions converge into a two-stage process of modernization: traditional values are replaced (or dominated) by secular-rational values* in the process of industrialization; values concerning self-expression become predominant during the transition from industrial to postindustrial (postmodern) societies.
>
> THORNE 2015; emphasis added

As a reminder, by "traditional" we should rather understand a universal set of values founding a deep bond with the community to which we belong and which transcends us, being logically and historically primary to us – whatever the historical costume they appear in. Denying "collectivism" together with "traditional society" is a classic case of throwing the baby out with the bathwater because love, solidarity, or loyalty are not inconsistent with individual rights. The problem we should focus upon is not the persistence of traditional values in "modernity," but their *harmonious connection* with the higher levels of hierarchically nested social organization. The negation of these values *opens the way to the exploitation of social resources*, which has been noticed and problematized first under the headlines of Corporate Social Responsibility, and subsequently of sustainable development.

3 The Scientific Project of Studying Society and Common Knowledge: the First Disruption

Aspiring to be called a "science," sociology had to design its object field as an order governed by objective, deterministic laws, that is, according to the Newtonian mechanics. And although this project was the cause of the founding schism in sociology into "positivist" and "interpretive" trends, the former gained the advantage, not only because of its greater "scientificity" but also because of the promise of manageability of social processes based on discovered laws, in short: social engineering. In his *Discours sur l'esprit positif* and *Discours sur l'ensemble du positivisme* (1973a, 1973b), Auguste Comte frequently quotes Francis Bacon's maxim that "knowledge is power," which Sloterdijk aptly sums as follows:

> This sentence brings to an end the tradition of a knowledge that, as its name indicates, was an erotic theory – the love of truth and the truth through love. From the corpse of philosophy arose the modern sciences

and theories of power in the nineteenth century in the form of political science, theory of class struggle, technocracy, vitalism, and in every form armed to the teeth. "Knowledge is power." This sentence fixed the course for the unavoidable politicization of thinking. Those who utter the sentence reveal the truth. However, with the utterance they want to achieve more than truth: they want to intervene in the game of power.
SLOTERDIJK 1987: XXVI–XXVII

If Sloterdijk is right, Comte's founding promise to discover the laws that govern society was an *entry into the game of power*. It is no wonder that positivist sociology gained greater recognition from important institutional actors than "interpretative sociology" did, as it renounces any ambition to predict, and even less to provide the basis for efficient governance. Circumstances also favored "positivist" sociology. First, the mass processes that characterize the formation of modern society were clearly neither planned nor predicted by anyone, which strengthened the impression that they were the result of objective laws operating similarly to the laws of nature, and thus beyond human intentionality and consciousness. Second, the process of individualization progressing both due to the lengthening and increasing complexity of interaction chains (Elias 1982) and the expansion of individual rights blurred the boundaries of groups and communities, creating the impression that "society" was increasingly moving into an associative mode, that is, becoming an aggregate of individuals operating on the market and in public spaces. Naturally, the community mode was noticed, but its role in the social whole seemed to weaken with the growing dependence of individuals on the market, and the takeover of various social competences by professionals and experts (Lasch 1977). Third, the reduction of "society" to individuals was facilitated by the perspective of state administration, which "sees" and registers only individuals. Hence, the first data that could be analyzed thanks to the development of statistics were available only at the individual level.

All these factors validated the model of society as an aggregate of individuals with measurable characteristics, operating in common public and economic spaces, and subject to common mechanisms that segment them on a macro scale into classes or layers. Over time, belonging to the community level was reduced to characteristics, or variables, such as gender, marital status, number of children, or place of residence. Indeed, looking at modern society from above – that is, from the perspective of state – one can actually see free individuals circulating in public spaces in the foreground. From this perspective, the community level does not seem to play a significant role, and in fact it sometimes is perceived as a ballast of the past that slows down modernization and limits the freedom of individuals. At best, it is postulated to change its mode of functioning from traditional/collectivist to modern/liberal – hence the promoted model of the liberal family, understood as an association of free individuals or a negotiation model of marriage.[4]

This model of understanding and examining society quickly brought the first measurable successes. It was in the field of demography – which is understandable, since the first "hard" data concerned marriages, births, and deaths – that the first models of population dynamics were created, and statistical regularities were discovered. Based on them, the first public policies were developed; in the nineteenth century, they were primarily focused on controlling reproductive behavior due to the first demographic transition resulting in an unprecedented population growth. When Karl Pearson documented a statistically significant relationship between the social class and the number of children – considerably more children were born in the lower classes than in the middle classes – and, additionally, thanks to medical examination of conscripts, a relationship was found between the social origin and the physical parameters and "fitness" of young men (Gawin 2006; Weeks 2018), a wave of fears about "population degeneration" began to sweep through England and then other European countries. Since more children were born in lower social classes, and these children grew up into "unfit" and sick adults, it was believed that these "unfit" people would dominate the populations of Great Britain and France in the future. As a remedy, Hygienic Societies and the infamous Eugenics Societies were established – not only in Great Britain, but throughout Western Europe – and the introduction of laws regulating marriage was seriously considered (Gawin 2006).

Eugenics is a vivid – and inglorious – example of translating scientific knowledge into public policies, although many other, more neutral examples can be given, such as the use of knowledge and social research by marketing.[5] What is most important here, however, is that scientists managed to prove that decisions made independently by individuals form regularities at the collective level. This can certainly be considered evidence of the existence of social

---

4 Richard Sennett, in an excellent essay (1978), shows that striving to base communities on associative values inevitably leads to the emergence of destructive communities (destructive *Gemeinschaft*).
5 According to estimates by the consulting agencies Redburn and PwC, in 2019, global investments in marketing amounted to USD 1.7 trillion (Dimitrioski 2019); this is an order of magnitude more than spending on scientific research, which, according to the UNESCO report, amounted to USD 1.767 billion in 2018 (Schneegans, Lewis, and Straza 2021).

laws and thus validates the model of "society" as an objective reality, acting "behind the backs" of individuals.

Thus, the constructed project of society also carries significant social consequences. First, its logical effect is the *radical separation of common social knowledge from scientific knowledge*. According to this model, "society" cannot be known from the bottom up, with an unaided eye, without statistical tools and theories available only to specialists. This triggers the process of acquiring competences in the production of valid social knowledge by specialists and professionals. The monopoly on valid knowledge about society is granted to sociology and other social sciences, among which economics undoubtedly enjoys the highest scientific prestige, viewing the market as a self-regulating universe of objective dependencies. Latour (2005) argues that each social group needs its advocates, who construct its identity in relation to other groups, define its boundaries, and thus maintain its existence in and through narrative. It was sociologists who became advocates of the existence and character of modern, mass society, as opposed to the "traditional" one, and "like new prophets, they mastered the art of predicting cause and effect" (Benjamin qtd. in Kusiak 2010: 73). Ordinary people were and are still unable to know, understand, or experience the "society" to which they belong. While the notion of "nation" allows everyone to easily imagine the community behind it, the notion of "society" is incomprehensible to anyone except sociologists. And if Elias (2010) is right, even for them this concept has become a worn-out coin that does not guarantee that we really understand each other.

The second implication is the *denial of the agency of acting subjects*, who actually provide empirical "input" to social phenomena and processes but lack cognitive skills to see them and to exercise control over them. Those who act "do not know what they are doing" or are mistaken about the meaning and motivation of their actions. For example, people nowadays believe that they get married for love, when in fact they implement the principle of marital homogamy. The denial of agency leads to the release of social life participants from responsibility for the reality they co-create. One can even say that – since the "invisible hand" can transform human flaws into the common good – the subject is freed from the moral tension that naturally accompanies the internal struggle of moral commands with selfish motives. Paradoxically, subjects gain influence on reality on a macro scale only *by refraining from action*. Since, for example, constituencies exist objectively and belonging to one of them is determined by the social position, the action of voters is limited to completing their own fate like the heroes of a Greek drama. However, if voters become overwhelmed by fatalism and do not go to the polls, it poses a real threat to democracy, even though the election result is valid regardless of turnout. It is difficult to maintain the narrative of "the will of the people" when the turnout is, say, below thirty percent. What is even more important, refraining from action overrides "impersonal forces", although putting democracy into crisis at the same time. That is why voting is presented as an obligation, not a right. Thus, even if voters have a complete sense of façade or do not see anyone worth their voices, they have an obligation to exercise their right. This sounds like a paradox, and, in fact, it is: forcing people to participate remains necessary for impersonal forces to act, thereby denying their agency.

Third, the orientation toward discovering general laws and relationships leads to the *decontextualization of social phenomena and – often methodologically invalid – generalizations*. As a result, it is difficult to relate scientific knowledge about society to one's own experience (Flyvbjerg 2001) or, to put it simply, to take it personally. This, I believe, is the reason for the lack of balance between the use of sociological knowledge by public institutions (institutional sociology as defined by Burawoy 2005) and its use by citizens and social organizations as a tool for emancipation. Institutions operate at the systemic level, and only they can implement public policies on a macro scale. People and social organizations operate locally and bottom-up, and therefore general and abstract knowledge about macro-scale relationships is of little use to them, especially in the face of the famous "ecological fallacy."

Fourth, the assumption that there are regularities governing social phenomena *makes us look for them, and modern statistical tools help to find them* – especially those that are designed for this purpose. Techniques for discovering hidden relationships, such as factor analysis, correspondence analysis, or cluster analysis, play an invaluable role here. When working with this type of tools, a lot of tests are usually carried out to obtain a reasonable result. Thus, although the outcome is presented as objective, it is in fact the outcome of a whole series of arbitrary decisions by the researcher. Therefore, it is not entirely certain whether sociology discovers relationships or creates them (Moore 2008; Halawa 2013) since its findings are pre-determined by the specific "scopic system" (Knorr-Cetina 2000). What is important in this context is the fact that scientific knowledge is usually not negotiated in social dialogue. Consequently, how can the studied reality provide feedback to the researcher if they do not give voice to the object they are talking about, and in the case of statistical dependencies, the concept of "falsifiability" as defined by Popper (2002) does not apply?

The separation of science from common knowledge is the first act of breaking the relation between society and social science. The second aspect is the *dichotomy between intentionality of the social action on the micro level and the quasi-deterministic nature of social reality on the macro scale.*

4 Intentionality and Determinism: the Second Disruption

Weber defines social action as an action which relates to other people's behaviors and carries a subjective meaning (Weber 1978: 6). Consequently, the starting point for every social action is giving meaning to a situation (Thomas and Thomas 1928), which makes the actions of all other actors meaningful and therefore – by virtue of the norms, traditions, or rules applicable in a given situation – predictable. This means that *the foundation of collective life is the knowledge of social world organized through shared categories of culture*. Many other authors representing interpretive trends in sociology could be cited here, although it seems that no one denies the intentionality of individuals' actions at the micro level. Positivist trends only deny the adequacy of semiotic categories for modeling social life on a macro scale. There is therefore a consensus that the basis of real, everyday social practices is common knowledge, which underlies the production and reproduction of social phenomena. To take the simplest example, the "family" exists only to the extent that its members share the understanding of this concept and to the extent that they are ready to voluntarily and consciously adhere to the meanings and norms contained in it. In this approach, social activities are intentional, meaningful, and voluntary, and social forms co-created by people – families, neighborhoods, peer groups, or villages – remain under their cognitive ("I know what it is and how it works") and actual control. Because people act on the basis of assumptions resulting from knowledge and experience, common knowledge is constantly verified in the process of social action, basically in a way analogous to the empirical testing of scientific theories – which makes it quite solid and robust.

Modernity has brought significant changes in the functioning of the associative mode, mainly under the influence of the rationalization process. Its essence, according to Max Weber (2004), is the introduction of metrics thanks to which previously incomparable goods, activities, or services can be compared, predicted, and calculated. This process concerns not only the market, but also the social sector, which the state bureaucracy standardizes and centralizes. Rationalization enabled the spread of instrumental rationality, understood as making a choice without reference to social values, but only based on comparing the effectiveness of available alternatives; this applies to both the economic field and the construction of public policies. The state played a key role in the rationalization process as the central regulator and guarantor of the implementation and execution of rules and laws.

This meant that the associative mode, previously emerging from the bottom up and locally, started to be organized top down and on a mass scale, encompassing everyone as citizens of the same state acting on the market. From the perspective of acting individuals, regulations constitute a system of external constraints beyond their control – although these constraints do not arise by themselves, just as the market and bureaucracy do not appear *deus ex machina*. This is what Benjamin's and Weber's (Kusiak 2010) intuitions express: behind the concept of "impersonal forces" operating in the economic and social realms there may lie a new incarnation of ancient gods.

Either way, on the one hand, the mass modern industrial society emerging in a real historical process and integrated at a higher level resembles nature, as mentioned above; on the other hand, it is recognized and projected scientifically as quasi-nature. However, the naturalization of society concerns only the associative mode because only in the spaces of the market and the state can individuals be seen as a mass of free, independently moving "atoms" whose actions form regular patterns even though the individuals neither know them nor are consciously guided by them. The model of society as quasi-nature cuts off the community mode, invisible from its perspective, and consequently loses sight of the entire hierarchically nested social system, flattening it and *reducing it to the space of the market and the state*. Thanks to this, however, it promises manageability. Knowing the cause-and-effect relationships and mechanisms responsible for the order of collective actions, it is possible to create constraints that steer individuals into the desired direction, analogously to the use of physical forces in machine technology.

This is where the disruption of the connection between the intentionality of social action and naturalized society occurs. Modern science, the assumptions of which are adopted by positivistic sociology, is founded on the Cartesian dualism, radically separating the subject and the object. Therefore, it is impossible to reconcile the objectivity attributed to society as the subject of research with the subjectivity of the participants co-creating it, or, in other words, the intentionality of human actions with the objectivity of social facts. No one falls in love with a person from the same social class to comply with the statistical principle of marital homogamy, and suicide is committed out of despair or for honorary reasons, the persons concerned being completely unaware of the combination of factors conducive to making such a decision (Durkheim 1997). Therefore, we need to answer the question of how the intentional actions of free individuals form regular patterns, for example, why we fall sincerely and passionately in love with a person of a similar social position.

The answer to this question is given in two ways: by assuming the existence of intermediary mechanisms, for instance, in the form of socialization, or by assigning rational-instrumental motivations to the acting individuals, thanks to which their choices are a consequence of an objectively existing system of boundary conditions. Thus, according to the assumption of mediating mechanisms, we fall in love with similar people because our preferences for a partner are pre-formed by cultural and social capital. According to the second explanation, those looking for a partner are – in the sense of the *homo economicus* model – rational actors who strive at least not to worsen their situation, which favors homogamy (Becker 1973, 1974).

In both cases, however, the subject's choices are largely determined, either by intervening social factors or by the "compulsion of rationality"; and this calls into question the intentionality and autonomy of the subject, who turns out to be a puppet controlled by impersonal forces. In this approach, the schism between positivistic and understanding sociology has an ethical dimension: either we recognize an individual's responsibility for the world they create or we release them from it; either we consider sense and meaning as the basis for creating social reality or we assume it is governed by laws; either we regard culture as a sphere of freedom or we view it as a cover for the compulsions of the material world. Choosing the first option restores people's agency and enables them to understand the social whole, but at the cost of giving up manageability. This means entrusting social sciences with a task other than discovering the laws that govern social reality and the indivisibility of the social world seen as a significant whole.

Social historian David Levine sees the task of social science as the search for experiences characteristic of various social formations because "in so doing we learn from the past not just to comprehend its totality but also to heighten our appreciation of both human behaviour and our own social experience" (1987: 3). Norbert Elias argues that the role of sociology is "to explore, and to make men understand, the patterns they form together, the nature and the changing configurations of all that binds them to each other" (1956: 234). According to Max Weber, socio-economic formations can only be understood by identifying the ideas of value that found them – frameworks of meaning – and the analytical construct of ideal types:

> An ideal type is formed by the one-sided accentuation of one or more points of view and by the synthesis of a great many diffuse, discrete, more or less present and occasionally absent concrete individual phenomena, which are arranged according to those onesidedly emphasized viewpoints into a unified analytical construct.
> WEBER 1978: 90

In all three cases, both the need to understand social reality as a whole and the emancipatory – rather than managerial – potential of sociology is emphasized.

5   The Process of Alienation of Scientific Knowledge about Society

Breaking the relation between common social knowledge and scientific knowledge leads to the inevitable divergences between how acting subjects perceive social reality and the image of social reality constructed by science. These divergences become apparent when scientific diagnoses concerning the condition of society enter the public discourse. Over time, the narrative of society becomes an important part of it, particularly if society deviates from the model desired by authorities or science. Sara Igo (2008), in a book about the process of legitimizing sociological surveys as a scientifically validated democratic practice of "giving society a voice," documents the protests caused by the first surveys on "representative samples" published in the press, as well as the protests of the "Middletown" inhabitants after the famous monograph was published. *The Washington Post*, which started to publish selected survey results in the regular "America Speaks" column, received letters from readers denying – based on their own experience – their veracity. However, the common sense represented by "ordinary" people had to lose in the confrontation with science. This was precisely how the readers were answered: that they did not have the competence to speak about society, or that their social knowledge was marginal. We regularly encountered this type of passionate opposition to scientific theses about society during the qualitative research we conducted on social self-knowledge (Giza 2013). After learning about the most common theses about what Polish society is like, one of the participants sighed and said, "They are not observing us properly" (Gołdys 2013). As a result, there is a common tendency to distance oneself from the "society," expressed by the widespread phrases "*this* society is difficult to" or "how to deal with *this* society," as if it were an external entity to which the speaker does not belong and does not want to belong.

This mental withdrawal from society and rejection of its scientific image leads to a split society, divided into "the mine" known from one's own experience and "the whole" known from the public narration by experts and publicists. When we conducted the above-mentioned qualitative research, our interlocutors carefully distinguished these two societies, asking whether we meant "the society I know" or "the Polish society" (Gołdys 2013). The consequences of knowledge dualism have been widely researched and described in social psychology (Deners-Ray and Epstein 1994) and common knowledge theory (Chwe 2013), from the well-known Asch experiment to the phenomenon of pluralistic ignorance (Prentice and Miller 1993) known from Christian Andersen's fairy tale about the emperor's new clothes. It consists in each individual believing X, as in "the emperor is naked," while thinking that all other people believe not X, namely "the emperor is wearing beautiful clothes." Pluralistic ignorance leads to several dysfunctional consequences, from collective hypocrisy through self-fulfilling prophecies in social relations (Vorauer and Ratner 1996) to passivity in the face of crisis situations. The belief in the divergence of one's own opinion and the opinion of the majority causes prison guards to mistreat prisoners, managers to refrain from expressing doubts as to the strategy announced by the management (Westphal and Bednar 2005), and ordinary citizens to avoid speaking out on complex public issues (Todorov and Mandisodza 2004). It also triggers a "spiral of silence" (Noelle-Neumann 1984) making respondents who have learnt they represent a minority refrain from declaring their opinion. According to Noelle-Neumann, due to this each subsequent public opinion poll becomes more and more distant from reality.

The dualism of knowledge also underlies social dimorphism (Tarkowska and Tarkowski 1994), when people use certain cognitive assumptions while acting inside their own social bubbles – "my society" – and different ones while interacting with the unknown people in the public space, in which case the "Polish society" assumptions are activated. As far as the image of the latter is negative, ascribing traits such as distrust, disinterested unkindness, or argumentativeness to its members, the social trap is triggered. Taking assumptions consistent with this image locks the interacting individuals in the prisoner's dilemma.

All these phenomena are symptoms of alienation, and the process of which they are the result meets its definitional conditions. As I have tried to show, alienation was triggered by the appropriation of cognitive competences – that is, means of producing social knowledge – by positivist social science. The mechanistic model of society underlying it leads to a disruption of the relation between the society (the whole) and the subjects who compose it (parts).

According to Marx, the alienation of labor occurs when a worker loses control over the production process and, consequently, contact with both its outcome/product and that part of his subjectivity that is involved in this process. Reduced to a technological element, a worker turns into an object. Analogically, with social sciences taking over the monopoly on organizing cognition and production of legitimate social knowledge, subjects/parts that produce and reproduce the social reality/the whole through their actions, lose control over this process, and their cognitive competences and agency are negated.

Leopold (2022) focuses on the philosophical and psychological dimensions of alienation, defining it as "the problematic disruption of the subject and the object that properly belong together." There are two important concepts in this definition that need to be explained: "properly belonging together" and "problematic disruption." As to the first one, the idea that people and society "properly" belong together was best expressed by Simmel, who – referring to Kant – indicated that

> what we call nature is a special way in which our intellect assembles, orders, and forms the sense-perception ... which are not in themselves inter-connected, [while] the *societary unity is realized by its elements without further mediation, and with no need of an observer, because these elements are consciously and synthetically active.*
>
> SIMMEL 1910: 372–373, emphasis added

Simplifying, the inter-connected social whole – "societary unity" – is ontologically and logically primary to its parts and exists priorly to and independently of cognition.

Disruption of the relation is "problematic," in turn, because it is relation that gives meaning, and thus identity, to its components. For example, one can only be a mother as the component of the motherhood (mother – child) relation. Disruption of the relation changes the identity of its relata and should be considered a case of semiotic corruption (McLaren 2015). Breaking a meaningful whole into pieces distorts their meaning and obscures the fact that they are elements of a complex, interconnected system. This opens the way to simplified and superficial analyzes.[6] McLaren (2015) argues that the decomposition of the diet into components – such as carbohydrates or fiber – has led to the obesity crisis not only because it generalized the components ignoring context-dependent differences, for example, between sugar in an apple and sugar in a carrot, but also because it opened the way to lobbying by processed food producers, who could present their products as healthy due to some of their ingredients, while ignoring other, for instance, by communicating fiber in breakfast cereals while keeping silent about sugar. Dysfunctions also affect the relation-isolated subject: opposed to the object with which they form a relational whole, they experience powerlessness, a sense of façade of their social roles, internal breakdown, and indifference (Leopold 2022). This kind of feeling and experience, and in particular the feeling of powerlessness, weakens and displaces values such as freedom and equality in the "risk society," resulting in withdrawal from participation (Beck 1992; Beck and Beck-Gernsheim 2002).

---

6 The meaning of the concept of "semiotic corruption" can be imagined as the decomposition of a significant whole, the essence of which is connections and relations (e.g. a puzzle), into elements (e.g. shapes and colors), and then analyzing them outside the context, making statements such as "thirty-one percent of the elements are pink, while only three percent are yellow."

This explains why people turn away from democracy and rebel against capitalism. Seeing and experiencing all its negative externalities, from growing inequalities to planetary crisis, they feel helpless in the face of "objective, impersonal forces" operating on a global scale. The silent consensus on the dogma of "modernization" as the only and best way of development and the dogma of the free market as the only way of growth and democracy, as imperfect as it may be but the best of the known systems, also explains why people are looking for political alternatives that give hope for regaining agency. Finally, the persistent legitimization of these dogmas by institutional science allows us to understand why people turn away from it. Social scientists often say that "this society" slides into irrationality because people do not want to listen to what science has to tell them. I would say the opposite is true: people slide into irrationality because they have listened to science for too long. Resistance and opposition are particularly strong in postcolonial and self-colonizing countries (cf. Głowacka-Grajper and Wawrzyniak in this volume) because the disruption between the subject and the object is accompanied there by a break in continuity with one's own past and the imposition of an alien model of "modern society." From this point of view, social trends in the countries of Central and Eastern Europe (CEE), including low voter turnout and strong support for right-wing parties, do not result, as is commonly claimed, from "immaturity" or weakness of the democratic tradition. On the contrary: it was in the countries undergoing transformation that the deficits of the "modern" social formation became apparent earlier and more clearly. We may and should treat them as a unique social laboratory where an in vivo experiment took place. Unfortunately, local social sciences did not take advantage of this opportunity, uncritically adopting the modernization model and focusing on tracking its progress, defined in accordance with this model (cf. Bukraba-Rylska in this volume).

Now we come to the crucial question: What if the dominant model of society that serves as the basis for governance, marketing, or designing public policies is an artifact? What if "we have never been modern" (Latour 2011), and the trivialized model of modernization, which assumes the death of *Gemeinschaft* along with "traditional values," is wrong? What if Durkheim (1961), Haidt (2012), Mestrovic (1992, 1995, 1997), and Shiling and Melor (1998) are right when they claim that the emotional experience of society as something that is bigger than us and the values associated with it are not relics of traditional society, but they are still present and active pillars of morality? According to the theorists mentioned, lack of the spaces for positively experiencing and expressing these values may lead to the "balkanization" of social life, and it certainly drives the search for "cracks" in which *effervescence collective* can be experienced, such as concerts, supporting sport teams or engaging in the new social movements; it certainly also fuels radical, nationalistic, and right-wing movements. Finally, what if the concept of "modernity" is one of the elements of colonizing the world and exploiting social resources (values) such as selflessness, sympathy, gratitude, or concern for the well-being of others?

All these issues have been raised, and cognitive alternatives have been formulated for a long time – in fact from the very beginning of the process of establishing social sciences. This is the last moment to take them seriously: only this can open the way to a different look at the crisis affecting us. One often hears the opinion that the social crisis currently being experienced – including decreasing support for democracy and the renaissance of right-wing movements, radicalism, and populism – is caused by people turning away from science: "They do not want to listen to us." In this text, I try to prove that the opposite is true: science has in many ways turned its back on people, and this has become the source of the crisis. Therefore, it is necessary to strengthen critical reflection in sociology on one's own cognitive assumptions and rethink the theory of modernity, involve participants in social life in research and dialogue, take responsibility for the quality of public discourse about "society," refrain from succumbing to the temptations of power, and get rid of besserwisserism and the sense of one's own cognitive superiority. Above all, it is necessary to start a real dialogue, based on respect and striving for understanding, both among us and with social partners.

References

Beck, U. (1992). *Risk society: Towards a new modernity*. SAGE Publications.
Beck, U., & Beck-Gernsheim, E. (2002). *Individualization: Institutionalized individualism and its social and political consequences*. SAGE Publications.
Becker, G. (1973). A theory of marriage: Part I. *Journal of Political Economy*, 81(4), 813–846.
Becker, G. (1974). A theory of marriage: Part II. *Journal of Political Economy*, 82(2), 11–26.
Benjamin, W. (1982). *Gesammelte Schriften*. Suhrkamp.
Bernstein, B. (1971). *Class, codes, and control*. Routledge.
Burawoy, M. (2005). For public sociology. *American Sociological Review*, 70(1), 4–28.
Chwe, M. Y. S. (2013). *Rational rituals: Culture, coordination, and common knowledge*. Princeton University Press.
Comte, A. (1973a). *Rozprawa o całokształcie pozytywizmu* (B. Skarga & W. Wojciechowska, Trans.). PWN (Original work published 1844).

Comte, A. (1973b). *Rozprawa o duchu filozofii pozytywnej* (B. Skarga & W. Wojciechowska, Trans.). PWN (Original work published 1844).
Denes-Raj, V., & Epstein, S. (1994). Conflict between intuitive and rational processing: When people behave against their better judgement. *Journal of Personality and Social Psychology, 66*, 819–829.
Dimitrioski, Z. (2019, February 13). How much money is in the global marketing industry – More than we believed. *Forbes.* https://www.forbes.com/sites/zarkodimitrioski/2019/02/13/how-much-money-is-in-the-global-marketing-industry-more-than-we-believed/.
Durkheim, E. (1961). *The elementary forms of the religious life.* Free Press.
Durkheim, E. (1997). *Suicide: A study in sociology.* Free Press.
Elias, N. (1956). Problems of involvement and detachment. *British Journal of Sociology, 7,* 226–252.
Elias, N. (1982). *The civilizing process: State formation and civilization* (E. Jephcott, Trans.). Basil Blackwell.
Elias, N. (2010). *Collected works: Vol. 10. The society of individuals* (E. Jephcott, Trans.). UCD Press.
Flyvbjerg, B. (2001). *Making social science matter: Why social inquiry fails and how it can succeed again.* Cambridge University Press.
Gawin, M. (2006). *Rasa i nowoczesność. Historia polskiego ruchu eugenicznego.* Neriton.
Giza, A. (2013). *Gabinet luster. O kształtowaniu samowiedzy Polaków w dyskursie publicznym.* Warszawa: Wydawnictwo Naukowe Scholar.
Gołdys, A. (2013). Po drugiej stronie lustra, czyli doświadczanie społeczeństwa. In A. Giza (Ed.), *Gabinet luster. O kształtowaniu samowiedzy Polaków w dyskursie publicznym* (pp. 356–429). Wydawnictwo Naukowe Scholar.
Haidt, J. (2012). *The righteous mind: Why good people are divided by politics and religion.* Pantheon.
Halawa, M. (2013). Tylu Polaków naraz widzieć. ... O statystycznym wytwarzaniu społeczeństwa. In A. Giza (Ed.), *Gabinet luster. O kształtowaniu samowiedzy Polaków w dyskursie publicznym* (pp. 34–67). Wydawnictwo Naukowe Scholar.
Hartmann, N. (2012). *New ways of ontology* (P. Cicovacki, Trans.). Transaction Publishers.
Heidegger, M. (1970). *Budować, mieszkać, myśleć* (K. Michalski, Trans.). Czytelnik.
Hoffman, P. T. (2017). *Why did Europe conquer the world?* Princeton University Press.
Husserl, E. (1989). *The crisis of European sciences and transcendental phenomenology: An introduction to phenomenological philosophy.* Northwestern University Press.
Igo, S. E. (2008). *The averaged American: Surveys, citizens, and the making of a mass public.* Harvard University Press.
Knorr-Cetina, K. (2000). *Epistemic cultures: How the science makes knowledge.* Harvard University Press.

Kusiak, J. (2010). Kto zamieszka w żelaznej klatce? Max Weber, Walter Benjamin i mitologie odczarowanej rzeczywistości. In P. Śpiewak (Ed.), *Dawne idee, nowe problemy* (pp. 67–89). Wydawnictwa Uniwersytetu Warszawskiego.

Lasch, C. (1977). *Haven in a heartless world: The family besieged.* W. W. Norton & Company.

Latour, B. (2005). *Reassembling the social: An introduction to actor–network-theory.* Oxford University Press.

Latour, B. (2011). *We have never been modern* (C. Porter, Trans.). Harvard University Press.

Leopold, D. (2022). Alienation. In E. N. Zalta & U. Nodelman (Eds.), *The Stanford encyclopedia of philosophy* (Winter 2022 Edition). Retrieved January 20, 2024, from https://plato.stanford.edu/archives/win2022/entries/alienation/.

Levine, D. (1987). *Reproducing families: The political economy of English population history.* Cambridge University Press.

Malinowski, S. (2023). Przyszłość. In K. Kasia & G. Markowski (Eds.), *Siedem życzeń. Rozmowy o źródłach nadziei* (pp. 63–98). Znak.

McLaren, G. (2015). The obesity crisis and semiotic corruption: Towards a unifying biosemiotic understanding of obesity. *Cosmos and History, 11*(1), 181–220.

Mestrovic, S. G. (1992). *Durkheim and postmodern culture.* Aldine de Gruyter.

Mestrovic, S. G. (1995). *The balkanization of the West.* Routledge.

Mestrovic, S. G. (1997). *Postemotional society.* SAGE Publications.

Mokrzycki, E. (1984). *Kryzys i schizma.* Vol. 1–2. Państwowy Instytut Wydawniczy.

Moore, D. (2008). *The opinion makers.* Beacon Press.

Noelle-Neumann, E. (1984). *The spiral of silence: Public opinion – our social skin.* The University of Chicago Press.

Popper, K. R. (2002). *The logic of scientific discovery.* Routledge.

Prentice, D. A., & Miller, D. T. (1993). Pluralistic ignorance and alcohol use on campus: Some consequences of misperceiving the social norm. *Journal of Personality and Social Psychology, 64,* 243–256.

Prigogine, I., & Stengers, I. (1984). *Order out of chaos: Man's new dialogue with nature.* Bantam Books.

Riesman, D. (1950). *The lonely crowd.* Yale University Press.

Schneegans, S., Lewis, J., & Straza, T. (Eds.) (2021). *UNESCO science report: The race against time for smarter development – Executive summary.* UNESCO Publishing.

Sennett, R. (1978). Destructive Gemeinschaft. In K. W. Back (Ed.), *In search for Community: Encounter groups and social change* (pp. 33–56). Routledge.

Shilling, C., & Mellor, P. (1998). Durkheim, morality and modernity: Collective effervescence, homo duplex and the sources of moral action. *The British Journal of Sociology, 49*(2), 193–209.

Siemek, Marek. J. (1983). "Nauka" i "naukowość" jako ideologiczne kategorie filozofii. *Studia Filozoficzne, nr 5–6,* 71–84.

Simmel, G. (1910). How is society possible? *American Journal of Sociology, 16*(3), 372–391.
Simmel, G. (1975). *Socjologia*. PWN.
Sloterdijk, P. (1987) *Critique of the cynical reason* (M. Eldred, Trans.). University of Minnesota Press.
Tarkowska, E., & Tarkowski, J. (1994). "Amoralny familizm," czyli o dezintegracji społecznej w Polsce lat osiemdziesiątych. In J. Tarkowski (Ed.), *Socjologia świata polityki. Władza i społeczeństwo w systemie autorytarnym* (Vol. 1, pp. 263–281). Instytut Studiów Politycznych PAN.
Thomas, W. I., & Thomas, D. S. (1928). *The child in America: Behavior problems and programs*. Knopf.
Thome, H. (2015). Values, Sociology of. In J. D. Wright (Ed.), *International encyclopedia of the social and behavioral sciences* (2nd ed., Vol. 25, pp. 47–53). Elsevier.
Todorov, A., & Mandisodza, A. N. (2004). Public opinion on foreign policy: The multilateral public that perceives itself as unilateral. *Public Opinion Quarterly, 68*, 325–348.
Vorauer, J., & Ratner, R. (1996). Who's going to make the first move? Pluralistic ignorance as an impediment to relationship formation. *Journal of Social and Personal Relationships, 13*, 483–503.
Weber, M. (1930). *The protestant ethic and the spirit of capitalism* (T. Parsons, Trans.). Scribner.
Weber, M. (1978) *Economy and society: An outline of the interpretative sociology*. University of California Press.
Weber, M. (2004). *Racjonalność, władza, odczarowanie. Wybór pism*. Wydawnictwo Poznańskie.
Weeks, J. (2018). *Sex, politics and society: The regulation of sexuality since 1800*. Routledge.
Westphal, J. D., & Bednar, M. K. (2005). Pluralistic ignorance in corporate boards and firms' strategic persistence in response to low firm performance. *Administrative Science Quarterly, 50*, 262–298.
Whitehead, A. N. (1925). *Science and the modern world: Lowell lectures*. Cambridge University Press.

CHAPTER 3

Sociology and Social Change: Polish Researchers and the Transformation

Izabella Bukraba-Rylska

1   Introduction

The relationships between sociology and the social phenomena it studies are manifold and by no means one-sided. Among the peculiarities of the social sciences analyzed by Stanisław Ossowski in the past (Ossowski 1967) – especially those related to the influence of research activities and research results on reality – one should add those describing the opposite relation, namely the influence of the researched reality on research activities and their results and the sociologists themselves. Certainly, in such an analysis one could use the assumptions of the sociology of knowledge – in its classical or non-classical version, that is, the inspiration of Peter Berger and Thomas Luckmann, the "strong program" of the Edinburgh School, or Michel Foucault's project – but it would probably be more interesting to trace the dependencies and mutual entanglements of knowledge and the context of its formation using the example of specific research practices. The achievements of Polish sociology over the past thirty years seem a convenient object for such an analysis. This is so not only because they concern a relatively recent and already completed period, but mainly because they refer to the process of intensive and profound transitions in Polish society, and it is precisely change (or dynamics) that constitutes one of the two fundamental objects of sociological reflection, perhaps even to a greater extent than the second one set by Auguste Comte at the very beginning: the study of duration (statics).

Far from the skepticism of historians, who, following Fernand Braudel, are inclined to claim that "there was never a total break, an absolute discontinuity between the past, even the very distant, and the present" (qtd. in Leszczyński MMXX: 524), sociologists – similar in this rather to Karol Irzykowski's "dolts"[1] (Irzykowski 1976: 524) – more often perceive fundamental breakthroughs and

---

1   Irzykowski coins the word *jełom*, which is a neologism constructed of *jełop* (dolt, dummy) and *przełom* (breakthrough), meaning that "a dolt is experiencing – or making for themself – a breakthrough" (Irzykowski 1976: 588). Translator's note.

turns, ends and beginnings, and affirm what is new, while they tend to call persistence stagnation. This attitude was undoubtedly influenced by the timing of the discipline's emergence: the disintegration of the old, agricultural-based feudal order and the birth of the new, industrial-capitalist order. As Jürgen Habermas writes, "sociology arose as the theory of bourgeois society; to it fell the task of explaining the course of the capitalist modernization of traditional societies and its anomie side effects" (Habermas 1985: xiii). The adopted attitude found reflection in numerous conceptions of social change, where the agrarian phase of the history, along with the peasant economy, was considered traditional, and the industrial and postindustrial phase was considered increasingly modern (e.g. Walt Rostow, Daniel Bell, or Daniel Thorner). According to this belief, the commonly used measures of socio-economic development assumed that the more significant the percentage of the population living in cities (urbanization), the more people employed in industry (industrialization), services, or the knowledge economy (cognitive capitalism), and the more modest the contribution to the GDP made by agriculture – the higher the level of civilization advancement a country presented. The chosen criteria and development indicators made the countryside and agriculture synonymous with backwardness, and progress was assumed to be measured by the rate and extent of shrinkage of the agrarian segment.

The second factor determining the specificity of sociology was, according to Immanuel Wallerstein (1999), the Enlightenment legacy with the overappreciation of the progress inherent in it. Changes were treated as progressive, and the terminology of development or modernization was used more often than the terminology of regression or retrogression. The opposition – put into handy dichotomies such as "traditional–modern" – organized sociological thinking, and a dynamic perspective emphasizing change became more attractive than a static one focused on continuity. The knowledge generated by sociology as a theory of the industrial age therefore assumed "the axiology of industrial culture and civilization of modern societies" (Poleszczuk 1990: 68) and questioned everything related to the countryside, agriculture, and peasant culture. This firm anti-ruralism was also taken up by rural sociology which did not offer a competing view of reality but fitted into the overarching paradigm. This has involved, among other things, adopting the optics of "urban chauvinism" (Bodenstedt 1998) and the imposition of the role of the rural areas as a service sector vis-à-vis large agglomerations (Kuvlesky and Coop 1983/1984). At the same time, rural communities were seen as a hotbed of conservative forces that were hostile to progress and were denied the ability to develop on their own, allowing only exogenous and externally induced change, which reduced the countryside to the role of an incomplete entity – passive and reactive, capable only of responding to applied stimuli and thus forced into a constant process of adaptation. The countryside was seen as merely "something passive, something that only lives and ruminates, rather than creates and strives," writes Władysław Grabski (2004: 77), one of those few who thought otherwise. Still, as many have observed, the category of progress serves sociology not only to describe and explain social trends, but also, so to speak, to impose an obligation on researchers to promote, accelerate, and even impose it if the opportunity to participate in the process arises, especially the opportunity to cooperate with the authorities. The distant-from-neutrality stance of engagement means that the "servile" role of the scientist, previously oriented toward using their objective and value-free analyses for understanding, and above all, the self-understanding of society, thereby changes into a subservient or even menial role (Bukraba-Rylska 2009). This occurs when a science professional begins to prioritize practical goals over cognitive ones and becomes an expert or advisor interested in social engineering goals. From this point on, their position – no longer so much a researcher, but a technocratically oriented reformer – is determined by their positioning between two polarities: "the intervention project" and "the worldview project" (Kurczewska 1989). The first one hinges on the conviction of the possibility of providing scientific solutions to all problems, the need for modernization, and the importance of professionals; the second one contains a considerable dose of utopian thinking, very close to extreme rationalism, which does not reckon with the conditions of a "specific place and time" (Hessen 2003: 3), and, thanks to the conviction of rightness, often becomes a terror of ideas, using the mechanisms of statist violence (Peshkov 2004). Shortly after the Second World War, the mission of the scientist-activist understood in this way was expressed in the words of Marxist philosopher Tadeusz Kroński: "We will teach people in this country to think rationally without alienation with our Soviet rifle butts" (Miłosz 1999: 318). After 1989, when the transformational process in Poland began to build a democratic liberal system and a free market economy, they acted according to a principle whose paradoxical nature was perfectly captured by Stefan Kisielewski: "You have to take society by the mouth and introduce this liberalism" (qtd. in Szacki 1994: 188). In both cases, however, it was not only a matter of imposing certain solutions, but also of the fact that these solutions were taken from outside, and this circumstance refers to another feature of the sociologist involved in the process of change.

When comparing the processes of modernization in the "leading" countries, that is, England and France of the eighteenth century, and the "follower" countries, Reinhard Bendix notes that while in the former the transformations occur gradually and are endogenous, and the governments and elites promoting them can be considered representatives of society, in the latter the changes are exogenous and the authorities apply them more or less shockingly (Bendix 1984), and this significantly affects the attitudes of researchers. As Zygmunt Bauman (1999) writes, sociologists in developed countries did not distance themselves from their societies, while in peripheral countries they manifested a tendency to adopt an external point of view and, having assimilated the patterns of modernity fulfilled elsewhere, they looked at their society "from a distance" and assessed it as underdeveloped, incapable of understanding the meaning of change, and stubborn in resistance. The personality type inherent in this attitude is best characterized by the figure of a "professional": someone who "trusts the so-called world solutions and does not consider how far they can be applied to local conditions. A principal person, but not their creator. One who believes in other people's rules and applies them uncritically" (Mikułowski-Pomorski 1999: 226). Like Oakeshott's rationalist, scholars of this kind thus place their society before the tribunal of the intellect (Oakeshott 1999) and, seeing nothing in the past but the "irrationalist scribblings of ancestors enslaved by tradition" (Chmielewski 2000: 55), seek to eliminate its remnants as a barrier to progress. The opinions, views, and attitudes they analyze are referred to as mental barriers, phobias, or stereotypes that must be exposed and eliminated.

Interestingly, Oakeshott attributes the attitude of the rationalist to people who are disenchanted, feel no ties with their society and lack familiarity with its values; these are people consumed by "a deep distrust of time, an impatient hunger for eternity and an easily revealed nervousness about everything local and transient" (Chmielewski 2002: 48). Such people are more likely to choose the path of the leftist thinker-analyst, who wants to make something new out of the existing world and therefore always moves their thoughts away from concrete existence, but not the conservative, who captures reality morphologically and wishes, as it were, to "praise being for being what it is" (Mannheim 1991: 278). People of this kind will never be able to admit what Edmund Burke believed, that "instead of casting away all our old prejudices, we cherish them to a very considerable degree, and, to take more shame to ourselves, we cherish them because they are prejudices; and the longer they have lasted and the more generally they have prevailed, the more we cherish them" (Burke 2005: 102). Sociologists of a peripheral country engaged in the process of transformation will therefore always remain "false" individualists, and not "true" ones in the sense Friedrich A. von Hayek (2018) gave to these terms, that is, those who feel a bond with the social group to which they belong and with their ancestral heritage. What deserves to be emphasized is that their preferences and the choices they make concerning society also project their attitude toward the domestic academic field, especially if it too begins to undergo intense changes: in the face of new patterns transplanted from outside, they become vulnerable by choosing either subordination or sterile declarations, and thus confirm the well-known regularity: "the revolution devours its children." The characteristics of the researcher of social change enumerated above can easily be found in the achievements of Polish sociologists of the time of transformation.

2 The Sociologist as an Old Aunt on the Couch

The point of departure for mainstream sociological reflection was the conviction expressed in a particularly vivid form by Marek Siemek, who saw the need for profound socio-economic, but also cultural changes as a simple choice between normality, rationality, and modernity on the one hand and stupidity, immaturity, and backwardness on the other hand. In his article, "On the New Europe and the East in Us," Siemek argues that

> the system of free-democratic civil society with its rule of law and enlightened culture, which has come into being in Western Europe, is the fullest realization of the modern form of humanity and socialization; "beyond" or "above" it there can be nothing that would not be a repeated fall into the chaos of stupidity, self-will, and violence.
>
> SIEMEK 2002: 333

It is easy to imagine what satisfaction the German readers of the first edition of the quoted article must have felt when a representative of the "sub-race" paid this tribute to the representatives of "the highest species of humanity," and, on top of that, in their language. However, what draws attention in Siemek's expression is not only the radical juxtaposition of Western European values and the "infantile mentality of the East," but also the certainty that modernization requires the rejection of everything that is found and the introduction of new elements in its place. There is no reference to any "third way," "equality of the Otherness of the Other," or "postmodern pluralism" – the accepted standard of occidental development gives his thinking a feature of non-alternativity and obvious finalism.

The way of reasoning presented by Siemek was widespread among sociologists, who criticized, in particular, the communitarianism, traditionalism, and religiousness of the Polish people – all of which were supposed to be a burden slowing down the desired transformations. Thus, Anita Miszalska postulated a complete "reconstruction" or even a complete "replacement" of the mental apparatus of Polish society (Miszalska 1996). Piotr Sztompka characterized two opposing types of culture in terms of the discourse: "real socialism" – collectivism, privacy, orientation to the past, reliance on fate, striving for isolation and autonomy, that is, "freedom from," inclination to mythology, and emphasis on justice and equality; and "the birth of capitalism" – individualism, openness to public affairs, orientation to the future, subjectivity, creative self-fashioning, or "freedom to," realism, and appreciation of merit and effectiveness (Sztompka 2000). Marek Ziółkowski saw the transformation as an opportunity to move from the old order described as "particularist, protective, creative, traditional, community-based, and egalitarian" to a new order seen as "universalist, market- and achievement-based, innovative, individualist, and anti-egalitarian" (Ziółkowski 2001). Thus, in their intransigent criticism, sociologists resembled an old aunt who does nothing but "sit on the couch and get it all wrong." However, the popular terms, used in various combinations, often revealed their narrow understanding and probably a rather selective reading of the works of foreign authors, who were otherwise often referred to. For instance, when it came to the issue of individualism treated as a necessary premise for political reconstruction, the conclusions derived from extensive international research were ignored. According to researchers, the ethos of competitive individualism negatively correlated with economic development, and no exception was established in this sphere (Hampden-Turner and Trompenaars 1998). The validity of these observations was also soon discovered in Poland. If in the 1990s the most important value was "essentially the ego, that is, egoistic self-realization rejecting everything that might hinder or limit it. What counts is an individual's success" (Bralczyk and Majkowska 2000: 43), it became apparent after just a few years of reforms that the individualism so strenuously promoted turned out to be an obstacle rather than a condition for creating mature capitalism. "Since the beginning of the transformation, Poland has been developing almost exclusively according to the molecular model," warned Janusz Czapiński, adding that "we are alien to communal development, for which an important condition is an adequate level of social capital" (Czapiński 2008: 62).

Unfortunately, the concept of "social capital" has been handled no better than individualism. The meaning of the term was most readily narrowed down to "associative" forms and "third sector" nongovernmental organizations (NGOs): bureaucratic institutions with a formal hierarchy, used to carry out public tasks as the state's "executive," or rather quangocrats – as Roger Scruton (2002: 54) calls them – and, contrary to their name, eager to use government funds (Szawiel 2006). Meanwhile, "second sector" organizations – not always registered, created from the bottom up in response to the immediate needs of a specific environment, and based on direct contacts – were overlooked and neglected. However, Robert Putnam, the author of the famous and oft-cited work *Bowling Alone*, explicitly emphasizes the fictitious "civic orientation" of so-called NGOs, which, according to him, are nothing more than "a failed replacement for the vanished social capital of traditional neighborhoods – sociological AstroTurf, suitable only where the real thing won't grow" (Putnam 2000: 107). Therefore, the researcher argues, it is more important to generate and multiply social capital to sit with buddies in the pub and play cards – because it is "a highly social way of spending leisure time" (Putnam 2000: 190) – than to be a member of nonprofit organizations, usually consisting only of donating an annual fee.

The momentousness and productivity of the community and family social capital in Poland was proved after February 24, 2022, when war broke out in Ukraine. Apart from a few government decisions on formal issues – assigning a personal ID number (PESEL), launching a system of allowances, or making health care and educational facilities available to refugee children – the entire burden of help was borne by Polish citizens: volunteers, people already involved in various associations or establishing cooperation among residents of one block or employees of a company, and above all, people ready to make their own homes available for foreign people and, with the support of their immediate family and neighbors, involved in organizing the daily lives of thousands of newcomers from across the eastern border. Thus, in these particular circumstances, the typical Polish "familism" turned out to be a "moral familism" as much as possible and went even beyond the framework of moral duties in many of its manifestations, since the decisions made at that time often belonged to "praiseworthy deeds," which are dealt with not by the science of morality, but by a somewhat forgotten dimension of reflection on ethics, called supererogation (Kaniowski 1999).

One more proof of the biased interpretation of fashionable terms of sociological discourse is provided by tracing the debate on trust, that category that has turned out to be an indispensable component of any understanding of social capital. As for Poland, researchers lamented over the mediocre quality of social capital and the low level of trust, which – presumably limited to relations in primary groups and blocking the establishment of external contacts – was, in their view, supposed to hinder the building of a truly civil society. While citing in their deliberations the findings in Francis Fukuyama's book with trust in its title, they did not benefit from his explanation of where exactly "good" social capital and trust come from and what guarantees their effectiveness. Still, Fukuyama argues that even in modern and rational societies, a considerable number of values is necessary, not modern by any means, but as traditional as possible, transmitted through religion and customs. As he writes: "Social capital, which is practiced as a matter of a rational habit and has its origins in 'irrational' phenomena like religion and traditional ethics, would appear to be necessary to permit the proper functioning of rational modern economic and political institutions" (Fukuyama 1995: 755). The condition for trust, in turn, according to him, is "the expectation that arises within a community of regular, honest, and cooperative behavior, based on commonly shared norms, on the part of other members of that community" (Fukuyama 1995: 74). It follows that the existence of shared beliefs and principles, especially those belonging to the broad cultural heritage of a given community, even when they do not conform to the spirit of the times, is a basic condition for the effective functioning of a group. It is also not without significance that a sense of being rooted in tradition strengthens self-esteem and makes it easier to face new challenges. The most useful thing in such situations turns out to be the nurturing of national megalomania, which, in addition to its negative side, most often emphasized by researchers, also has a huge positive meaning. Jan Bystroń, the author of a dissertation with national megalomania in its title, points out that "faith in own strength is a necessary condition for success both for individuals and for entire social groups; the maintenance of this faith among society must always be the persistent concern of its managers" (Bystroń 1935: 9). However, Polish sociologists understood their role in an utterly distinct way after 1989, persistently trying to foster attitudes of micromania and guilt among Poles and awaken complexes toward the West (Legutko 2008). In doing so, they ignored any testimony that might contradict the simplistic statements and failed to see the obvious, empirically confirmed fact that the past can be useful in building the future, and that appealing to traditionalism or communitarianism not only provides better guarantees for development, but would also allow for building a more interesting and original paradigm of transformation than the one developed in Polish sociology and pursued by the Polish elite.

Both the assumptions cited above, which speak of the need for a fundamental change, and all the resulting proposals were characterized by a similar schematism, a truly Manichean dualism and a high suggestiveness of striking contrasts, based, however, more on the rhetorical power of persuasion than on logic and scientific argumentation. The simplistic, black-and-white perception of reality used in the cited diagnoses was due, among other things, to the confusion of two plans: the ideal and the real. Concerning Western societies, textbook assumptions about the nature of ideal types were followed, while Polish society was described in terms of "real socialism." Bogdan Mach (1998) aptly calls the essence of transformation conceived in this way the model of "imitation and substitution," lamenting that it effectively supplanted reflection on other possible paths of transformation: the model of "transplantation," "recombination," or "retrogression."

The preference for a copycat model of transformation was combined with the acceptance of radical and immediate decisions. As Mach (1998: 19) notes, "economic, social, and cultural big bang was promoted as the best cure for ills." This was indeed the case: "It's now or never," argued the author of "shock therapy," Leszek Balcerowicz, in a very romantic style, stating: "You have to close your eyes and jump down, without checking either the water at the bottom or the height of the cliff" (qtd. in Kowalik 2009: 71). In line with this slogan, many sociologists pointed out that the country's significant civilizational backwardness should prompt the mobilization of forces and the earliest possible closing of the gap between Poland and Western countries: "Poland is about thirty years behind on this universal path of development compared to the most highly developed countries of Europe. There is nothing left to do but to walk this road at an accelerated pace" (Kolarska-Bobińska, Rosner, and Wilkin 2001: 12). In this kind of statement, it would be possible to find all the relics of nineteenth-century evolutionist thinking, with its Eurocentric conviction about the unilineal evolution and finalism of modernization, the optimal shape and highest level of which was supposedly achieved in Western Europe. There was also no room for the reflection that Feliks Koneczny expressed immediately after Poland regained its independence in 1918 when pondering the choice of the country's development path. In his work *Polskie Logos a Ethos* (Polish Logos and Ethos), Koneczny was skeptical both of uncritical drawing on other people's models and of accelerating the historical process, because, as he notes, "it is not necessarily desirable to have the greatest possible historical vivacity. What is desirable is such as a given society can bear" (Koneczny 1921: 55). Probably, it was precisely this kind of attitude of the elite, but also of intellectuals and sociologists, that Jan Szczepański (1999) had in mind when he defined transformation as a process of making changes in a state of trance, that is, of weakened will and clouded consciousness, and therefore – of incomplete sanity.

Sociologists formulate theoretical assumptions, but the actual course of the transformation also brings to mind the specific type of change typical of Eastern European – strictly speaking, Russian – culture, as analyzed by Juri Lotman in his book *Culture and Explosion*, which is fundamentally different from that belonging to Western European culture. The basic difference between the two boils down to the way of valuing the most essential elements that determine the order and at the same time the perception of the world. Russian culture realizes, according to Lotman, the principle of binarity – only good or evil, old or new, sinful or holy is possible there. Any change is thus seen in terms of mutually exclusive members of an alternative, and the new order must mean the destruction of the old:

> In binary systems, the explosion penetrates life in its entirety. The ruthless nature of this experiment is not immediately apparent. First of all it attracts the most maximalist layers of society by virtue of its radicalism and a poetic subscription to the immediate construction of "a new earth and a new sky." The price to be paid for such a utopia is only revealed at the next stage.
> LOTMAN 2009: 166

For Lotman, there was no doubt that after the collapse of communism, Russia went through a process of transition from traditional thinking and organizing reality, which is proper to the Russian mentality, to a ternary one. However, he saw a notable contradiction in these efforts: "the journey itself is thought of using the traditional concepts of binarism" (Lotman 2009: 171). The withdrawal from the failed historical experiment and the switch to "natural" development is thus carried out in an atmosphere of "rushing history" and "catching up" with the liberal West, but with the preservation of the previous methods, that is, the dominant role of the state. "Even when we are talking of gradual development, we want to accomplish this using explosive techniques. This, however, is not the result of some lack of thought, but rather the severe dictates of a binary historical structure," Lotman (2009: 174) concludes with dispassion. His conclusions can also be applied to the Polish situation, in which case the exposure of the traditional binary scheme of transformation aspiring to create a modern ternary system used by sociologists reveals their entrenchment in a mentality typical of Eastern culture.

A derivative of radical thinking and a sense of alienation from the society was another characteristic feature of the discourse conducted in Poland after 1989, both public and academic, namely the stigmatization of all the "transformation losers." Although it was precisely them – the large-industry workers, but also the peasants who formed the core of the "Solidarity" Independent Self-Governing Trade Union of Individual Farmers and demanded typically capitalist regulations: guarantees for individual ownership, the right of inheritance of farms, or the free circulation of land – who fought against the previous system, immediately after its overthrow they became synonymous with the relics of the old system and, ironically, began to be referred to as *homo sovieticus*. According to the intentions of the creator of the term, Alexander Zinovyev, it was intended to refer to people who were "bearers and apologists of socialist society," that is, "Soviet people" with "a relatively high level of culture and education, found among the most socially active part of the population, especially in the sphere of management, science, propaganda, culture, and education." They were all characterized by "stunning self-confidence," "pathological conceit," and "amazing narrow-mindedness," due to which they exhibited high adaptability, or, to put it in simple terms, extreme conformism. Moreover, each of them had "their share of privileges, power, and freedom," so "nobody threatened, stupefied, or morally corrupted them; rather, they did it to others" (Zinovyev 1986: 152).

Nonetheless, on the grounds of Polish sociology, this concept was significantly redefined, or rather distorted, as it began to be applied to those who were victims of the previous system, fought against it, and overthrew it. Meanwhile, as research of the 1980s showed, it was urban residents, primarily members of the Polish United Workers' Party (PUWP), rather than "Solidarity," and certainly not those associated with peasant agriculture, who declared obedience to the people's government, support for government policies, or condemnation of strikes (Adamski 1986: 525), and so it was rather to these circles that such a pejorative term should have been applied. Dawid Wildstein and Kasia Majchrowska rightly write about this distortion of reality:

> Today's Poland is a country of perverse evolutions. They are subject not only to people or institutions, but also to concepts. ... They do not serve to describe reality as neutrally as possible but are meant to stigmatize or glorify. In public debate, they usually have normative functions. It is the communities that define themselves as leftist or liberal, associated with today's ruling camp, communities that orient their ideological identity around a positive interpretation of the Round Table and the transformation, which have managed to impose new ways of defining these concepts.
> WILDSTEIN and MAJCHROWSKA 2013: 16

In other words, it was those who once again showed the appropriate flexibility and opportunism, who demonstrated the ability to adapt, as Zinovyev writes, to "any historical necessity, be it class struggle or Europeanization," that is, the true "Soviet people," who called those who did not deserve it so. The assimilation of this mechanism of interpretation falsification and manipulation by sociology shows how far scientific objectivity has been abandoned and how far the principle of "freedom from valuation" has been violated.

The process of labeling and degrading working people carried out through liberal political elites and intellectuals, but also many academics, was aptly summarized by David Ost. In his book *The Defeat of Solidarity*, the American researcher writes that in just a decade, "the undisputed vanguard of a nonviolent revolution" was considered the main obstacle to the implementation of the new order: no longer "a harbinger of the new, they were reinterpreted as a specter from the past" (Ost 2018: 37). They were categorized as "thief-beggar classes" who feel entitled, cultivate "learned helplessness" and want to live at the cost of the rest of society. It has been alleged that they have "stopped in the process of evolution to capitalist normality" (Winiecki 2001) and manifest numerous "mental barriers" (Kośmicki 2000), "irrational phobias" (Perepeczko 2000), and clear deficits in "civilizational competence" (Sztompka 1993). Criticism was levelled at the widespread lack of understanding of democracy and free market principles in Polish society, the lack of civic qualifications and "amoral familism," and especially the tendency to authoritarianism, which was supposed to make these groups the electorate of anti-democratic, populist, and fascist factions. In making these accusations, however, it was forgotten that Theodor Adorno qualified the very tendency to make such accusations as an indicator of fascist attitudes. As he writes in *The Authoritarian Personality*,

> abolition of the dole, rejection of state interference with the "natural" play of supply and demand on the labor market, the spirit of the adage "who does not work, shall not eat" belong to the traditional wisdom of economic rugged individualism and are stressed by all those who regard the liberal system as being endangered by socialism. At the same time, the ideas involved have a tinge of punitiveness and authoritarian aggressiveness which makes them ideal receptacles of some typical psychological urges of the prejudiced character. Here goes, for example, the conviction that people would not work unless subject to pressure – a way of reasoning closely related to vilification of human nature and cynicism. The mechanism of projectivity is also involved: the potentially fascist character blames the poor who need assistance for the very same passivity and greediness which he has learnt not to admit to his own consciousness.
> ADORNO 2019: 88–89

Thus, as can be seen, the language of public debate and even the terms used in scientific publications can be considered not only as a tool for describing reality – although in this case probably more as a tool for creating that reality – but also as an indicator of the views and inclinations of those who operate it.

Rural residents, especially small farmers, still known as peasants, became the object of particularly harsh and often indiscriminate attacks. Quite seriously, fears were expressed that they could become "the gravedigger of the liberal state and the market economy" (Rychard 1993: 27) and that their inherent rootedness in "ethnicity, distinct local culture, and religiosity" would "separate people from each other" and "hamper the common effort toward European citizenship" (Lamentowicz 1995: 121). For sociologists, the entire rural area was an environment marked by deep anomie and pathology: "The Polish countryside, with its destroyed village solidarity, devoid of intellectual elites, undereducated and debauched, with a disjointed system of moral values, did not meet the demands of the new times and still is unable to adapt" (Kocik 2002: 91). The Polish peasants were excluded from society by classifying them as an underclass and claiming that by the way they farmed, and the attitudes and opinions they presented, they were merely an archaic, unnecessary, and harmful relic. Thus, it was considered that they "do not fit into the structure of a given society," "are contradictory [to it]," and "do not fit into its logic" because they are stuck in an "anachronistic niche reaching deep into the past," and the very fact of their existence "is today a testimony to the backwardness of the country" (Mokrzycki 2001: 53). The researchers' diagnoses were eagerly picked up by the media, and press texts quoted statements by recognized scientific authorities: "The Polish countryside does not currently represent anything of value in terms of customs, culture, or morality. On the contrary, it is a specter of moral decay and Lumpenproletarianization" (Łagowski 2003: 17); "the clearest manifestation of the backwardness of Polish society is the high percentage of the rural population, which lives at the expense of the rest of society and is the crutch of Polish society" (Majcherek 2008: 21); "small farmers are citizens of special care, as they are unable to bear even part of their civic duties, or even to support themselves" (Solska 2010: 21); "peasants are doomed to extinction, and their days are numbered, as these people are agricultural survivors on the verge of extinction, a ticking time bomb and ballast that we should get rid of as soon as possible because there is no use for them." In this context, there appeared phrases such as "the inevitable end of the peasants" and "the annihilation of the peasants," or – more elegantly – "we no longer need the peasants" (Łazarewicz 2008: 38).

The words and terms used in both academic and media discourse, as well as the evaluation criteria behind them, belong to the conceptual apparatus of "cow sociology," as such a term was proposed by Daniel Bell to describe a discipline disposed contemptuously toward the groups studied and evaluating them solely from the point of view of economic productivity (Stachowiak 2020: 113). But the manners used during the transition period to define all "losers" were also qualified in other ways – as obvious manifestations of "hate speech" (Bukraba-Rylska 2010), "Orientalizing society" (Buchowski 2008), or "neoliberal racist discourse" (Bobako 2010). Such rhetorical strategies used means considered unacceptable in modern social sciences: they appealed to generalizations and even stereotypes, essentialized and naturalized traits attributed to a given group, and considered them permanent, culturally inherited, and innate, as it were. Adam Kuper notes that, nowadays, talking about culture often plays the role of a euphemistic reference to the no longer popular term of race (Kuper 2005: 207–208), which refers to the original understanding of this concept, defined not by anthropological, but precisely cultural factors (Balibar and Wallerstein 1991). In one form or another, this line of argumentation is meant to prove that the place allotted to certain groups and the way they are treated is as adequate as possible because of what they represent, so they have no right to expect anything more or to protest.

The frequent reference in the transformation debate to the term "ballast" leads to other, even more sinister associations. This is because it is reminiscent of the term *ballastexistenzen*, which a century ago was introduced by German scientists – internationally respected professors of law, medicine, but also economics, demography, or urban planning – who argued that this ballast, or "population surplus," should be eliminated. They included here not only the sick, disabled, or those belonging to "inferior races," such as Jews, the Romani, or Slavs but also anyone insufficiently efficient and productive who would be a burden in the ambitious project undertaken by the Third Reich to modernize the economy and society as a whole. It was the extremely economized topos of productivity, "rational" calculation and accompanying utilitarian rhetoric, and not merely racial considerations or traditional "popular" anti-Semitism, which lay at the root of the "final solution" to eliminate all the "worthless," that is, those whose cost of living outweighed their utility (Diner 2023). Such were the plans floated by "Nazi elites with academic backgrounds," those "forerunners of extermination" with the goals of economic recovery, modernization of society, and thorough modernization of the state (Peukert 1994). As can be seen, not only the language they used but also their vision of the desired changes turn out to be disturbingly close to the ambitions of Polish sociologists of the transition period. In Poland, too, proposals were formulated on how to get rid of the unnecessary "ballast." One of the ideas, of course, was not a radical project of a "final solution," but a proposal for the "last emigration." Its authors predicted that the permanent departure from the country of approximately three million peasants constituting an "unnecessary demographic surplus" and a "difficult-to-manage labor resource" would provide a major boost to the economy and a significant relief to the rest of society. It was claimed that small farmers represented "value systems and habits incommensurate with the needs of development," and were therefore "an inhibitor of modernization processes in Poland," and attempts to adapt them would only mean "incurring excessive costs that limit development opportunities" (Grabowska-Lusińska and Okólski

2009). The "last emigration" project, vividly reminiscent of the plans considered in the interwar period to relocate the Jewish population to Madagascar, was part of the logic of modern thinking, perfectly characterized by Bauman:

> Declaring that a particular category of people has no room in the future order is to say that this category is beyond redemption – cannot be reformed, adapted, or forced to adapt itself. The Other is not a sinner, who can still repent or mend his way. He is a diseased organism, "both ill and infectious, both damaged and damaging." He is fit only for a surgical operation; better still, for fumigation and poisoning. He must be destroyed so that the rest of the social body may retain its health. His destruction is a matter of medicine and sanitation.
> BAUMAN 2013: 45

3   Polish Sociologists toward Their Academic Field

The Polish sociologists also manifested a similar attitude to the public toward their discipline. Besides, disregard for native traditions and fascination with foreign innovations were by no means unprecedented. As early as 1917, Jan Stanislaw Bystroń diagnosed this permanent, as it later turned out, feature of sociology in Poland. According to him, it has "not a historical development, but a purely logical one: authors in Poland are always in living contact with foreign theories, being mostly unfamiliar with previous Polish work" (Bystroń 1995: 540). Also, during the communist period, despite the officially reigning Marxism, the prevailing attitude was to treat Western science as the leading sphere whose achievements should be assimilated and applied at home. American sociology was held in particular esteem, using the concepts of neo-positivism, social psychology, and functionalism in the middle of the twentieth century, which, combined with the survey method, gave hope for the realization of the ideal of a social science close to the universalism of the natural sciences. What was overlooked was that the dominant academic field was thus imposing its way of doing sociology on local fields, while seemingly neutral methodologies and theories promoted American values – to which perhaps only Jan Strzelecki proved to be immune – and often concealed geopolitical interests (Warczok 2016: 175). Thus, invitations to reside in the USA were eagerly accepted: selected scholars were given internships there or were employed as lecturers so that they could then promote the acquired knowledge in their home countries. It was during this period that Polish sociology, as Jarosław Kilias observed, although present in international circulation – but mainly the institutional one: organization of and participation in conferences, membership in scientific associations – actually had little scope for original scientific work, and Polish researchers were treated rather condescendingly in the West. A verbose account by Władysław Markiewicz states:

> We were treated like monkeys who speak human. Seemingly from socialist countries, seemingly Marxists, and you can talk to them. They know the issues, they know their stuff, they know us. Americans could not get out of admiration that Poles know American sociology better than many Western European sociologists.
> KILIAS 2017: 246

The sociological community assessed its situation during the transition period no differently. The best expression of this was Piotr Sztompka's polemic with Michael Burawoy. According to the Western-centric conviction expressed by Max Weber that "only in the West does science exist at a stage of development which we recognize today as 'valid'" (Weber 1992: xxviii), the Polish researcher argued as follows: Here is somewhere in the West, specifically in the USA, that "normal sociology" is being practiced – the only one that is acceptable and universally valid because it represents the highest scientific level, and the mechanisms of social change are essentially the same everywhere. Any national varieties of the discipline created in the rest of the world are therefore at best "indigenous" versions of this exemplary science. As such, they can be evaluated as "better" or "worse" mutations, but in no way are they entitled to the status of equal schools of sociological analysis. Such pipe dreams are nothing more than "anti-scientific obscurantism" (Sztompka 2011). Significantly, such a view was expressed by a researcher coming from precisely those flawed and backward peripheries, while a researcher situated in the very heart of the center and perhaps therefore able to see its limitations and deficits took a completely different view. He argued that it dealt primarily with its society, and not even all of it, since it focused its attention on its middle class, in an unauthorized way relating the assumptions and conceptual grid developed with such a fragmented and specific area to the rest of the world. Sztompka's uncritical admiration for America, including the science practiced there, was explained by the peculiarities of the Polish context, which molded his views more than he could have wished. It is simply hard to imagine, Burawoy writes, that something like this could have been written by any American author (Burawoy 2011). The myth of Western science, supposedly offering an objective and universal approach to all social phenomena, was accurately documented a few years ago by Grzegorz Zabłocki in his analysis of the "world sociology of the countryside" (Zabłocki

2014). It would be helpful if such beneficial work were done in the field of other sub-disciplines as well, exposing the baselessness of the claims made by scientists from the periphery. Otherwise, the vision of science as a competition, where the concepts created are both a tool for distinguishing oneself from others and achieving hegemony, will continue to be alien to Polish researchers, and the realistic picture outlined by Randall Collins presenting it as a space filled with people shouting, "Listen to me, listen to me!" (Collins 2014: xxi) will still prefer to substitute a hierarchical vision and be content to cry out, "We listen to you, we listen to you!"

Marked by a provincial complex, the infatuation with Western science is expressed by Polish researchers in two ways. Primarily, they do not see its obvious errors and weaknesses, noticed by representatives of other disciplines. Serious shortcomings in the American textbooks from which students learn – as it is common practice at universities there to lecture from ready-made scripts rather than construct an original course on their own (Winkin 2001) – are lamented, for instance, by historians appalled by examples such as that Piłsudski was a fascist, the Warsaw Ghetto Uprising broke out in 1943, and the Polish-Soviet War never happened. That is why lecturers at prestigious American universities need to be given special refresher courses by Polish researchers to make them aware of basic facts, such as that in the First Polish Republic, the parliament was already functioning 300 years before the USA gained independence (Rzeczkowski 2008: 8). That said, there is no shortage of similarly embarrassing displays of sheer ignorance in other fields as well, including sociology. Theodore Abel reports the misinterpretation of Weber by Talcott Parsons (Abel 1970: 167), Steven Lukes mentions the "selective misreading" of Durkheim by American social scientists (Lukes 1985: 338), Ewa Domańska points to Rorty's "thorough misinterpretation" of Gadamer (Domańska 2010: 200), while Bruno Latour (Latour 2007: 86) and Scott Lash (Lash 1994: 135–137) discuss misinterpretations of Foucault and Adorno, respectively. At this point, it is also worth briefly mentioning other embarrassing slip-ups of Western researchers: "What the professor at the Collège de France has to say about dialogicality can be called a fairy tale," writes Danuta Bakalarczyk in her review (Bakalarczyk 2011: 11). For a certain Swiss doctoral student and, to make matters worse, also for her promoter, a well-known French historian, Numa Denis Fustel de Coulanges, raptly becomes two people – Fustel de Coulanges and Numa Denis, as Antoni Mączak notes with some consternation in his book on clientelism (Mączak 2003: 86–87). On the other hand, Judith Shklar, professor of political thought at Harvard, attributes Montaigne's "Pyrrho's pig" to Pyrrhus, thereby betraying the serious shortcomings of her education (Shklar 1997: 14).

The second manifestation of the lack of skepticism toward Western science among Polish researchers is their disregard for native achievements, which are often pioneering compared to analyses by foreign authors and are even now recognized by many international authors as inspiring. After all, it was the world-famous theorist of civilization, Arnold Toynbee, and later Samuel Huntington, who used the thoughts of Feliks Koneczny, about whom hardly anyone in Poland remembers today, while in contemporary academic publications, his original name "Koneczny" is twisted and written as "Konieczny." To take another example, it was the reflection of Ludwik Fleck, the author of the concepts of "thought styles" and "thought collectives," that paved the way for Thomas Kuhn's famous concept of scientific paradigms. But ironically, it is only from foreign books that the Polish reader has a chance to learn that in today's world anthropology the interpretation of the prohibition of incest which is gaining popularity is not the cultural one proposed by Lévi-Strauss but the demographic-materialist one put forward much earlier by Ludwik Krzywicki, and that it paved the way for the now-so-important interest in "minor events," for example, in the theory of genetic drift, where the theory of natural selection is being pushed out of its hitherto privileged position (Kurczewski 2012). Furthermore, it turns out that to appreciate the novelty of the work by Franciszek Bujak, the author of numerous monographs of villages and entire counties in Poland from the early twentieth century, one also needs the perspective of a foreign researcher, since none of the Polish authors has recognized that it predates the research of the well-known French historian Philippe Ariès. Only Etsuo Yoshino, a Japanese economist fascinated by the Polish rural areas, unhesitatingly rates Bujak's studies more highly, calling them "a pioneering achievement in the field of historical demography," in addition made half a century before the Frenchman's analysis (Yoshino 1997: 9). And whose name, in particular, is mentioned in Jean-Claude Kaufmann's well-known *Ego: Pour une sociologie de l'individu*, a book that opens new perspectives in thinking about the relationship between the individual and society? The name of a researcher unknown – Kaufmann writes – after whom a few yellowed copies of a text remain in French libraries, happily translated once into French but now forgotten like its author, Edward Abramowski (Kaufmann 2001). Honestly, do Polish sociologists only have to learn from foreign publications what great authors Polish science once had? Why do they not reach out to their works, which are lying in libraries, and in addition – are written in Polish? If they had systematically read these works, developed the inspirations contained therein, and propagated them, maybe Polish science would lead the world today, and not American or French science, which, after all, uses Polish achievements. If they did so, perhaps the level of world science would also be higher because important and truly revealing ideas would take the place of the famous concepts of Beck, Giddens, Castells, and many other "public intellectuals," who, according to the prominent British sociologist John Goldthorpe, present "intellectual bluff and bluster" rather than serious achievements (Goldthorpe 2001: 115).

As a result of this negligence, the uncritical admiration for everything foreign and the completely unjustified and very harmful micromania when it comes to scientific achievements, Polish sociology is indisputably placed in the peripheral academic field, which leads to many unfavorable consequences. Primarily, the memory of indigenous traditions of research and the findings made on their basis is fading. This means not only a lack of familiarity with the methods once developed – after all, the monographic and diary methods were once considered the "showpieces" of Polish sociology in world science – but also a lack of knowledge about their society. These two circumstances make up the situation envisioned by Bujak when, on the threshold of regained independence, in his work *Nauka a społeczeństwo* (Science and Society), he deplored the fascination with other people's innovations and called for independent solutions to scientific problems. In 1920, he wrote:

> We value higher and know better the scientific work of foreign nations than our own national one. It is insufficient; one cannot effectively use only the science of other nations. It is necessary to grow it ourselves at home. A society limiting itself to drawing on foreign sources and cultural resources could not develop its individuality, but, on the contrary, would have to become part of its spiritual host and educator, would have to look at the world and itself through foreign eyes.
> BUJAK 1976: 230–231

Exactly such consequences can be observed during the transition period when Polish society began to be judged almost exclusively through the prism of the problems associated with regime change, that is, the construction of a market economy, democracy, and civic attitudes. It was then that sharp criticism emerged disparaging the resources found: Piotr Sztompka writes about "civilizational incompetence" (Sztompka 1993), Mirosława Marody tracks down "socialist residuals" (Marody 1996), Edmund Wnuk-Lipiński condemns "learned helplessness" (Wnuk-Lipiński 1996), and Maria Lewicka analyzes the popular issue of alleged "entitlement" (Lewicka 2006). The focus on these and not other issues was derived from the use of conceptual apparatus taken from abstract Western theories, such as modernization theory, and thus detached from the local context. The danger of such an approach is aptly pointed out by Maria Wieruszewska in a text devoted to current discourses on the Polish countryside:

> The desire to keep up with the "slipping world" easily absolves one from abandoning old tools and vocabularies. Seduction by fashionable concepts, so to speak, "ahead" of the empirical testimonies of the present moment, creates insufficiency. There remain undeveloped fields of former interest.
> WIERUSZEWSKA 2005: 211

Another unfavorable consequence of believing in the superiority of Western science is being satisfied with prefabricated theories and content to illustrate them with empirical data from local realities, as has been seen repeatedly. According to Daniel Płatek, Polish scientific communities

> rarely produce knowledge that contributes to this global field of sociological knowledge. Instead, they reproduce the available stock of theoretical knowledge and reinterpret it in local conditions. The work of scholars consists mainly of deduction within the framework of already existing theories. It is difficult to observe original research and theoretical contributions to the field in question.
> PŁATEK 2016: 190

The asymmetry of such a division of labor and the resulting dependence on the hegemonic center, which leads to a loss of subjectivity and autonomy by local academic fields, is also pointed out by other contributors:

> Polish social sciences, as in other countries in the region, have become mainly providers of empirical data about their own countries to Western researchers, who have taken over the entire burden of theoretical work. In other words, there is a growing – previously visible but not so strong – asymmetry in most global scientific fields between the hegemonic core monopolizing most theoretical considerations and the periphery focused on implementation work and empirical data collection.
> TURKOWSKI and ZARYCKI 2022: 291

This activity, which can be compared to filling in coloring books, does lead to the development of the discipline, but only intensively, not extensively. Indeed, many case studies are appearing, but their ambition is only to describe phenomena with the help of selected categories, not to explain them, and therefore they deserve at best to be called tourism sociography, but not real sociology. "Polish sociology stops at reproducing reality, instead of trying to explain it," Henryk Domański stresses (Domański 2006: 32), and Marek Czyżewski adds that contemporary sociology "does not critically analyze reality but handles it" (qtd. in Kaźmierska 2012: 10). This results in the risk of losing its independence in the sense pointed out by Pierre Bourdieu. Subjected to the pressure to answer all questions on social issues, sociology deals with them without having done the prior work of transforming them into sociological problems, and then the researcher becomes a tool in the hands of what they consider as the object of their thought (Bourdieu 2001: 237). However, the observed extensive development of the discipline not only means the exploitation of reality devoid of scientific ambition, but at the same time poses the risk that existing concepts will be misused, and this results in the phenomenon known as "intellectual degeneration" of research programs. Imre Lakatos understood by this term the loss of a theory's potential to predict new facts, since this ability is manifested only by "progressive" research programs. Exploitation of stagnant theories, on the other hand, leads to the fact that they only enable the absorption of facts already known, which can only be confirmed, while in the face of facts incompatible with the conceptual framework, these theories will remain immunized. At the same time, the distinction between "progressive" and "degenerating" research programs serves Lakatos as a criterion for distinguishing science from pseudoscience, and thus scientific progress from intellectual decline (Lakatos 1974: 3–4).

A third consequence of the peculiar situatedness of scientists between the central academic field and their society is the ambiguous role they must play not only in the transfer of knowledge but also in the material and financial means of acquiring it. Thus, on the one hand, even representatives of the scientific elite essentially play the role of salesmen and retailers distributing products manufactured elsewhere in their field, but on the other hand – in the face of the misery of science funding in their own country – they have to reckon with the necessity of also getting the funds for their livelihood and activities externally by conducting research, publishing articles and books, or participating in international conferences (Płatek 2016: 197), whereas this limits their ability to critically verify the concepts they use and explains their general subservience to the trends of Western science. The scientific elites in the peripheral countries thus share the fate of the intelligentsia and cultural elites by becoming part of the comprador sector performing services for the global center (Dębska 2016). Consequently, the agreement to perform such an ambiguous function influences the formulation of scientific claims that include a certain vision of society and the desired changes, accompanied – according to the adopted quasi-religious symbolism – by the identification of the "modern," accepting progress and equipped with the necessary competencies, and therefore deserving of salvation, and all "traditionalists," mentally and materially backward, and therefore doomed to damnation (Alexander 2010). However, the combination of epistemological, moral, and eschatological perspectives plays a decisive role not only in the perception and appropriate qualification of social groups but also in the evaluation of representatives of one's scientific community. The choice of specific criteria of scientific excellence dictates specific prescriptions for purging the environment of all the inefficient and unproductive and promotes academic cannibalism. An example of an idea for such a radical change in the academic field is Radosław Markowski's proposals for reforming the Polish Academy of Sciences: fire sixty to eighty percent of the current academics, about whom the world knows nothing, introduce global standards for evaluating employees, and thus, within twenty years make the institution competitive with the best in the world (qtd. in Warczok and Zarycki 2016: 211).

Therefore, a comparison of the attitude of Polish sociologists to the Polish society on the one hand and to their scientific community on the other shows notable analogies. In both cases, the fundamental impulse turns out to be a specific vision of change: progress proceeding according to universal, "mundane" principles. The example of the ideal state, the fulfillment of the "evolutionary-eschatological" perspective (Strzelecki 1989), always appears to be the Western countries, from which it is necessary to take examples to eliminate the distance that prejudices lagging. This process should proceed as quickly as possible, and all obstacles – groups formed in the old fashion and individuals thinking differently – should be eliminated. Only in this way will society and its intellectual elites become more like the West. The imitative model of political transformation thus finds its counterpart in the imitative project of remodeling the academic field, and both constructs are evidence of imitative thinking incapable of creating original ideas of their own.

The outlined picture would be too pessimistic if it were not supplemented by voices indicating that such a state of affairs is also objectionable. After all, there are opinions whose authors do not agree with the loss of sovereignty of Polish social sciences and humanities. This is particularly emphatically expressed by Ewa Domańska, who condemns "the impotence of Polish researchers to create their own theoretical approaches" and warns that

> by treating theories created in Western Europe and the USA as ready-to-use toolboxes, we carry out intellectual self-colonization, provincialize ourselves, confirming – using the language of post-colonialists – that the

center provides theories, and the periphery provides research material and case studies.

DOMAŃSKA 2012: 176

Also opposing the "imperialism of Western science" is Krzysztof Abriszewski, who calls for "epistemic patriotism," "epistemic disobedience," and practicing "slow science" (Abriszewski 2013). Their appeals turn out to be very close to the calls made in other countries as well, where demands are being made to break with postcolonial "mental subordination" and the creation of "branches of sociology from a metropolis," and instead develop "indigenous" sociologies that will not apply the perspective of the center to describe the periphery, but will propose theories which are "dirty" because of contamination with local details but remain their own theories (Connell 2007). Hints as to how these intentions can be realized are provided by Andrzej Szahaj, who admonishes the creation of "interpretive communities" capable of forming new concepts, which subsequently – through the construction of local "metrological chains" – conventionalize a given interpretation, ensure its "objectivity," and then share it (Szahaj 1997). What is at stake here is not only the autonomy of scientific disciplines but also the creation of narratives that bear the potential of giving meaning to local experiences of reality and enabling its subjective, not merely imitative, shaping by Polish society (Janion 2006). In other words, as Stanisław Brzozowski writes, it is about intellectualizing the attitudes developed in a given society to give them significance, all for the purpose of ensuring that nations, even peripheral ones, do not have to remain "nations without significance" (Brzozowski 1990). It is easy to see that the postulate of intellectual sovereignty turns out to be identical to national sovereignty. Awareness of this fact should become common among Polish sociologists.

Translated by Grupa Mowa

References

Abel, T. (1970). *The foundation of sociological theory*. Random House.
Abriszewski, K. (2013). *Kulturowe funkcje filozofowania*. Wydawnictwo Naukowe UMK.
Adamski, W. (1986). Społeczeństwo wobec władzy i polityki. In W. Adamski, K. Jasiewicz, & A. Rychard (Eds.), *Polacy '84. Dynamika konfliktu i konsensusu* (Vol. 2, pp. 461–531). Wydawnictwa Uniwersytetu Warszawskiego.
Adorno, T. W. (2019). *The authoritarian personality*. Verso.
Alexander, J. (2010). *Znaczenia społeczne. Studia z socjologii kulturowej*. Nomos.

Bakalarczyk, D. (2011). Teoria literatury i jej niewygody. *Nowe Książki, 7*, 11.
Balibar, E., & Wallerstein, I. (1991). *Race, nation, class: Ambiguous identities*. Verso.
Bauman, Z. (1999). Po co komu teoria zmiany? In J. Kurczewska (Ed.), *Zmiana społeczna. Teoria i doświadczenia polskie*. IFiS PAN.
Bauman, Z. (2013). *Modernity and ambivalence*. Polity Press.
Bendix, R. (1984). Nowe spojrzenie na tradycję i nowoczesność. In J. Szacki & J. Kurczewska (Eds.), *Tradycja i nowoczesność*. Czytelnik.
Bobako, M. (2010). Konstruowanie odmienności klasowej jako urasowianie. Przypadek Polski po 1989 r. In P. Żuk (Ed.), *Podziały klasowe i nierówności społeczne*. Oficyna Naukowa.
Bodenstedt, A. (1998). Rolnictwo Europy – wspólne dziedzictwo czy kość niezgody? In Z. T. Wierzbicki & A. Kaleta (Eds.), *Rolnictwo i wieś europejska*. Wydawnictwo Naukowe UMK.
Bourdieu, P. (2001). *Zaproszenie do socjologii refleksyjnej*. Oficyna Naukowa.
Bralczyk J., & Majkowska, G. (2000). Język mediów – perspektywa aksjologiczna. In J. Bralczyk (Ed.), *Język w mediach. Upowszechnianie Nauki – Oświata „UN-O"*.
Brzozowski, S. (1990). *Idee. Wstęp do filozofii dziejowej*. Wydawnictwo Literackie.
Buchowski, M. (2008). Widmo orientalizmu w Europie. Od egzotycznego Innego do napiętnowanego swojego. *Recykling Idei 10*.
Bujak, F. (1976). Nauki społeczne i historyczne. In F. Bujak, *Wybór pism* (Vol. 1). PWN.
Bukraba-Rylska, I. (2009). *Służebna i służalcza rola socjologii oraz inne kwestie*. Tadex.
Bukraba-Rylska, I. (2010). Współczesna kwestia wiejska: od mowy nienawiści do ostatecznego rozwiązania? In. B. Fedyszak-Radziejowska (Ed.), *Wieś i rolnictwo w debacie publicznej – stereotypy, polityka, wiarygodność*. Kancelaria Sejmu.
Burawoy, M. (2011). The last positivist. *Contemporary Sociology, 40*(4).
Burke, E. (2005). Revolution in France. In E. J. Payne (Ed.), *Burke: Select Works*. The Lawbook Exchange.
Bystroń, J. S. (1935). *Megalomania narodowa*. Towarzystwo Wydawnicze „Rój".
Bystroń, J. S. (1995). Rozwój problemu socjologicznego w nauce polskiej. In J. Szacki (Ed.), *Sto lat socjologii polskiej*. PWN.
Chmielewski, A. (2000). Racjonalizm i antyracjonalizm w filozofii politycznej. In J. Miklaszewska (Ed.), *Rozum a porządek społeczny*. Księgarnia Akademicka.
Collings, R. (2014). *Interaction ritual chains*. Princeton University Press.
Connell, R. (2007). *Southern theory: Social science and the global dynamics of knowledge*. Polity Press.
Czapiński, J. (2008). Molekularny rozwój Polski. In J. Szomburg (Ed.), *Modernizacja Polski. Kody kulturowe i mity*. Instytut Badań nad Gospodarką Rynkową.
Dębska, H. (2016). Strategia wielopozycyjności w półperyferyjnym polu prawnym. Homo academicus na rynku. In T. Zarycki (Ed.), *Polska jako peryferie*. Scholar.

Diner, D. (2023). *Beyond conceivable: Studies on Germany, Nazism, and the Holocaust*. University of California Press.
Domańska, E. (2010). *Teoria wiedzy o przeszłości*. Wydawnictwo Poznańskie.
Domańska, E. (2012). *Historia egzystencjalna*. Wydawnictwo Naukowe PWN.
Domański, H. (2006). Niektóre zagrożenia profesjonalizacji. In P. Kierzek (Ed.), *Polskie nauki humanistyczne i społeczne w nowym stuleciu i nowej Europie*. IBL PAN.
Fukuyama, F. (1995). *Trust: The social virtues and the creation of prosperity*. The Free Press.
Goldthorpe, J. (2001). *On sociology* (Vol. 1). Oxford University Press.
Grabowska-Lusińska, I., & Okólski, M. (2009). *Emigracja ostatnia?* Scholar.
Grabski, W. (2004). System socjologii wsi. In W. Grabski, *Prace socjologiczne*. SGGW.
Habermas, J. (1985). *The theory of communicative action* (Vol. 1; T. McCarthy, Trans.). Heinemann Educational.
Hampden-Turner, C., & Trompenaars, A. (1998). *Siedem kultur kapitalizmu*. Oficyna Ekonomiczna.
Hayek, F. A. (2018). Indywidualizm prawdziwy i fałszywy. In F. A. Hayek, *Indywidualizm i porządek ekonomiczny*. Aletheia.
Hessen, S. (2003). *Państwo prawa i socjalizm*. IFiS PAN.
Irzykowski, K. (1976). *Słoń wśród porcelany. Lżejszy kaliber*. Wydawnictwo Literackie.
Janion, M. (2006). Nowa opowieść humanistyki. In P. Kierzek (Ed.), *Polskie nauki humanistyczne i społeczne w nowym stuleciu, w nowej Europie*. IBL PAN.
Kaniowski, A.M. (1999). *Supererogacja. Zapomniany wymiar etyki*. Oficyna Naukowa.
Kaufmann, J.-C. (2001). *Ego: pour une sociologie de l'individu*. Nathan Université.
Kaźmierska, K. (2012). Wstęp. In K. Kaźmierska (Ed.), *Metoda biograficzna w socjologii. Antologia tekstów*. Nomos.
Kilias, J. (2017). *Goście ze Wschodu. Socjologia polska lat sześćdziesiątych XX wieku a nauka światowa*. Nomos.
Kocik, L. (2002). Anomia moralno-obyczajowa wsi polskiej. In J. Mariański (Ed.), *Kondycja moralna społeczeństwa polskiego*. WAM.
Kolarska-Bobińska, L., Rosner, A., & Wilkin, J. (2001). *Przyszłość wsi polskiej. Wizje, strategie, koncepcje*. Instytut Spraw Publicznych.
Koneczny, F. (1921). *Polskie Logos a Ethos. Roztrząsania o znaczeniu i celu Polski* (Vol. 2). Księgarnia Św. Wojciecha.
Kośmicki, E. (Ed.). (2000). *Problem barier świadomościowych na wsi wobec integracji Polski*. Akademia Rolnicza.
Kowalik, T. (2009). *Polska transformacja*. MUZA SA.
Kuper, A. (2005). *Kultura. Model antropologiczny*. WUJ.
Kurczewska, J. (1989). *Technokraci i świat społeczny*. IFiS PAN.
Kurczewski, J. (2012). Antropologia Ludwika Krzywickiego. In J. Hrynkiewicz (Ed.), *Wizjoner i realista. Szkice o Ludwiku Krzywickim*. WUW.

Kuvlesky, W. P., & Coop, J. H. (1983/1984). Rozwój wiejskiej części Ameryki: perspektywy alternatywne. *Roczniki Socjologii Wsi xx*.

Lakatos, I. (1974). Science and pseudoscience. Retrieved January 28, 2024, from https://www.inf.fu-berlin.de/lehre/pmo/eng/Lakatos-Science.pdf.

Lamentowicz, W. (1995). Obywatelstwo w integrującej się Europie. In M. Szyszkowska (Ed.), *Człowiek jako obywatel*. ISP PAN.

Lash, S. (1994). Reflexivity and its doubles: Structure, aesthetics, community. In U. Beck, A. Giddens, & S. Lash (Eds.), *Reflexive modernization*. Stanford University Press.

Latour, B. (2007). *Reassembling the social*. Oxford University Press.

Legutko, R. (2008). *Esej o duszy polskiej*. Ośrodek Myśli Politycznej.

Leszczyński, A. (MMXX). *Ludowa historia Polski*. WAB.

Lewicka, M. (2006). Fakty i mity o polskiej roszczeniowości. In K. Szafraniec (Ed.), *Jednostkowe i społeczne zasoby wsi*. IRWiR PAN.

Lotman, J. (2009). *Culture and explosion* (W. Clark, Trans.). Walter de Gruyter.

Lukes, S. (1985). *Emile Durkheim: His life and work*. Stanford University Press.

Łagowski, B. (2003). Pomyłki. *Przegląd, 1*.

Łazarewicz, C. (2008). Chłopom już dziękujemy. *Polityka, 38*.

Mach, B. (1998). *Transformacja ustrojowa a mentalne dziedzictwo socjalizmu*. ISP PAN.

Majcherek, J. (2008, June 30). Kula u polskiej nogi. *Gazeta Wyborcza*.

Mannheim, K. (1991). *Ideology and utopia: An introduction to the sociology of knowledge*. Routledge.

Marody, M. (1996). Między realnym socjalizmem a realną demokracją. In M. Marody (Ed.), *Oswajanie rzeczywistości*. ISS UW.

Mączak, A. (2003). *Nierówna przyjaźń. Układy klientalne w perspektywie historycznej*. Wydawnictwo Uniwersytetu Wrocławskiego.

Mikułowski-Pomorski, J. (1999). Niepokój a potrzeba ładu: współczesna polska transformacja wobec zmiany świadomości. In P. Sztompka (Ed.), *Imponderabilia wielkiej zmiany*. PWN.

Miłosz, C. (1999). *Zaraz po wojnie. Korespondencja z pisarzami*. Znak.

Miszalska, A. (1996). *Reakcje społeczne na przemiany ustrojowe*. Uniwersytet Łódzki.

Mokrzycki, E. (2001). Klasa z przeszłości. In E. Mokrzycki, *Bilans niesentymentalny*. IFiS PAN.

Oakeshott, M. (1999). *Wieża Babel i inne eseje*. Aletheia.

Ossowski, S. (1967). O osobliwościach nauk społecznych. In S. Ossowski, *Dzieła* (Vol. 4). PWN.

Ost, D. (2018). *The defeat of solidarity: Anger and politics in postcommunist Europe*. Cornell University Press.

Perepeczko, B. (2000). Rolnicy polscy wobec UE. In F. Kośmicki (Ed.), *Problem barier świadomościowych na wsi wobec integracji Polski z UE*. Akademia Rolnicza.

Peshkov, I. (2004). *Etatyzm i przemoc w teoriach zacofania gospodarczego*. WSB.

Peukert, D. (1994). The genesis of the "Final Solution" from the spirit of science. In T. Childers & J. Caplan (Eds.), *Reevaluating the Third Reich*. Holmes and Meier.

Płatek, D. (2016). Centra i peryferie polskiej socjologii ruchów społecznych. In T. Zarycki (Ed.), *Polska jako peryferie*. Scholar.

Poleszczuk, J. (1990). Społeczno-kulturowa geneza współczesnej socjologii empirycznej. In A. Giza-Poleszczuk & E. Mokrzycki (Eds.), *Teoria i praktyka socjologii empirycznej*. IFiS PAN.

Putnam, R. (2000). *Bowling alone: The collapse and revival of American community*. Simon and Schuster.

Rychard, A. (1993). Społeczeństwo w transformacji: koncepcje i próba syntezy. In A. Rychard & M. Federowicz (Eds.), *Społeczeństwo w transformacji*. IFiS PAN.

Rzeczkowski, G. (2008, December 15). Polska historia bez błędów. *Dziennik*.

Scruton, R. (2002). *Co znaczy konserwatyzm*. Zysk i S-ka.

Shklar, J. (1997). *Zwyczajne przywary*. Znak.

Siemek, M. (2002). O nowej Europie i Wschodzie w nas. In M. Siemek, *Wolność, rozum, intersubiektywność*. Oficyna Naukowa.

Solska, J. (2010). Obywatele specjalnej troski. *Polityka, 46*.

Stachowiak, J. (2020). *Czynnik ludzki. O cywilizowaniu uprzedmiotowienia*. Sedno.

Strzelecki, J. (1989). *Socjalizmu model liryczny*. Czytelnik.

Szacki, J. (1994). *Liberalizm po komunizmie*. Znak.

Szahaj, A. (1997). Wstęp. In A. Szahaj & T. Komendziński (Eds.), *Filozofia amerykańska dziś*. UMK.

Szawiel, T. (2006). Społeczeństwo obywatelskie i kapitał społeczny w Polsce na przełomie wieków. In A. Miszalska & A. Piotrowski (Eds.), *Obszary ładu i anomii. Konsekwencje i kierunki polskich przemian*. Uniwersytet Łódzki.

Szczepański, J. (1999). *Reformy, rewolucje, transformacje*. IFiS PAN.

Sztompka, P. (1993). Civilizational incompetence: The trap of post-communist societies. *Zeitschrift für Soziologie 22*(2).

Sztompka, P. (2000). *Trauma wielkiej zmiany. Społeczne koszty transformacji*. ISP PAN.

Sztompka, P. (2011). Another sociological utopia. *Contemporary Sociology, 40*(4).

Turkowski, A., & Zarycki, T. (2022). Od paradygmatu zależności do neoliberalizmu. Niedostrzeżona rewolucja w polskim polu nauk społecznych. In T. Zarycki (Ed.), *Polskie nauki społeczne w kontekście relacji władzy i zależności międzynarodowych*. WUW.

Wallerstein, I. (1999). *The end of the world as we know it: Social science for the twenty-first century*. University of Minnesota Press.

Warczok, T. (2016). Globalne pole nauk społecznych a socjologia polska. In T. Zarycki (Ed.), *Polska* jako peryferie. Scholar.

Warczok, T., & Zarycki, T. (2016). *Gra peryferyjna. Polska politologia w globalnym polu nauk społecznych*. Scholar.

Weber, M. (1992). *The protestant ethics and the spirit of capitalism*. Routledge.
Wieruszewska, M. (2005). Współczesne dyskursy na temat wsi i rolnictwa – główne osie sporu. In P. Kowalski (Ed.), *Polacy o sobie. Współczesna autorefleksja: jednostka, społeczeństwo, historia*. Oficyna Wydawnicza Stopka.
Wildstein, D., & Majchrowska, K. (2013). Obywatelska Polska "B." *Kontakt, 24*.
Winiecki, J. (2001). Historia polskiego marginesu. *Rzeczpospolita, 303*.
Winkin, Y. (2001). *Anthropologie de la communication: De la théorie au terrain*. Éditions du Seuil.
Wnuk-Lipiński, E. (1996). *Demokratyczna rekonstrukcja. Z socjologii radykalnej zmiany społecznej*. Wydawnictwo Naukowe PWN.
Yoshino, E. (1997). *Polscy chłopi w XX wieku. Podejście mikrodeskryptywne*. Semper.
Zabłocki, G. (2014). Od światowej socjologii wsi do polityki wobec nauk społecznych i humanistyki. *Wieś i Rolnictwo, 1*(162).
Zinovyev, A. (1986). *Homo Sovieticus*. Grove/Atlantic.
Ziółkowski, M. (2001). Tendencje zmian w podstawowych sferach życia społecznego. In E. Wnuk-Lipiński & M. Ziółkowski (Eds.), *Pierwsza dekada niepodległości*. ISP PAN.

CHAPTER 4

Postcolonial Parallels, Global Entanglements, and Practices of Decolonization: Varieties of Postcolonial Discourses on Poland

Joanna Wawrzyniak and Małgorzata Głowacka-Grajper

> It is no doubt that there is, on this planet, not a single square meter of inhabited land that has not been, at one time or another, colonized and the postcolonial.
>
> MOORE 2001: 113

> The notion of postcolonial theory has been floating around the Polish intellectual scene for the last ten years like a colorful balloon that nobody can ever quite capture or claim.
>
> BILL 2014: 1

1 Introduction

Recent years have seen a resurgence of interest in postcolonial discourses in Central and Eastern Europe (CEE). The actors in the debates are diverse and include conservative politicians, progressive activists, heritage practitioners, public intellectuals, and so forth. The contexts of reference to postcolonialism and decolonization are as different as the full-scale Russian invasion of Ukraine, right-wing governments' political negotiations with Brussels, the Black Lives Matter movement, a new historiography of serfdom, nineteenth-century empires, and the Polish-Lithuanian Commonwealth. The opening quotes from Africanist David C. Moore and UK-based Slavist Stanley Bill draw attention to the existence of a profound disagreement on postcolonialism among scholars of the region and beyond. While a growing number of authors see CEE as an area affected by internal colonization(s) or are eager to reconceptualize this region's history within a global (post)imperial framework, others claim that scholars have overstretched and overused postcolonial theory, rendering it unable to add any further value to discussions on the region's past, present, and future. Instead of taking a definite stance in this discussion, this chapter differentiates several existing approaches that use the terms "(post)colonial" and "decolonial" in relation to Poland and CEE to highlight the differences in their overall perspectives. Poland shares with other CEE countries the sense of in-betweenness (Kubik 2019) and inter-imperiality (Parvulescu and Boatcă 2022), resulting from being part of the projects of several historical empires. Poland's own imperial aspirations give another reason for implementing postcolonial categories for researching its past and present relations with neighboring nations and minority groups. These different experiences with imperial practices have, in turn, contributed to a variety of postcolonial discourses.

In this chapter, we present different ways of looking at the case of Poland as a CEE country in the context of postcolonial studies. By reviewing the literature written over the last three decades, we examine how researchers apply and transform concepts related to postcolonialism to interpret the history of Poland and its current sociopolitical and cultural condition. We identified three main approaches in which scholars use these concepts: *colonial parallels, global entanglements*, and *decolonial practices*. The first perspective posits that CEE societies underwent *similar* processes to those of Europe's overseas colonies. Such canonical authors in the global field as Frantz Fanon, Edward Said, Dipesh Chakrabarty, Gayatri Chakravorty Spivak, Leela Gandhi, Homi K. Bhabha, and Robert Young have inspired postcolonial approaches to CEE. Following the publication of their works, the researchers of CEE began to apply arguments by *analogy*, using concepts such as orientalization, altering, resistance, delegitimization, and hybridization to their region of interest. In terms of Poland's geographical location, it is possible to identify the analogy argument in at least three colonizing forces: the West (specifically, German-speaking countries and, in general, European/global modernity), the East (Russia and the Soviet Union), and Poland itself. The second perspective, which is pursued by historians today, places CEE within a broader, global framework of colonization and decolonization processes. Some scholars "go beyond noting parallels between colonialism and Nazism and … [have] begun to chart the material and discursive means of transmission that link them" (Rothberg 2009: 104). Others study various connections between the decolonized world and the Soviet Union and its satellites. Both perspectives help to draw attention to processes overshadowed by more conventional notions used by the historiography of the region, such as partitions (of nineteenth-century Poland), foreign occupations, nation-building, totalitarianism, the concept of "Second World," (post)Cold War, transformation, (post)communism, (post)socialism, and others. Finally, the decolonial perspective focuses on practices aimed at implementing political, social, and cultural transformations beyond the dichotomies of the postcolonial approach. Overall, the chapter offers a road map that should enable researchers to find their way through a tangle of discourses on Poland's postcolonial condition that are simultaneously international and local, academic and public, and descriptive and normative.

2 (Post)colonial Parallels

One of the key components of the postcolonial paradigm is criticism of Eurocentrism (McLennan 2003). However, this narrative presents a tacit assumption of Europe as a self-evident and coherent geographical entity that exercised colonialism outside its borders. Scholars first applied postcolonial categories to relations between European countries in regard to Ireland, portrayed as the subject of the colonial practices of Great Britain (Cavanagh 2004). Scholars found this concept of European internal colonization useful when describing and analyzing the situation of the CEE countries after the collapse of the Soviet Union (Stefanescu 2013). Observers sometimes saw the differences between postcolonial and postsocialist situatedness as an obstacle to applying the postcolonial paradigm. Responding to those challenges, Radim Hladik proposed to see postcolonial theory as a traveling one:

> The similarity or dissimilarity of post-colonial and post-socialist contexts seems to depend more on the perspective and the level of abstraction adopted by a theoretician than on the substantive identity of social, political, or cultural elements. ... If, however, we admit that a theory can ... move from one particular place and historical constellation to another, the differences are no longer insurmountable nor something to be minimized.
>
> HLADIK 2011: 578–579

Taking into account the complex history of the region, the postcolonial approach broadened its focus on the Soviet Union also in relation to the imperial powers such as Tsarist Russia, Bismarckian and Nazi Germany, the Ottoman Empire, and Austria-Hungary. Scholars argued that these empires pursued colonial policies *inside* Europe, and those affected by their politics are examples of postcolonial subaltern groups. Terms such as Germany's "adjacent colonialism" (Nelson 2009), a "subaltern empire" (Morozov 2013), Russia's internal class-based colonization (Etkind 2011), Poland's "impressive post-colonial credentials" (Cavanagh 2004), the "self-colonising cultures of Eastern Europe" (Kiossev 1999; Sowa 2011), "the interface periphery" (Zarycki 2011), the "internal periphery" (Zarycki 2016) or the notion of Ukraine as an "inner colony" and its "post-colonial syndrome" (Riabczuk 2015) have now permanently entered the academic discourse of CEE. In the last decade, the literature has been growing exponentially, especially in the Baltic states, Ukraine, Balkan countries, Poland, Czechia, and Russia (see Hladik 2011: 582–583), engaging representatives of different disciplines (including literary scholars, sociologists, anthropologists, cultural theorists, Slavists, and historians).

Public and academic debates point to differences in the definitions of the phenomenon of "internal European colonization." These depend on the colonizer under investigation. For example, while Bulgaria was grappling with the influence of the Ottoman Empire, it saw in Russia a European country that could support it during its struggle with a colonizer that was more distant in terms of culture and religion. By contrast, other societies looked to Western Europe for support against Russia. Russia itself was both a colonizer and a subject to Western Europe's colonial (primarily cultural, but also economic) influence. Among several empires that conquered and controlled CEE throughout hundreds of years of its history, the Habsburg empire's "colonial" status seems to be the most questionable. However, even in this case, scholars are paying attention to the new possibilities that the postcolonial perspective opens in research on various regions of the empire, such as Galicia (Kaps and Surman 2012) or the Balkans (Bobinac 2014; Rexhepi 2018). Focusing on internal European colonization should not obscure the fact that although we may perceive CEE as a region shaped by imperial conquests, it has also played a role in overseas colonization. At various times, Prussian, Russian, Austrian, or even Polish or Czech cultural and political elites had either conquered and exploited non-European territories or had fantasies to do so (Feichtinger, Prutschand, and Csáky 2003; Kałczewiak and Kozłowska 2022), which further complicates the analysis of the already complex colonial and postcolonial practices. In the case of Poland, it is possible to distinguish three (sometimes interrelated) areas of study for applying postcolonial categories: colonization by the West, colonization by Russia/Soviet Union, and the colonial practices of Poland itself.

2.1   *The West as the Colonizer*

The canonical book in this field is Larry Wolf's *Inventing Eastern Europe* (1994). Echoing Said (1978), for whom Orientalism was, above all, a web of discursive practices through which the West constructed the East, Wolf examined the Enlightenment vision of the world and claimed that at that time the North-South divide which separated the "savage" from the "civilized" was complemented by a new cultural construct: the East-West divide, similarly tainted by dichotomies such as civilization-barbarity, culture-nature, cleanliness-dirtiness, laziness-industriousness, and others. Several authors later followed and nuanced Wolff's ideas, one of them being Maria Todorova (1997), who wrote an exceptionally successful book on the Balkans.

Similarly, several research projects have sought the Enlightenment roots of the German concept of *Mitteleuropa*: "a space between East and West ... for conversion, civilization, modernization, while its inhabitants, who were basically different, foreign half-animal, would be the objects of a humanizing operation" (Neuger 2007: 25). In the Polish case, German-speaking countries have always been the main colonizing Western "other" (Kopp 2012). "All the hallmarks of the new imperialism of the nineteenth century, as well as both its more murderous and more informal manifestations in the twentieth century, exist in the history of Germany and Eastern Europe" claims Robert Nelson (2009: 6–7), adding that one needs no "salted sea between Berlin and Warsaw" to see another chapter of colonialism. Taking such a perspective as a point of departure, several authors have depicted how German cultural chauvinism of the nineteenth century evolved into the extreme version of biological racism associated with the twentieth century and how CEE became a colonial space and laboratory for Nazi social and racial experiments (for summaries, see Nelson 2009; Surynt 2006; Keim 2014; more can also be found in the section on entanglements in this chapter).

A branch of postcolonial theory, cultivated by critical humanities and social sciences that complemented "postsocialist"/"post-Soviet" studies, depicted the consequences of the pivotal year of 1989 on the history of CEE in quite a distinct manner. Although different groups of scholars developed this approach, it still engaged with the way of imposing the notion of Western modernity on the region. In particular, it characterized the situation of "transition" societies – evolving from socialism to capitalism and dictatorship to democracy – as "postcolonial" due to the teleological, modernizing, and globalizing neoliberal tendencies that enjoyed a hegemonic position in the region at the time and also today (see Kušić, Lottholz, and Manolova 2019). Observers have also referred to the situation of CEE societies as "neocolonial" due to the influence of international organizations such as the International Monetary Fund, World Bank, NATO, and the European Union that advocated liberalization, democratization, and marketization in the region. These concepts, focused on the "colonial oppressor–victim" dichotomy, were so popular that they also became attractive for a nationalist reading of the postcolonial theories. As Kołodziejczyk and Huigen state: "postcolonial concepts have become in some cases tools legitimating right-wing populist politics, providing the vocabularies of decolonisation, of a national insurgency against the hostile hegemony of the West, of the deprivation of national agency resulting in a domination by hegemonic states within the EU" (2023: 22).

These critical studies claimed that neo-Oriental figures dominated international discourse and "creolized" local elites, who became exponents of "the West." However, such observations were also omnipresent in the "postcolonial nationalism" of some Polish scholars dealing with the concepts of postcolonialism (Uffelman 2020) and were sometimes echoed by the conservative right in different countries of the region. From this perspective, local intellectual traditions were erased in favor of international English-speaking cultures, and this whole process contributed to the orientalization and the downgrading of those who were the biggest losers of the transition, in particular, the poor, the unemployed, and the "civilizationally incompetent," leading to the circulation of patronizing figures of speech and dichotomies such as "modern-backward" (Buchowski 2004; Buchowski 2006; Csepely, Örkény, and Scheppele 1996).

The concept of "self-colonizing cultures" emerged during the development of this critical discourse. The concept attempted to investigate "colonial influences" on CEE while accommodating the local ideologies that social conditions fueled internally. An excellent example of such an analysis is a book by a Polish sociologist, Jan Sowa, who attempts to show the modernizing influence that colonizers – be they German speakers or Russians – had on the Polish economy and society. At the same time, he perceives Polish self-identification with the West as a form of self-colonization that becomes a choice for societies devoid of their own cultural or social accomplishments (Sowa 2011). Concepts of self-colonization may also be traced in the works of scholars from other CEE countries (Kiossev 1999) and Russia (Morozov 2013).

2.2 Russia/the Soviet Union as the Colonizer

For decades, Russia/the Soviet Union has been absent from postcolonial studies of imperial colonizers. Madina Tlostanova, a scholar specializing in decolonization in Eurasia, explained why these empires fail to appear in the mainstream postcolonial paradigm:

> Most decolonial thinkers ... equated modernity with capitalism and Christianity with Catholicism and Protestantism. The rivalry with the empires of lighter weight categories (non-capitalist, non-Christian, or with a "wrong" Christianity, alphabetically non-Latin, non-modern, and non-European or questionably modern and European) such as Russia or the Ottoman Sultanate – was beyond the interest or competence of most decolonial thinkers. The Soviet and post-Soviet experience tinted with characteristically ideological deceptions only added to the decolonial

> reluctance to venture into analyzing Eurasia, especially that some of decolonial theorists had decidedly Marxist origins and refused to see the Soviet Union as a colonial empire, while others tended to see Russia and the Soviet Union as a blurred zone of semi-periphery or even a colonial zone comparable to India and Latin America and not to Britain or Spain.
>
> TLOSTANOVA 2015: 270–271

Today, scholars point out that Tsarist Russia and the Soviet Union as (an) imperial power(s) colonized not only CEE but also parts of Southeast Europe, Eurasia, and the borderlands of Transcaucasia. In the case of nineteenth-century Russia, researchers draw colonial analogies, such as the acquisition of territory; exercising military power; subordination of local administrations to a metropolitan power; limited or absent political rights of populations settled on the acquired territories; boosting colonial settlements with special privileges for colonists; economic exploitation of natural and human resources; industrial and agricultural specialization at the behest of a metropolitan power; the dominant position of the Russian language; orientalist, racist or patronizing attitudes towards local populations; resistance to Russian control and the cooperation of local elites; turning different ethnic and political groups against each other according to the principle of "divide and rule"; and also some positive contributions to healthcare and education (e.g. Carey and Raciborski 2004; Thompson 2000; 2010; Tlostanova 2010, 2015).

In his nuanced study of Poland's place in nineteenth-century imperial Russia, German historian Malte Rolf (2014) focuses on the circulation of ideas and practices between the center and the empire's periphery. In his view, Poland became a laboratory in the Western part of the empire for modern administrative practices that penetrated the inner empire and supported the consolidation of its bureaucracy. Rolf uses this example to argue against the sweeping generalizations of oversimplified colonial analogies. Instead, he proposes to apply a multiple modernities perspective. He shows that, on the one hand, as was the case with other European colonial powers, knowledge and practices acquired from the Polish periphery influenced the Russian metropolis. On the other hand, in stark contrast to the situation of other European overseas territories, Poland was Russia's "window on the West," and some modernization processes reached the Romanov Empire via its Polish periphery. These trends also had their opponents in Moscow and Saint Petersburg, where the struggle against Polish ideas inspired by Latin Europe strengthened the position of those who supported Russia's own civilizational project and its distinct developmental path (see also Buruma and Margalit 2004; Kola 2004).

A recurring perception of Imperial Russia's successor, the Soviet Union, is of a colonial power that concealed its colonial ambitions behind a "smokescreen" of progressive ideology and the support it granted to decolonization movements in Asia, Africa, and Latin America. In fact, the Soviet empire reinforced tendencies such as Russification; exploitation of non-Russian republics and peoples; domination of countries in CEE; deportations and ethnic cleansing; forced labor and crimes against indigenous people (see Kolarz 1952; Korek 2007; Stefanescu 2012; Tlostanova 2012, 2017). Carey and Raciborski (2004) identified several types of Soviet colonialism: classical colonies in Central Asia, which witnessed brutal suppressions of Muslim communities; inner colonies comprising two subgroups: the Transcaucasian and the European republics (the Baltic States, Belarus, Ukraine, and Moldova); and semi-colonies, i.e. Soviet satellites in Central and Eastern and Southeastern Europe. On this basis, they argued that the overall effects of the transition from socialism differed in different parts of the empire due to historical and political-institutional path dependencies.

However, regardless of crucial differences, the decay and fall of the Soviet Union, much like the fall of other colonial empires, unleashed processes such as anti-colonial nationalism (facilitated by the preceding Soviet-sponsored development of limited nationalism among various groups), revolutions in power and social structures, tendencies favoring "the rule by law rather than the rule of law" combined with low levels of trust towards the state as well as judiciary institutions and politicians (Carey and Raciborski 2004). One important indirect outcome of the empire's fall has been a specific memory of "colonialism and decolonization" and the way it affects contemporary cultural and political identities. In countries like Poland or the Baltic states, public memory preserves mainly negative representations of imperial Russia and the Soviet Union (Kalnačs 2020). The political and cultural realms have often seen attempts to silence the stories of the cohabitation and collaboration of Russians with local societies (Carey and Raciborski 2004; Zarycki 2004).

In Poland, sociologists point out that one of the legacies of Soviet times was the image of Russia as a country of supposed inferiority. The capitalist and democratic milestone of 1989 enabled the Polish public discourse to exploit Russia as a point of reference that smooths over Polish shortcomings, a trend which Tomasz Zarycki summarizes as follows: "the key role of Russia in Polish political discourse directed both at the foreign and internal public is that of rescaling of Poland's weaknesses. Russia serves as the key reference criterion, allowing [participants in the Polish political discourse] to reduce the scope of their own problems while at the same time not hiding or forgetting them. ... This comparison of weakness ... plays an important role both in strengthening the self-confidence of Poles in their confrontations with foreigners as well as in healing their frustrations at home." (Zarycki 2004: 599–600). Such an approach presents Russia in a manner typical of the orientalist approach described by Edward Said, that is, as an undifferentiated "Other" that is civilisationally inferior, wild, and unpredictable (Cobel-Tokarska 2021).

The category of colonialism referring to Russia's imperial policy, such as "the post-imperial resentment" (Morozov 2015), has become particularly relevant after Vladimir Putin started the war in Ukraine in 2014 and expanded it into a full-scale invasion in February 2022 (Barkavi 2022; Korolov 2023; Mälksoo 2023). Researchers dealing with Ukraine, but also representatives of Ukrainian society, began to define the situation of this country in post-colonial terms on an extended scale (Gerasimov 2014; Törnquist-Plewa and Yurchuk 2019; Eppinger 2022). They developed the notion of Ukraine as a "double subaltern" (Korablyova 2022) and conducted studies searching for parallels between Ukraine and other European colonized nations (Velychenko, Ruane, and Hrynevych 2022). The field of culture and social life saw many attempts to decolonize Ukraine by rejecting Russian and Soviet symbols, monuments as well as literary and artistic works (Betlii 2022). Today, Ukrainian scholars make the most significant contributions to (post)colonial and (post)Soviet studies.

2.3 *Poland as the Colonizer*

Another (post)colonial approach relates to Poland's imperial ambitions. It makes Poland an example of a *multilevel colonial situation* – not only was it a state colonized by neighboring empires, but it was also a colonizer to groups living in its eastern borderlands. During the Early Modern Era, when it was at the peak of its territorial development, the Polish-Lithuanian Commonwealth covered the greater part of today's Baltic states, Belarus, Ukraine, and parts of Russia. That makes Poland not only a subject of orientalization pursued by the West but also an orientalizing actor towards its neighboring Ottoman Empire and other nations within the Russian Empire:

> For several hundred years the Polish-Lithuanian Commonwealth bordered the Ottoman Empire and was involved in the process of cross-border cultural exchange. Imperial Russia developed a means of colonizing "its" Orient by conquering and managing the Crimea, the Caucasus, Central Asia, and Siberia. In that sense, both Poland and Russia were simultaneously "perpetrators" and "victims" of Orientalist debates on Easternness, and both emerged as complex case studies that afford us better insight into the intricacies of European Orientalism.
>
> KAŁCZEWIAK AND KOZŁOWSKA 2022: 5

Moreover, historians point to the internal colonization in the sense of a serfdom-based economy and claim that divisions of its social structure among the gentry and peasants, and the cultural effects of these divisions were similar to those of the slave economies of colonial powers (Leszczyński 2022; Gliński 2015). They also stress the orientalization or forced Polonization of various minorities, in particular, the Ruthenians, Belarusians, Ukrainians, and Jews (see Fiut 2003; Bakuła 2006; Mayblin et al. 2016). The Commonwealth and the Second Polish Republic's acquisition of space and employment of cultural and racial stereotypes accompanied the propagation of the myth of Poland's exceptionality as a bulwark of Christian civilization and the defender of Europe against the Ottoman Empire or the Bolsheviks. The country's expansion to the East has contributed to the popular (until today) mythic notion of the Polish Eastern Borderlands (Kresy). The notion contains different and often conflicting images such as, on the one hand, Kresy as a zone of contact with enemy forces and a site for the forging of a heroic Polish-Catholic identity and, on the other, a nostalgic Polonocentric vision of Kresy as a land of peaceful co-existence among various ethnic and religious groups under the allegedly tolerant roof of the multinational Commonwealth and the Second Polish Republic (Zarycki 2014).

In addition, the cultural and political elites of the end of the nineteenth century, and particularly those of the Second Polish Republic, contributed to the circulation of fantasies of Poland acquiring colonies in Africa (Kowalski 2010) or teaching various Muslim countries "how to build a European state" (see Borawski and Dubiński 1986). In the interwar period, Poland, like other countries in the region, tried unsuccessfully to enter the global balance of power as a holder of overseas colonies (Puchalski 2022). This occurred as a form of compensation for the fragility and poverty of the Second Polish Republic (Kałczewiak and Kozłowska 2022: 8). Revealing these tendencies deprives Poland of "colonial innocence" (Rampley 2021) and indicates the internalization of thinking by its elite in colonial terms about their Europeanness and relations with others (Kałczewiak and Kozłowska 2022: 8).

Scholars increasingly use the postcolonial perspective to revise, deconstruct, and historicize national myths present in culture and social behavior. The perspective calls for a critical and deconstructive approach to national historiography and public history (Nakoneczny 2020) and proposes an alternative to the topoi of Poland as an eternal victim of German or Russian colonialism. Within this discourse, Poland has been depicted as imitating the colonization practices of other states while internalizing the orientalizing gaze of the West, being subjugated to Russian military supremacy and tending to transfer its inferiority complex to the lower strata (Zarycki 2008) or other ethnicities, in particular, Jews, Belarusians, and Ukrainians (see Bakuła 2011; Borkowska 2007; Gosk 2008; Sowa 2011; Snochowska-Gonzalez 2012; Zarycki 2013).

3 Global Entanglements

Global historians have helped elaborate on the second central perspective of seeing Poland in reference to colonialism. This perspective concentrates on actual, historical *entanglements* between Eastern Europe and other parts of the world rather than on their postcolonial analogies. This recent literature follows many earlier intuitions, such as those exposed by Hannah Arendt in *The Origins of Totalitarianism* (1951) and Aimé Césaire in *Discourse on Colonialism* (1955[2000]) about the precursive role that imperialism in Africa played in the rise of National Socialism and the Holocaust (Sznaider 2022); or by W. E. B. Du Bois in his essay on *The Negro and the Warsaw Ghetto* (1952), in which he revised his idea of the "color line" to accommodate all instances of racial segregation, which, for him, was the main problem of the twentieth century. As Michael Rothberg (2009: 101) opined, "it has taken scholars half a century to catch up to these early insights."

One of the most active recent proponents of the thesis on the direct links between German colonial expansion in Africa and Eastern Europe is German scholar Jürgen Zimmerer. In numerous texts, including a book bearing the telling title *From Windhoek to Auschwitz* (2011), Zimmerer claims that the Holocaust and CEE historians tend to overlook the lasting backdrop to the Nazi policies created by a purported need for *Lebensraum* in Eastern Europe. By pointing to such background in the colonial practices of the Wilhelmine Period, he shows how the rise in popularity of global geography in the late nineteenth century accompanied colonial projects, which, in turn, provoked growing interest in and enthusiasm for colonial expansion (Zimmerer 2004a). By highlighting the continuities of ideas, practices, and people, Zimmerer underlines the extent to which the concept of space – especially in relation to race – was key to both German colonialism in Africa and Nazi imperial strategies in Eastern Europe. The space won through "the discovery and conquest had to be developed and civilized and made ready for the settlers." Above all, Zimmerer points to connections between the genocidal aspects of both projects. The Herero and Nama genocide in German South West Africa (1904–1908) was German imperialism's first attempt at practicing methods of mass killing and dehumanization. The Holocaust became the largest genocidal atrocity, but it was not without precedent, as other ethnic groups had also fallen victim to "dual legal systems" that separated colonizers from the colonized based on racial criteria.

The key to Zimmerer's argument is that the Third Reich's policies in the East were neither analogous with nor sought to emulate the conquests of the Americas, Australia, Asia, or Africa by Europeans. Instead, they were a radicalized variant of these conquests based on bureaucratic organization and the involvement of the state apparatus. According to Zimmerer, "The German war against Poland and the USSR was without doubt the largest colonial war of conquest in history" due to the number of people and resources mobilized, people murdered, and the sheer size of the envisaged empire, which was to reach far beyond the Ural Mountains. After all, Hitler said "The Russian territory is our India" (Zimmerer 2004b: 49). Although Zimmerer received criticism for not giving enough evidence to his claims about connectivities between German colonization in Africa and the Nazi genocidal policies in CEE, several other authors have been independently pursuing a similar course with a research focus on different aspects of the Nazi colonial empire and German administrative and military culture (Lower 2005; Hull 2005).

Another research venue is the linkages between various post-imperial independence movements. For instance, Mark and Slobodian (2018) believe that the CEE, in a sense, led the way in decolonization processes that followed the fall of empires after the First World War. They observed that "the very term 'decolonization' was first used in English in the 1930s to connect the already-achieved independent state in Eastern Europe with an argument about the inevitability of the liberation of nations in Africa and Asia in the near future" (2018:2).

Authors studying various forms of socialism and postsocialism have developed yet another type of entanglement argument. In the foundation article, anthropologists Sharad Chari and Katherine Verdery (2009) called for the liberation of "the Cold War from the ghetto of Soviet area studies and postcolonial thought from the ghetto of Third World and colonial studies." They proposed the rejection of both terms – "postsocialism" and "postcolonialism" – in favor of working on a single broader framework enabling the exploration of the effects of Cold War ideology worldwide:

> Not only were Eastern Europe and much of the former Soviet Union under a form of colonial domination, but numerous other "Third World" countries – Cuba, Mozambique, Ethiopia, South Yemen, Laos, and so on – had entered the Soviet orbit as part of establishing their independence from one or another western imperial power. To think about these geopolitical peripheries with tools from both postcolonial and postsocialist

studies enables thinking critically about colonial relationships together with market and democratic transitions.
CHARI and VERDERY 2009: 12

The team behind the project "Socialism Goes Global: Cold War Connections Between the 'Second' and 'Third Worlds,'" led by British historian James Mark, shared similar concerns. The focal point of this project was the position of the socialist bloc in the decolonization processes of the second half of the twentieth century. The scholars gathered around Mark traced the Soviet empire's double life. One life was represented by reinstating the colonizing pattern prevailing in Tsarist Russia; the other was evident in the support the Soviet Union granted to the liberation tendencies of the Third World. By the mid-1970s, a period of global appeasement enabled greater cooperation between socialist and capitalist states on various projects in Africa and the Middle East, influencing new international entanglements. The project traced multiple links between the Global South and Eastern Europe and Eurasia with regard to the circulation of ideas, people, capital, and goods (Mark, Kalinovsky, and Marung 2020). In a similar vein, historians and sociologists showed how, in socialist Poland, politicians, journalists, writers, literary critics, historians, and the reading public were both fascinated with decolonization processes and contributed to those processes (Kola 2018; Mazurek 2018).

4 Decolonial Practices

As a term and an approach, "decolonization" merits a separate discussion from the abovementioned perspectives on analogies and entanglements. Madina Tlostanova (2019) argues that "postcolonialism" primarily refers to a post-dependent situation, while "decolonization" refers to the agency of social actors who are dealing with the consequences of this situation. Thus, decolonization usually connotes some sort of political, cultural, or social action/practice, but the term has different associations. Among the most frequent are decolonization movements for national independence, on the one hand, and cultural practices of heritage decolonization, on the other. Often, they only have loose links with each other. Notably, the current wave of decolonizing museums encompasses requests ranging from returning cultural artifacts to former colonies, working on new "relational ethics" between those colonies and former centers, to changing the Eurocentric, white-centric museum narratives which for years have disregarded the sensitivities of non-elite, non-white members of increasingly multicultural European societies (e.g. Ariese and Wróblewska 2021; Sarr and Savoy 2018; Sieg 2021; Lehrer and Wawrzyniak 2023).

The situation in Poland can serve as a reflection of both. As discussed in previous sections, Poles have historically fought for independence, but they have also colonized other nations. Along with a group of co-authors, one of us analyzed critical artistic projects in Poland to develop the notion of the "duality of decolonization." This concept refers to the cultural practice that addresses the legacies of foreign dependencies while also destabilizing nationally framed "memory regimes" that have emerged as a result of those dependencies. A dual decolonial approach can serve as a critical heuristic tool for studying examples from the CEE region and beyond. We can apply this approach to cases where the nationalistic framing of heritage and memory is the default decolonial response to the fall of empires and their aftermaths (Bukowiecki, Wawrzyniak, and Wróblewska 2020).

Yet, the question arises of whether the application of the "(de)colonial approach" to the region does not equate to "colonizing the minds" of its inhabitants with categories and assumptions developed elsewhere. It is also worth remembering that the colonial worldview also exists in the language of post-colonialism, as Ashar notes:

> The decolonial project, having found expression in nationalist movements, in political and epistemic resistance, and in reform and revival, nevertheless continues to be undertaken in the language of coloniality. This language – one in which we continue to attempt to make sense of ourselves and fight our silent battle against coloniality – is a problematic one. It not only facilitates a regeneration of the discourses of coloniality but also is otiose and obscures all that resides outside of the imperial worldview.
>
> ASHAR 2015: 263

In response to this type of criticism, in some theoretical formulations, the "decolonial option" transgresses postcolonial discourses, breaking away from them in its quest to establish a new balance of power (Mignolo 2011). As Tlostanova notes, "The advantages of the decolonial option in this respect lie in its radical conceptual stance, given the way that it touches upon and destabilizes the very mechanisms of knowledge production and institutional assumptions in an attempt to shift the geography of reasoning" (Tlostanova 2015: 280). She adds that this proposal has become especially important in the face of globalization: "The decolonial option has been steadily globalizing in the last decade, finding parallels and responses in the sensibilities of the people from seemingly quite different local histories of Eastern and Western Europe, South-East Asia, Africa, the Arab world, Russia, and the post-Soviet countries" (2015: 279).

The decolonial proposal, thus conceived, enables us to break free of existing subjugation/dependency narratives and seek new links that might not have been obvious before. As Kušić, Lottholz, and Manolova state:

> a decolonial project would start with reconstructing experiences, thoughts, and ways of being and living locally ... This emphasis on locality does not imply another revival of area studies and parochial conclusions, but points to the need for approaching modernity/coloniality from specific locations and viewpoints that have so far been excluded.
> KUŠIĆ, LOTTHO LZ, MANOLOVA 2019: 16

Therefore, pursuing the decolonial option may also mean abandoning a language connected with colonialism/postcolonialism to concentrate on local heritage (with all its multilateralism) and the ways of its understanding, creation, management, and presentation. Researching the past of local heritage, its vernacular understanding, and its contemporary reading may unveil complex colonial and postcolonial parallels and entanglements in the region and individual countries. In his analysis of Czech art history, Matthew Rampley states:

> In his account of the presumption of colonial exceptionalism on the part of many Czechs, Filip Herza stresses that decolonizing should not be seen merely as an attribution of colonial 'guilt' or as singling out individuals as meriting censure. Rather, it is concerned with a broader examination of how the construction of Czech culture and identity has been (and remains) shaped by the legacy of this complex past, in order to then dismantle it.
> RAMPLEY 2021: 23

Reflecting on Polish postcolonial studies, Marta Cobel-Tokarska (2021: 152) emphasizes that its paradoxical problems lie in the inability to admit that Poland, seen through a postcolonial lens, may be the same subject of subordination and peripheralization as the nations of Africa or Asia which Polish discourse continues to orientalize. Researching complex pasts without implementing global hierarchies is a necessary approach. Thus, discovering the colonial past's complexity and its influences on the contemporary situation is a necessary step to evade postcolonial dichotomies and the social positions they create (such as perpetrator and victim).

In this context, Ewa Łukaszyk proposes to replace "postcoloniality" with "transcoloniality":

> postcoloniality is a state of mental dependence, a state of incomplete and unfinished separation from the metropolis, to which the so-called 'return shipment' was sent – a message containing regrets unspeakable in the past. This settlement with the former colonizer who has gone, has been going on for some time, which can be observed on the example of any divorce, but eventually expires. ... Transcoloniality may mean freeing oneself from the psychological compulsion of reckoning with a former colonizer, which created a spectral umbilical cord, more supportive than breaking the past dependence. At the same time, it combines with the settlement of domestic violence instances or abuses within the postcolonial state.
> ŁUKASZYK 2016: 95–96

Thus, in the decolonial approach, the existence of postcolonial ways of thinking is not pre-assumed, and scholars may search for emic categories used in social space and locate them in the global context. At the same time, this approach retains its critical potential, not limited to researching the consequences of the past but with an eye on the future, and it can also contribute to social transformation.

5 Instead of Conclusions: Whither Postcolonialism?

As we have shown in this chapter, the postcolonial paradigm has anchored well in CEE over the last thirty years. We can provisionally indicate two explanations for the paradigm's popularity in this region. First, the postcolonial perspective allows the incorporation of the history of CEE into the context of reflection on global relations of power and subjugation and their varied consequences. Second, this perspective has political potential and a moral dimension.

The latter explanation is connected with the popularity of this approach in Poland and the attempts to employ it in public discourse, intriguingly, as both a progressive liberal and a conservative right-wing project, a phenomenon that Tomasz Zarycki (2014: 89–114) analyzes in detail in his book. The progressive tones of postcolonialism come as no surprise because they are part of postcolonialism as critical theory. Nonetheless, it is important to note that in Poland, researchers and public intellectuals with left-wing sympathies primarily employ the postcolonial perspective as a tool for criticizing the contemporary Polish right and deconstructing national myths. "The task is usually defined as a moral mission in service of both Poland and the wider European community, which can be threatened by unchecked outbursts of nationalism," writes Zarycki (2014: 106). Therefore, for the public intellectuals on the left, postcolonialism is becoming one of several tools for criticizing various manifestations of Polish ethnocentrism. Along with this focus on the critique of ethnocentrism and xenophobia, researchers of Poland have started to develop the critical analysis of coloniality seen as "embedded firmly into the constitution of modernity: colonial forms of living and knowing continue to structure contemporary formations of capital, race, and gender" (Kušić, Lottholz, and Manolova 2019: 13).

Furthermore, Zarycki notes that the conflict between Poland and Russia over the primacy of their respective "Europeanness" mirrors the internal conflicts within the Polish elites and the place the vision of East and West occupies in them:

> Just as Polish liberals deny their conservative opponents the right to represent modernity and identify with Europe, Poles, as a nation, also question Russian credentials in this respect. Polish conservatives see themselves as not only true patriots, but also as true Europeans, faithful to the old continent's Christian roots. In the same way, Russians often see themselves as more European and modern than backward, neo-feudal and Russophobic Poland.
> ZARYCKI 2014: 263

Therefore, the public Polish debate is one of several examples of the postcolonial approach being incapable of resisting its "appropriation by the right." The approach is becoming a useful tool for Poles to communicate their unique historical traumas that also complements nationalist anti-communist, anti-Soviet, anti-Russian, anti-German, anti-European (and currently also anti-immigration) discourses (Balogun 2023; Bucholc 2022; Fomina 2019; Kalmar 2022; Kościańska 2022; Skórczewski 2020; Zarycki 2014, 2023). In one author's view, Polish postcolonialism is simply an "aberration of nationalism and martyrdom" (Snochowska-Gonzales 2012: 709). Postcolonialism is also becoming a way of producing nostalgic content, myths, and cultural illusions and legitimizing fictions. For example, right-wing publicists often use the illusion of an authentic, wealthy, mighty, and tolerant Poland "stolen" from the Poles that they find in pre-partition times. A frequently cited example within this context is the positive reception Poland gave to Ewa M. Thompson's book *Imperial Knowledge: Russian Literature and Colonialism* (2000), in which the author, influenced by Said, defined Russian literature as an imperial discourse of power creating objects of its own knowledge to enable their subjugation. In this case, the anti-imperial discourse serves to bolster nationalist resentments to reclaim Poland as a colonized and continuously oppressed nation.

Generally, before the full-scale Russian invasion of Ukraine in 2022, accusations directed against Russia appeared most frequently on the right side of the Polish debate, as did accusations against the West, perceived as a hegemon allegedly marginalizing Poland's role in the European political and cultural realm. However, in the latter case, the intention of advocates of a postcolonial approach was not, as Neil Lazarus noted, to "unthink Eurocentrism," "provincialize Europe," or promote a "post-European perspective" or some version of "post-Occidentalism." On the contrary, the primary concern of the conservative elites is "to seek to install oneself at the very heart of 'Europe' – as 'core European' – by way of emphasizing not only one's modernity ... but also, and however paradoxical this might sound, one's postcoloniality, which is inextricably bound up with the victim syndrome" (Lazarus 2012:126).

Consequently, the position of a "subaltern" and a victim of colonialism is a moral position enabling the building of moral capital to be subsequently employed in internal and international policy. The Polish sociologist Michał Łuczewski draws on Pierre Bourdieu's categories to define this capital as follows: "Moral capital is a reserve of attributes of individuals or groups that, in the public perception, grant them moral status, moral value, or also moral character" (2017:113). Memory of victims has a moral dimension that makes it difficult to dispute unless the indication is that the victims are also perpetrators, as occurs in the German-Jewish-Polish case or in complex German-Soviet-Ukrainian-Polish relations. This all leads to a "victimhood contest" and the monopolization of suffering by refusing other groups the right to commemorate it, which leads, by the same token, to "victimhood nationalism" (Lim 2010).

This kind of nationalism is the main challenge in implementing critical postcolonial theories into Polish academic discourse. As argued by Marta Cobel-Tokarska, "the biggest problem of the Polish version of postcolonial studies is 'Polonocentrism.' Polish scholars tend to automatically take an interest in Poland and treat other Central and Eastern European countries merely as background" (Cobel-Tokarska: 150). This "postcolonial nationalism" (Uffelman 2020) is especially visible in the works focusing on Poland as a victim of colonialism (primarily Russian/Soviet), which fail to recognize Poland's broad colonial relations within the region and the globe. Dirk Uffelman points out that anti-nationalist researchers trying to develop "post-dependencies studies" as a new methodology not imitating Western postcolonial studies are also focused on Polonocentric essentialism: "Thus, despite their explicit antinationalist statements, the advocates of post-dependence studies share with their adversary, Ewa Thompson, a desire for national specificity, both an 'originality of Polish culture' ... and of Polish research in the humanities" (Uffelman 2020: 146). Focusing on Poland as a dependent country that is subject to colonization led to the creation of a vicious circle of reflection on the various dimensions of this oppression. On the whole, in the Polish case, the postcolonial approach's robust entanglement with national discourse and the critique of this discourse leads to both the conservative and progressive variants of the approach frequently falling into the trap of essentialism and epistemological contradictions (Bill 2014; Kołodziejczyk 2010; Lazarus 2012). Although many classical authors associated with the postcolonial trend, from Frantz Fanon to Leela Gandhi, have underlined that nationalism is an important component of decolonization that enables anticolonial identities to crystallize, they have also made clear that this is not the ultimate goal because once nationalism assumes free rein, it becomes little more than a copy of oppressive colonial ideologies.

The overriding objective of postcolonial research is deconstruction, "the decolonization of minds," and the stimulation of continuous intellectual, political, and cultural negotiations among variously situated actors. Researchers taking part in Polish postcolonial debates should keep this in mind so as not to fall into the trap of using the language of postcolonialism to essentialize identities within dichotomous divisions. The classics of postcolonialism clearly perceived this danger and warned against describing the relationship between colonizers and the colonized "as a simple, undialectical one in which the rule and mind-set of the one either wholly reconstructs that of the other in its own image, or by contrast unleashes a 'pure' form of resistance and oppositional consciousness" (McLennan 2003). Therefore, the postcolonial approach should identify and deconstruct colonial categories and, above all, propose new ones in order to encompass ambivalences, hybrids, subjectivity, and new agencies. The global perspective of thinking about different and sometimes unexpected entanglements seems to be the source of new knowledge and ways of interpretation: "the value of the postcolonial perspective lies in the way in which it opens a global perspective of interconnections and develops new ways for tracking, analysing, and understanding the nature of changes after the dismantling of the bipolar world order, rather than in proving the postcolonial status to East Central Europe" (Kołodziejczyk and Huigen 2023: 15). In this sense, to close this chapter with the author whom we cited at the beginning, it is not particularly helpful "to judge whether place X 'is postcolonial or not'." It is better to question whether "postcolonial hermeneutics might add richness to studies of place ... X or Y or Z" (Moore 2001: 127).

References

Arendt, H. (1951). *Origins of totalitarianism*. Harcourt, Brace and Co.
Ariese, C. E. & Wróblewska, M. (2021). *Practising decoloniality in museums: A guide with global examples*. Amsterdam University Press.
Ashar, M. (2015). Decolonizing what? Categories, concepts and the enduring "not yet." *Cultural Dynamics* 27(2): 253–265.
Bakuła, B. (2011). Polska i kolonialna przeszłość dzisiaj. *Nowa Krytyka 26–27*: 145–180.
Bakuła, B. (2006). Kolonialne i postkolonialne aspekty polskiego dyskursu kresoznawczego (zarys problematyki). *Teksty Drugie 6*: 11–33.
Balogun, B. (2023). *Race and the colour-line: The boundaries of Europeanness in Poland*. Routledge.
Barkavi, T. (2022). War and decolonization in Ukraine. *New Perspectives 30*(4): 317–322.
Betlii, O. (2022). The identity politics of heritage: Decommunization, decolonization, and derussification of Kyiv monuments after Russia's full-scale invasion of Ukraine. *Journal of Applied History 4*(1/2): 149–169.
Bill, S. (2014). Seeking the authentic: Polish culture and the nature of postcolonial theory. *nonstite.org*. 12. https://nonsite.org/article/seeking-the-authentic-polish-culture-and-the-nature-of-postcolonial-theory.
Bobinac, M. (2014). Cultural transfer in the Habsburg Empire: Croatia and German-language culture from a postcolonial perspective. In Göttsche D. & Dunker A. *(Post-)colonialism across Europe: Transcultural history and national memory*. Aisthesis, 305–319.
Borawski, P. & Dubiński A. (1986). *Tatarzy polscy. Dzieje, obrzędy, legendy, tradycje*. Iskry.
Borkowska, G. (2007). Polskie doświadczenie kolonialne. *Teksty Drugie 4*: 15–2.
Bucholc, M. (2022). Schengen and the rosary: Catholic religion and the postcolonial syndrome in Polish national habitus. *Historical Social Research 45*(1): 153–181, https://doi.org/10.12759/hsr.45.2020.1.153-181.
Buchowski, M. (2004). Hierarchies of knowledge in Central-Eastern European anthropology. *Anthropology of East Europe Review 22*(2): 5–14.
Buchowski, M. (2006). The Specter of Orientalism in Europe: From exotic other to stigmatized brother. *Anthropological Quarterly 79*(3): 463–82.
Bukowiecki, Ł., Wawrzyniak, J. & Wróblewska, M. (2020). Duality of decolonizing: Artists' memory activism in Warsaw. *Heritage & Society 13*(1–2): 32–52, DOI: 10.1080/2159032X.2021.1898076

Buruma, I, & Margalit A. (2004). *Occidentalism: The West in the eyes of its enemies.* Penguin.

Carey, H.F., & Raciborski, R. (2004). Postcolonialism: A valid paradigm for the former Sovietized states and Yugoslavia? *East European Politics and Societies 18*(2): 191–235.

Cavanagh, C. (2004). Postcolonial Poland: An empty space on the map of current theory. *Common Knowledge 10*(1): 82–92.

Césaire, A. (1955[2000]). *Discourse on colonialism.* Monthly Review Press.

Chari, S. & Verdery, K. (2009). Thinking between the posts: Postcolonialism, postsocialism, and ethnography after the Cold War. *Comparative Studies in Society and History 51*(1): 6–34.

Cobel-Tokarska, M. (2021). Problems and contradictions in Polish postcolonial thought in relation to Central and Eastern Europe. *Postcolonial Studies 24*(1): 139–158.

Csepeli, G., Örkény, A. & Scheppelle, K.L. (1996). Acquired immune deficiency syndrome in social science in Eastern Europe. *Social Research 63*(2): 487–509.

Du Bois, W. E. B. (1952). The Negro and the Warsaw Ghetto. *Jewish Life.*

Eppinger, M. (2022). From "limited sovereignty" to decolonization in Ukraine. *FHAU: Journal of Ethnographic Theory 12*(3): 659–667.

Etkind, A. (2011). *Internal colonization: Russia's imperial experience.* Polity Press.

Feichtinger, J., Prutschand U. & Csáky, M. (Eds.). (2003). *Habsburg postcolonial: Machtstrukturen und kollektives Gedächtnis.* StudienVerlag.

Fiut, A. (2003). Polonizacja? Kolonizacja? *Teksty Drugie 6*: 150–156.

Fomina, J. (2019). European integration as self-colonization? The appropriation of postcolonial theory by Polish eurosceptics. *Czas Kultury 4*: 18–31.

Gerasimov, I. (2014). Ukraine 2014: The first postcolonial revolution. *Ab Imperio 3*: 22–44.

Glinski, M. (2015). *Slavery vs. serfdom, or was Poland a colonial empire?* https://culture.pl/en/article/slavery-vs-serfdom-or-was-poland-a-colonial-empire.

Gosk, H. (2008). Polski dyskurs kresowy w niefikcjonalnych zapisach międzywojennych. Próba lektury w perspektywie postcolonial studies. *Teksty Drugie 6*: 20–33.

Hladík, R. (2011). A Theory's travelogue: Post-colonial theory in post-socialist space. *Teorie Vědy /Theory of Science 33*(4): 561–90.

Hull, I. (2005). *Absolute destruction: Military culture and the practices of war in imperial Germany.* Cornell University Press.

Kalmar, I. (2022). *White but not quite: Central Europe's illiberal revolt.* Bristol University Press.

Kalnačs, B. (2020). Latvian multiculturalism and postcolonialism. In Albrecht M. (Ed.), *Postcolonialism cross-examined: Multidirectional perspectives on imperial and colonial pasts and the neocolonial present.* Routledge, 255–268.

Kałczewiak, M. & Kozłowska, M. (2022). Introduction. In Kałczewiak M. & Kozłowska M. (Eds.), *The World beyond the West: Perspectives from Eastern Europe*. Berghahn Books.

Kaps, K. & Surman, J. (2012). Postcolonial or post-colonial? Post(-)colonial perspectives on Habsburg Galicia. *Historyka. Studia metodologiczne XLII*: 7–36.

Keim, W. (2014). Conceptualizing circulation of knowledge in the social sciences. In Keim, Wiebke et al. (Eds.), *Global knowledge in the social sciences: Made in circulation*. Ashgate, 87–113.

Kiossev, A. (1999). Notes on self-colonising cultures. In Pejic B. & Elliott D. (Eds.), *After the wall: Art and culture in post-communist Europe*.

Kola, A. (2004). *Słowianofilstwo czeskie i rosyjskie w ujęciu porównawczym*. Ibidem.

Kola, A. (2018). *Socjalistyczny postkolonializm. Rekonsolidacja pamięci*. Wydawnictwo Naukowe UMK.

Kolarz, W. (1952). *Russia and her colonies*. Frederick A. Praeger.

Kołodziejczyk, D. (2010). Postkolonialny transfer na Europę Środkowo-Wschodnią. *Teksty Drugie 5*: 22–39.

Kołodziejczyk, D. & Huigen, S. (2023). East Central Europe between the colonial and the postcolonial: A critical introduction. In Huigen S. & Kołodziejczyk D. (Eds.), *East Central Europe between the colonial and the postcolonial in the twentieth century*. Palgrave MacMillan, 1–31.

Kopp, K. (2012). *Germany's wild east: Constructing Poland as colonial space*. University of Michigan Press.

Korablyova, V. (2022). Russia vs. Ukraine: A subaltern empire against the "populism of hope." *Acta Universitatis Carolinae Studia Territorialia* 2: 39–60.

Korek, J. ed. (2007). *From sovietology to postcoloniality: Poland and Ukraine from a postcolonial perspective*. Södertörns högskola.

Korolov, G. (2023). Playing with the past: Does the decolonisation of the history of Ukraine make sense? *New Eastern Europe* 2: 177–183.

Kościańska, A. & Petryk, M. (2022). *Odejdź. Rzecz o polskim rasizmie*. Wydawnictwo Krytyki Politycznej.

Kowalski, M. A. (2010). *Dyskurs kolonialny w drugiej Rzeczypospolitej*. DiG.

Kubik, J. (2019) How to think about "area" in area studies? In Milutinovic Z. (Ed.), *The rebirth of area studies: Challenges for history, politics and international relations in the 21st century*. Bloomsbury, 53–90.

Kušić, K., Lottholz, P. & Manolova P. (2019). From dialogue to practice: Pathways towards decoloniality in Southeast Europe. *Diversia* 3: 7–30.

Lazarus, N. (2012). Spectres haunting: Postcommunism and postcolonialism. *Journal of Postcolonial Writing* 48(2): 117–29.

Leher, E. & Wawrzyniak, J. (2023). *Decolonial museology in East-Central Europe: A preliminary to-do list*. https://www.europenowjournal.org/2023/02/24/decolonial-museology-in-east-central-europe-a-preliminary-to-do-list/.

Leszczynski, A. (2022). *Ludowa historia Polski*. Wydawnictwo W.A.B.

Lim, J.-H. (2010). Victimhood nationalism in contested memories: National mourning and global accountability. In Assmann A. & Conrad S. (Eds.), *Memory in a global age*. Palgrave Macmillan, 138–162.

Lower, W. (2005). *Nazi empire-building and the Holocaust in Ukraine*. University of North Carolina Press.

Łuczewski, M. (2017). *Kapitał moralny. Polityki historyczne w późnej nowoczesności*. Ośrodek Myśli Politycznej.

Łukaszyk, E. (2016). Od podległości do horyzontalnego diagramu relacji. Studium procesów trans kolonialnych. In Kieniewicz J. (Ed.), *Perspektywy postkolonializmu w Polsce, Polska w perspektywie postkolonialnej*. Artes Liberales, 87–104.

Mark, J., Kalinovsky, A. M. & Marung, S. (2020). *Alternative globalizations: Eastern Europe and the postcolonial world*. Indiana University Press.

Mark, J. & Slobodian, Q. (2018). Eastern Europe in the global history of decolonization. In Thomas M. & Thompson A. (Eds.), *The Oxford handbook of the ends of empire*. Oxford University Press.

Mayblin, L., Piekut, A. & Gill, V. (2016). "Other" posts in "other" places: Poland through a postcolonial lens? *Sociology 50*(1): 60–76.

Mazurek, M. (2018). Polish economists in Nehru's India: Making science for the Third World in an era of de-stalinization and decolonization. *Slavic Review 77*(3): 588–610.

Mälksoo, M. (2023). The Postcolonial moment in Russia's war against Ukraine. *Journal of Genocide Research 25*(3–4): 471–481, DOI: 10.1080/14623528.2022.2074947.

McLennan, G. (2003). Sociology, eurocentrism and postcolonial theory. *European Journal of Social Theory 6*(1): 69–86.

Mignolo, W. (2011). *The darker side of Western modernity: Global futures, decolonial options*. Duke University Press.

Moore, D. C. (2001). Is the post- in postcolonial the post- in post-Soviet? Toward a global postcolonial critique. *PMLA 116*(1): 111–28.

Morozov, V. (2015). *Russia's postcolonial identity: Subaltern empire in a eurocentric world*. Palgrave MacMillan.

Morozov, V. (2013). Subaltern empire? Toward a postcolonial approach to Russian foreign policy. *Problems of Post-Communism 60*(6): 16–28.

Nakoneczny, T. (2020). Dyskurs postkolonialny wobec historii Polski. *Przegląd Historyczny CXI*(4): 928–953.

Nelson, R. L. (Ed.). (2009). *Germans, Poland, and colonial expansion to the East: 1850 through the present*. Palgrave Macmillan.

Neuger, L. (2007). Central Europe as a problem. In Korek, J. (Ed.), *From Sovietology to postcoloniality: Poland and Ukraine from a postcolonial perspective*. Södertörns högskola, 23–33.

Parvulescu, A. & Boatcă, M. (2022). *Creolizing the modern: Transylvania across empires*. Cornell University Press.

Puchalski, P.. (2022). *Poland in a colonial world order: Adjustments and aspirations*. Routledge.

Rampley, M. (2021). Decolonizing Central Europe: Czech art and the question of "colonial innocence." *Visual Resources 37*(1): 1–30, DOI: 10.1080/01973762.2022.2087168.

Rexhepi, P. (2018). The politics of postcolonial erasure in Sarajevo. *Intervention*s *20*(6): 930–945, DOI: 10.1080/1369801X.2018.1487320.

Riabczuk, M. (2015). *Ukraina. Syndrom postkolonialny*. Kolegium Europy Wschodniej.

Rolf, M, (2014). *Imperiale Herrschaft im Weichselland: Das Königreich Polen im Russischen Imperium (1864–1915)*. Oldenbour.

Rothberg, M. (2009). *Multidirectional memory: Remembering the Holocaust in the age of decolonization*. Stanford University Press.

Said, E. (1978). *Orientalism*. Pantheon.

Sarr, F. & Savoy, B. (2018). *The restitution of African cultural heritage: Toward a new relational ethics*. Philippe Rey/Seuil.

Sieg, K. (2021). *Decolonizing German and European history at the museum*. University of Michigan Press.

Skorczewski, D. (2020). *Polish literature and national identity: A postcolonial perspective*. University of Rochester Press.

Snochowska-Gonzalez, C. (2012). Post-colonial Poland: On an unavoidable misuse. *East European Politics and Societies and Cultures 26*(4): 708–23.

Sowa, J. (2011). *Fantomowe ciało króla. Peryferyjne zmagania z nowoczesną formą*. Universitas.

Ştefănescu, B. (2012). Reluctant siblings: Methodological musings on the complicated relationship between postcoloanislim and postcommunism. *Word and Text* 2(1): 13–26.

Ştefănescu, B. (2013). *Postcommunism/postcolonialism: Siblings in subalternity*. Editura Universităţii din Bucureşti.

Surynt, I. (2006). *Postęp, kultura i kolonializm. Polska a niemiecki projekt europejskiego Wschodu w dyskursach publicznych XIX wieku*. Centrum Studiów Niemieckich i Europejskich im. Willy Brandta Uniwersytetu Wrocławskiego.

Sznaider, N. (2022). *Fluchtpunkte der Erinnerung. Über die Gegenwart von Holocaust und Kolonialismus*.

Thompson, E. (2010). Whose discourse? Telling the story in post-communist Poland. *The Other Shore l* (1): 1–18.

Thompson, E. (2000). *Imperial knowledge: Russian literature and colonialism*. Bloomsbury.
Tlostanova, M. (2010). *Gender epistemologies and Eurasian Borderlands*. Palgrave MacMillan.
Tlostanova, M. (2012). Postsocialist ≠ postcolonial? On post-Soviet imaginary and global coloniality. *Journal of Postcolonial Writing, 48*(2): 130–142.
Tlostanova, M. (2015). Between the Russian/Soviet dependencies, neoliberal delusions, dewesternizing options, and decolonial drives. *Cultural Dynamics 27*(2): 267–83.
Tlostanova, M. (2017). *Postcolonialism and postsocialism in fiction and art: Resistance and re-existence*. Palgrave Macmillan.
Tlostanova, M. (2019). The postcolonial condition, the decolonial option and the postsocialist intervention. In Albrecht M. (Ed.), *Postcolonialism cross-examined: Multidirectional perspectives on imperial and colonial pasts and the new-colonial present*. Routledge, 165–178.
Todorova, M. (1997). *Imagining the Balkans*. Oxford University Press.
Törnquist-Plewa, B. & Yurchuk, Y. (2019). Memory politics in contemporary Ukraine: Reflections from the postcolonial perspective. *Memory Studies 12*(6): 699–720.
Uffelman, D. (2020). Postcolonial theory as post-colonial nationalism. In Albrecht M. (Ed.), *Postcolonialism cross-examined: Multidirectional perspectives on imperial and colonial pasts and the neocolonial present*. Routledge, 135–152.
Velychenko, S., Ruane, J. & Hrynevych, L. (2022). *Ireland and Ukraine: Studies in comparative imperial and national history*. Columbia University Press.
Wolff, L. (1994). *Inventing Eastern Europe: The map of civilization on the mind of the Enlightenment*. Stanford University Press.
Zarycki, T. (2004). Uses of Russia: The role of Russia in the modern Polish national identity. *East European Politics and Societies 18*(4): 595–627.
Zarycki, T. (2008). *Kapitał kulturowy. Inteligencja w Polsce i w Rosji*. WUW.
Zarycki, T. (2011). Eastern Poland in a center-periphery perspective. In Stefański M. (Ed.), *Strategic issues of the development of the Lublin region*. Innovatio Press: 95–112.
Zarycki, T. (Ed). (2013). *Polska Wschodnia i orientalizm*. Wydawnictwo Naukowe Scholar.
Zarycki, T. (2014). *Ideologies of eastness in Central and Eastern Europe*. Routledge.
Zarycki, T. (Ed). (2016). *Polska jako peryferie*. Wydawnictwo Naukowe Scholar.
Zarycki, T. (2023). Polish stereotypes of the East: Old and new mechanisms of orientalisation in the regional and transnational dimensions. In Huigen S. & Kołodziejczyk D. (Eds.), *East Central Europe between the colonial and the postcolonial in the twentieth century*. Palgrave MacMillan, 57–85.
Zimmerer, J. (2004a). Im Dienste des Imperiums: Die Geographen der Berliner Universität zwischen Kolonialwissenschaften und Ostforschung. *Jahrbuch für Universitätsgeschichte 7*: 73–99.

Zimmerer, J. (2004b). Colonialism and the Holocaust: Towards an archaeology of genocide. In Moses, A. D. (Ed.), *Genocide and settler society: Frontier violence and stolen indigenous children in Australian history*. Berghahn Books, 49–76.

Zimmerer, J. (Ed.). (2011). *Von Windhuk nach Ausschwitz? Beiträge zum Verhältnis von Kolonialismus und Holocaust*. LIT.

CHAPTER 5

The Absent Bourgeoisie: Implications of the Relative Weakness of the Polish Economic Elite in the Long Twentieth Century

Tomasz Zarycki

1 The Rise and Fall of the Bourgeoisie at the Turn of the Nineteenth and Twentieth Centuries[1]

The starting point of this chapter is an observation that the dominant accounts of Polish history typically underestimate the dynamic development of the bourgeoisie and, more broadly, of modern capitalism that took place on Polish soil in the second half of the nineteenth century. That period of dynamic development and accumulation of capital by what can be seen as the modern economic elite of its time encompassed extremely important events in Polish social history, even though the process did not last long and mainly concerned the Russian sector of Polish lands. Indeed, the end of the nineteenth century was a period of capital accumulation – unprecedented in modern Polish history – in the hands of elites residing primarily in the Russian-controlled part of the Polish territory, as Rosa Luxemburg in particular pointed out already in her doctoral thesis (Luxemburg 1898). It can be argued that during this period the Polish lands, although on average poorer than Western Europe, developed a social structure similar to that of the Western European states.

On the one hand, the ranks of the working class were multiplying, while the ranks of the educated middle class were also mounting, and finally the bourgeoisie was growing rapidly richer. On the other hand, industrial plants and financial institutions were mushrooming in Warsaw, Łódź, and the Dąbrowa Basin. Their influence was beginning to extend beyond the Russian-controlled Congress Kingdom of Poland. Thus, it can be said that Polish society briefly approached Western societies in its structure, only to diverge from them significantly in later years. This paradoxical trajectory in the development of Polish society seems to be rarely noticed, although it explains many of the

---

1 This chapter was written as part of research project funded by the National Science Center of Poland (NCN) project no. 2020/39/B/HS6/00211.

nonobvious effects of its dissimilarity. In particular, it is the pronounced weakness of its economic elites, whose role in what Pierre Bourdieu calls the field of power is largely being replaced by cultural elites. At the same time, this weakness, I will argue, should primarily be considered in terms of the ability of economic elites to accumulate capital.

Thus, after a period of dynamic growth in the second half of the nineteenth century, the Polish bourgeoisie began to rapidly lose its capital starting with the beginning of the First World War. The turning points of this decline included the Bolshevik Revolution, the Treaty of Riga, the cutting off of the newly formed Polish state from Russian markets, and finally the tariff wars with Germany from the mid-1920s. The history of the original Polish bourgeoisie ended with the Second World War and the nationalizations carried out by the Stalinist authorities. These marked the disappearance of the bourgeoisie as a social class, but, interestingly, they also caused a rapid disappearance of the memory of it. The dominant actors in the Polish field of power then became the communist nomenklatura and the intelligentsia. The former, after the Stalinist period, slowly began to lose its previously overwhelming influence, and finally left the field of power in 1989. The disappearance of the memory of the bourgeoisie as a historical elite can be contrasted with the much greater persistence of the social memory of landed gentry and aristocracy – groups which, despite the loss of all their property, have retained some social visibility. The circles nurturing their remembrance have also survived (Smoczyński and Zarycki 2021). Thus, while the average educated Pole knows the names of the great Polish aristocratic families, they have usually not heard of any of the richest Polish industrialist and banker families of the late nineteenth and early twentieth centuries.

The disappearance of the memory of the dominant role played by the bourgeoisie in Polish society until 1918 has also shaped the way the social sciences view Poland's past. In particular, it can be noted that the significance of the phenomenon under discussion – the dynamic development of the bourgeoisie in the Polish lands in the late nineteenth century – is often underestimated, and therefore depreciated in large parts of the historiographical literature as well as in the sociological, economic, or political sciences studies. The main reasons for this phenomenon include first and foremost the intelligentsia-centric perspective of Polish historiography, that is, the tendency to write Polish history from the point of view of intelligentsia as its main actor. It can also be considered a form of presentism, especially based on the assumption that the intelligentsia has always been the dominant force in Poland's modern history, or at least was historically determined to become one.

The second factor conditioning the weak memory of the history of the Polish bourgeoisie is the Polish-centric perspective of the national historiography, which depreciates the relatively positive aspects of the development of the Polish lands under the Partitions of Poland in the nineteenth century. Instead, it is oriented toward appreciating the achievements of the independent Polish state, especially the Second Polish Republic (1918–1939). In particular, it can be noted that the concentration of economic development processes at the turn of the nineteenth and twentieth centuries in the Russian part of the country, which became the most dynamically developing region of Poland, does not harmonize with the dominant Polish stereotypes according to which Russia's influence on Poland was only negative (Zarycki 2004). Especially the Russian Partition is usually seen as the most backward part of the country, while the history of Prussian and especially Austrian rule in the southern and western parts of the Polish lands is shown much more favorably (Zarycki 2007). The arguments about the positive role of the Prussian and Austrian governments in the second half of the nineteenth century are, of course, true to a considerable degree, particularly with regard to the level of infrastructure or educational development, but neither in the Austrian nor in the Prussian part of Poland did the bourgeoisie and, more broadly, modern economy (industry and finance) develop as dynamically as in the Russian part. This was largely determined by the peripheral location of the Polish lands in the Austrian Empire and the Kingdom of Prussia and their opposite location in Russia. In the latter, they were the empire's westernmost region close to Western Europe's core and simultaneously had the advantage of access to the huge Russian market (Kochanowicz 2006).

The characteristic aspects of the intelligentsia historians' depreciation of the development enjoyed by the Polish bourgeoisie in the late nineteenth century also include overestimating the role of the non-Polish bourgeoisie and of landed gentry and aristocracy in the economic development at the time. The non-Polish roots of a considerable part of the bourgeoisie in the Polish lands are supposed to depreciate its image and make it an insignificant foreign actor. In turn, the ties of the new economic elite to landed gentry and aristocracy are supposed to undermine the aspirations of this faction of the elite to the status of the engine of modernity. In other words, the historical Polish bourgeoisie, according to today's intelligentsia images, is actually hardly Polish because it was mainly of Jewish and German origin and hardly modern because it was dominated by landed gentry and aristocracy.

It may be noted that the first argument carries a somewhat nationalistic character, while the second is rather classist in nature as it assumes that the feudal origins of certain members of the new elite condemn them to backwardness.

In turn, both arguments abstract from the broader global context. First, the global economic elites of the time, as they do today, had multinational and multireligious origins in many other European countries as well. Second, the Western economic elites were also based on an alliance of the "new" bourgeoisie and the "old" feudal and landed elites allocating their capitals to more modern industries, particularly financial ventures (Charle 1990). An important element of this alliance was mixed marriages, a typical aspect of which was the exchange of "old" aristocratic titles for "new" financial fortunes. It also involved the purchase by the growing industrial elite of landed estates, whose role was becoming increasingly symbolic.

Furthermore, one should note in this context the strong Polonization of the bourgeois elite in the late nineteenth century. This was especially true for its main center, which was Warsaw, and, to a lesser extent, the second largest city of Russian Poland – Łódź. As Joanna Hensel points out, the national and religious differences in the then-consolidating business elite of the Congress Kingdom of Poland began to blur at the end of the nineteenth century. Consequently, one could speak of a partnership of different national groups (Hensel 1979). Following Witold Kula, Hensel also observes that the nationality of capital is determined primarily by its place of disposition and use (Kula 1983). Be that as it may, the Warsaw bourgeois elite of the second half of the nineteenth century firmly chose Polish culture as their dominant identity, and they contributed significant sums to the development of that culture. For instance, the mass printings of Polish literature, magazines, and scientific works would not have been published without this support. Specifically, Henryk Sienkiewicz's *The Trilogy* was financed by banker Hipolit Wawelberg. Scientific research was then supported by financially powerful institutions of the Polish bourgeoisie such as the Mianowski Foundation.

Thus, the present intelligentsia's attempts at a secondary "depolonization" of the bourgeoisie living in the Polish lands at the turn of the nineteenth and twentieth centuries seem hardly justified, as do the attempts to feudalize its historical picture. As mentioned, they can be interpreted as efforts by the currently dominant intelligentsia elites to diminish the historical significance of the Polish bourgeoisie as its historical and, potentially, future opponent. This is because the history of the development of the Polish bourgeoisie at the turn of the nineteenth and twentieth centuries may be seen as inconvenient to a considerable part of contemporary Polish intelligentsia. This tension might constitute an aspect of a struggle for the status of the leader of the modernization process in the Polish lands. The modern intelligentsia wants to be perceived as the only true guide of the Polish nation toward modernity. This, of course, assumes that modernity is seen as the main stake in the struggle for legitimacy of domination in the modern Polish field of power.

Intelligentsia, in particular in its form which emerged and accumulated wealth after 1989, is considered as the only legitimate elite and the only proper incarnation of the Polish upper class. The earlier ones were either insufficiently Polish and democratic or excessively backward, feudal, and traditionalist. Such arguments are demonstrated very clearly by Marcin Piatkowski, a well-known Polish economist working, among others, for the International Monetary Fund (IMF) and the World Bank (WB), in his acclaimed book *Europe's Growth Champion: Insights from the Economic Rise of Poland* (Piatkowski 2018). Piatkowski's work presents an intelligentsia perspective in which only after 1989 did Poland step on the track of full-fledged economic development and quit its previous role of a feudal country ruled by "extractive" elites. Piatkowski's vision, which has enjoyed quite a positive reception (the book was also published in Polish), seems to illustrate very well the dominant intelligentsia's common sense.

2   The Power of the Intelligentsia and Its Narrative

Contrary to numerous laments about the decline of the intelligentsia, it can be argued that after 1989 one is witnessing its final victory and the establishment of what I propose to call the intelligentsia's hegemony (Zarycki, Smoczyński, and Warczok 2017). This was the completion of the long process of the intelligentsia taking over the dominant position in the Polish field of power from the economic elite, that is, landed gentry and the bourgeoisie, and later from the nomenklatura. For the landed and bourgeois elites, the main blow turned out to be, as already mentioned, the Bolshevik Revolution. They lost most of their property: both capital, as it was connected with the financial markets of the Russian Empire, and land, since it was located east of the Polish–Soviet border established by the Treaty of Riga in 1921. In the interwar period, they still retained some property, but it was usually the remnants of the land and capital resources they had owned until the outbreak of the First World War. In the Second Polish Republic, meanwhile, it was the intelligentsia that had already assumed dominant roles in the state. At the same time, it largely ignored the interests of the former economic elite.

A perfect example of the antagonism between these two factions of the elite was the dispute over the outcome of the Treaty of Riga, which ended the Polish–Soviet war and established the border between Poland and the USSR in 1921. On the one hand, the landed elite considered the results of the treaty a betrayal of national interests. On the other hand, the intelligentsia elite perceived the economic interest of landed gentry as unrelated to the national interest. Good examples of this dispute are the statements of Zdzisław Grocholski (1929) as a representative of the landed elite on the one hand and Władysław Grabski (2016) as a representative of the intelligentsia elite on the other. Grabski, former Prime Minister of the Second Polish Republic, argued in his book first published in 1935 that Poland cannot be identified "with the state of possession" of the landed elite. He saw its interests not as a desire to defend the nation's wealth, but as "a desire to secure their narrow group's economic interests" (Grabski 2016: 84). This opinion can be read as an expression of the stance held by the dominant part of the intelligentsia elite of the Second Polish Republic and its rejection of legitimacy for large landownership rights. On the contrary, Zdzisław Grocholski, as a representative of the landowners who had lost their estates in the territories ceded to the Soviet Union by the Treaty of Riga, pointed out that the course of political borders was a secondary issue to the far more important one of property rights. He suggested that the possessions of Polish landowners should be seen as part of the economic resources of the entire nation. He also mentioned that his circle had advocated Poland's support for an independent Ukrainian state as early as 1917, implying that the creation of an independent but Polish-friendly Ukraine at that time would allow most of the landed estates in that part of the former Russian Empire to remain in Polish hands. Meanwhile, as is well known, they were nationalized in 1918, and now, in the process of privatization, are passing into the ownership of large agricultural holdings controlled mostly by global capital (Mousseau and Devillers 2023).

Be that as it may, the loss of landed estates in the territories that came under Soviet control in 1918 and then in 1944, combined with the partial nationalization of large-landed estates in the Second Polish Republic, resulted in the economic decline of the Polish landed gentry in the interwar period. Its wealthiest elite still owned significant estates and retained certain public visibility as a traditional elite with an aristocratic status until 1939. However, as a broader stratum, it was already an impoverished group without strong political influence (Mich 2000). The same was true of the entrepreneurial class, which was largely active thanks to some of its surviving capitals and companies from before the Bolshevik Revolution. However, most of those were already very much truncated, and the cutoff from the Russian and German markets hindered more serious economic development and expansion. Finally, the Second World War also proved to be a total economic disaster for the former economic elites, particularly the remnants of the bourgeoisie. After 1945, they were completely expropriated.

It should be noted here that the intelligentsia is understood here in a way that differs from its conventional definitions dominant in Poland, which are usually based on an identity perspective. In their understanding, intelligentsia members are people who can be characterized by intelligentsia ethos, patriotism, intellectual skills, and good knowledge of higher culture. Instead, I adopt here a structural understanding of intelligentsia following Ivan Szelényi and his co-authors (Eyal, Szelényi, and Townsley 1998). In this view, intelligentsia is defined as a part of the elite for which the main source of social status is their cultural capital (that is, their education, erudition, or knowledge of manners), as well as country-specific social capital, in particular, membership in the elite networks of Poland's cultural elite. Such individuals may periodically enter the political elite and thus gain political capital, or they may accept highly lucrative positions in the private or state sectors and thus gain economic capital. However, their main permanent resource, and therefore one that multigenerationally defines their status, is cultural capital. It is this specific capital that they are able to accumulate and transmit between generations, and also convert into material income in periods of opportunity – for example, in the form of employment in managerial positions in public or private institutions.

The post-1989 period can be thus considered as the transition of most intelligentsia elites from their positions in the field of cultural, scientific, or, more broadly, symbolic production to the economic field. A case study in this area is my paper co-authored with Andrzej Turkowski (Turkowski and Zarycki 2023), in which we analyzed the careers of the Polish economic historians circle, developing the paradigm of the dependency theory. Most of them moved from the academic field to economy and politics after 1989, sometimes abandoning academic careers altogether, sometimes retaining academic posts, but usually not conducting serious research. In other words, the transition of a significant part of the intelligentsia from the intellectual and scientific fields to business or politics after 1989 should not be seen as the final collapse of the intelligentsia. Rather, it was its adaptation to changing socio-economic conditions and its movement to the most attractive fields that allow for the reproduction of status and the beneficial conversion of previously held resources – especially the conversion of cultural capital into economic capital. These fields now enable them to reap significant material benefits, but this does not mean that capital accumulation on a larger scale has become possible. The intelligentsia elite remains mostly managers, rather than becoming the owner elite of the Polish economy, which would mean its transformation into bourgeoisie. Indeed, its capital resources on an international scale are rather limited, as will be discussed in greater detail below.

3 Dependent Development

The relatively modest wealth of the Polish economic elite can be linked primarily to the ownership transformation process that took place in Poland after 1989. It was associated first and foremost with the sale of a significant portion of public assets to foreign investors. At the same time, however, the intelligentsia elite members who seized power in 1989 tried to prevent former members of the communist elite from taking over large changes of the public assets, as happened, for example, in Ukraine or Russia. This effect was achieved, among other things, with the aforementioned privatization aimed primarily at Western investors. As a result, one can speak of the unique configuration of elites in Poland, where no group of oligarchs has emerged, as was the case even in the Czech Republic. More broadly, Poland has not developed a strong economic elite capable of projecting its far-reaching interests on politics and other spheres, including science or culture. This thesis seems to be confirmed by studies which show that political connections in Poland are of relatively low importance for the functioning of the economic elite (Sałach and Brzeziński 2020). In other words, one can speak of the relative insignificance of political capital in the formation and functioning of the contemporary Polish economic elite.

The interpretation of the post-1989 transformation presented below relies heavily on the already mentioned dependent development paradigm (Palma 2008). At the same time, what will be proposed here is its combination with the critical approach of David Harvey, in particular his vision of the global-scale process of dispossession. The perspective of studies of wealth inequalities on a global scale, well represented by Thomas Piketty, will be also adopted here. In particular, Piketty argues that

> after the collapse of communism, Western investors did gradually become owners of much of the capital of the former Eastern bloc: about a quarter if one considers the entire capital stock (including real estate) but more than half if one looks only at firms (and even greater if one considers only large firms). National accounts data indicate that outflows from profits and other capital income (e.g. interest or dividends) net of corresponding inflows averaged 4–7 percent of GDP between 2010 and 2016, which substantially exceeds the inward flow of EU funds in Poland, Hungary, the Czech Republic, and Slovakia.
> PIKETTY 2020: 640

This asymmetry is not greatest for Poland but, interestingly, for the Czech Republic, from which almost four times more capital flowed out in 2010–2015 than flowed in through the European Union's (EU's) structural aid and related sources. This dependence has been, of course, noted earlier by some researchers who have pointed out that it gives rise to a number of asymmetries not only in the purely economic sphere, but also in related realms such as politics or culture. Andreas Nölke and Arjan Vliegenthart, who paid particular attention to the unprecedented scale of external ownership in these economies, have therefore proposed to describe the economic nature of Central European countries with the use of a separate category of "dependent market economy" (Nölke and Vliegenthart 2009).

Accurate data on the acquisition of property by foreign capital and its current holders by the owners' country of origin is difficult to access as no systematic records are kept for the whole of Poland in this regard. Rather, what we have at our disposal is fragmentary and mostly estimated data, which nevertheless give some indirect picture of the scale of foreign capital's control over Polish economy. For example, Krzysztof Jasiecki quotes the 2011 data on the ownership structure of the largest companies in the region, stating that fifty-six percent of them have foreign owners (Jasiecki 2013: 229). Interesting information is also provided by the work of Martin Myant, who estimates that companies owned by foreign capital in Poland were responsible for twenty-four percent of employment in 2010 (Myant 2018) and, according to the 2016 data, for forty-four percent of the total value of Polish exports, and in the automotive industry for as much as ninety percent of the value of exports (Myant 2018: 299). This and other authors (Gál and Lux 2022) point out that external ownership rates are still significantly lower in Poland than in the Czech Republic, Hungary, and Slovakia.

The fact that privatization and other ownership transformations in most Central European countries have resulted in foreign ownership on such a spectacular, perhaps unprecedented, scale seems to be an important but not always appreciated aspect of the transformation. The influence of this factor cannot be overestimated for many reasons. Specifically, it hinders the accumulation of investment capital and extremely lowers the wealth indicators of Poles. When one focuses on indicators such as the gross domestic product (GDP) per capita, the country's development dynamics may even look spectacularly positive. This becomes even more visible if one adopts 1989 – the moment of a total collapse of the Polish economic system – as the starting point of the analysis. The international income inequality between Central and Western Europe has thus been reduced many times over the past three decades. The level of

Poland's GDP per capita is slowly approaching that of Greece and currently amounts to approximately one third of that of Germany.

However, the initial estimates regarding wealth inequality in the late 1990s were many times lower, indicating capital assets per capita stock up to fifty times lower than Germany's (Deloitte 2015). Later, the statistics improved, but the overall assets of Polish elite are small compared to those of the economic elites in Russia or even the Czech Republic. Moreover, they are heavily dependent on fluctuations in the global economy. Although the financial crisis of 2008 did not affect the Polish economy as such too strongly, the wealth of the 100 richest Poles according to *Forbes'* ranking melted at that time by as much as forty percent (Jasiecki 2010). This seems to confirm the very high dependence of development processes in Poland on the cycles of the global economy. In 2009, the total wealth of the 100 richest Polish millionaires was valued at an equivalent of about fifty billion USD. In a similar period, as estimated by Russian researchers, Mikhail Khodorkovsky's wealth was about twenty-four billion USD, while Roman Abramovich's assets amounted to around twelve billion USD (Guriev and Rachinsky 2005).

More recent estimates of global wealth by the Credit Suisse Research Institute (2022) for 2021 give much more optimistic results. Simultaneously, however, according to the same source, the degree of concentration of these resources in the hands of the richest in Poland and the size of superrich elite is small compared to Western countries. Thus, in 2021, the number of people owning more than USD 100 million was 108 in Poland, 1741 in Russia, 3672 in Germany, and 1095 in Sweden, which is almost ten times more. Sweden is a good contrast to Poland here because, although some of the large fortunes there were nationalized in the early twentieth century, a large part of the national wealth has been controlled by just a few families for many generations (Agnblad et al. 2001). Most of those have owned their fortunes since at least the nineteenth century and have been able to secure a reputation as responsible stewards of the national economic resource. As is well known, in addition to Sweden's rise after the Second World War to the ranks of the world's wealthiest countries, part of this legitimacy is formed by the relatively high level of income redistribution by the state. It has provided the Kingdom of Sweden with an image as one of the most socially just countries for many decades.

The data on the private wealth management market cited by Jasiecki (2010) are also interesting in this regard. Thus, in 2003, the CEE market accounted for only 1.6 percent of the total European wealth market. What is even more remarkable is that, according to Jasiecki, the typical private banking client in Poland is usually a manager who has earned most of their income from employment in a global company. This standard profile of a Polish private banking client fits into a picture in which the role of the economic elite in Poland tends to be played by the intelligentsia – people who mainly sell their cultural and social capital to companies as managers – rather than the bourgeoisie, who would live mainly off accumulated economic capital. This may, of course, be related to the significant degree of foreign ownership in the Polish economy as discussed above and explain the already mentioned weakness of the bourgeoisie in modern Poland.

4 Dispossession in Central and Eastern Europe

What will be argued here is that this state of affairs – the high degree of dependence of the Polish economy on foreign ownership and the low level of capital accumulation, particularly in private hands – has its roots in processes that, in the perspective of long duration and in terms of critical sociology, can be interpreted as dispossession of the Polish economic elite following the interpretation of the notion as proposed by David Harvey. Thus, they primarily involved the loss of property during the First World War and in its aftermath, first and foremost to the Soviet state. Subsequently, Polish owners were deprived of property by the occupying forces during the Second World War. The communist authorities nationalized private property after 1945 but did not turn it over to foreign hands. However, the process of the Polish economy becoming dependent on Western capital began as early as the 1970s. Harvey (2003) points out that the IMF adjustment programs, such as those used in Latin America in the 1980s, had a clear aspect of ownership transfer from public hands to those of global capital, and it was already at that time that Poland and Hungary became dependent on foreign capital. The demands of global financial institutions involved forcing various types of reforms and deregulations, which led to the low-cost seizure of resources in indebted countries by global financial corporations thus finding a place to utilize their surplus capital.

After the wave of reforms in Latin America, the next stage in the involvement of global financial institutions in similar activities on the periphery of the world system was their entry into former communist countries, particularly those in Central and Eastern Europe (CEE). This began even before the collapse of the communist system; in the case of Poland, for example, the symbolic moment was its formal return to IMF membership as early as in 1986. So far, the economic and political transformation after the collapse of communism has been discussed most systemically in such a critical perspective primarily in the context of Hungary (Gerőcs and Pinkasz 2018). The role of international financial institutions has also been studied in the context of the

Polish transition (Tyszka 2019), although usually without a systematic identification of its broader global context. Particularly noteworthy is the work of Jacek Tittenbrun, who was one of the first to point out the involvement of the IMF and the WB in the planning of Poland's ownership transformation from the early 1980s onward, and later studied its course in detail (Tittenbrun 1993). No less important contributions to the critical examination of the process of Polish assets takeover by foreign capital were made by Tadeusz Kowalik. His work not only discusses in detail the privatization process and its broader international context, but also points to the role played by the intelligentsia elite, which provided this transformation with crucial legitimacy (Kowalik 2012).

As Hungarian researchers point out, already the first credit wave of the 1970s, which also benefited Poland, could be considered part of the mechanisms described by Harvey. At the time, it did not yet lead to significant acquisitions of property by international capital, but it prepared the ground for this process, which reached the critical moment after the final collapse of communism in 1989. Indeed, the first credit wave generated debts that were difficult to repay or even service and brought the countries of the region, led by Poland and Hungary, to a multidimensional crisis that occurred in the early 1980s (Tyszka 2019). This crisis, which was also facilitated by the USA's sanctions imposed on the Polish People's Republic after the declaration of martial law, led to conditions that were extremely favorable to privatization in 1989 and created an unprecedented demand for external capital necessary both to service debts and to launch any development processes in the economy. Hungarian researchers believe that because of their country's dependence on the Western credit in the late 1970s, the conditions under which it was reintegrated into the global economy in the early 1990s proved particularly unfavorable. In the ensuing years of the first postcommunist decade, Hungary, seeing no other alternatives for attracting the Western capital increasingly necessary for development, reinforced a system of asymmetric privileges for global investors which were gradually taking over large chunks of economy (Gagyi and Gerőcs 2022). These factors also allowed a part of industrial production to be moved to the region from Western Europe, mainly from its inner southern periphery (Meardi 2014). Hungary could be an extreme case in several respects, notably the level of debt to the West, but analogous mechanisms were at work throughout the region and the effect was similar in most countries – a phenomenon which certain more radical researchers call a state of economic colonization (Švihlíková 2022).

The global capital obtained significant market shares and ownership of assets as well as asymmetric privileges vis-à-vis local entrepreneurs in all the Central European countries. As a result, local business leaders proved relatively weak players at the level of each country's elite, or the field of power. A more detailed analysis of economic elites reveals significant differences between countries. In the Czech Republic, an oligarchic group of local businesspeople capable of influencing politics and the media has emerged (Slačálek and Šitera 2022), in Hungary, Prime Minister Viktor Orbán's project of building a "national bourgeoisie" is being implemented (Scheiring 2022), while in Poland, a group of managers formerly working for multinational corporations has formed as an important proponent of adopting national developmental policies (Naczyk 2021). However, the overall advantage of large foreign corporations over local business owners, primarily in the dimension of strategic lobbying and influence on the national and EU policy making, seems to be widespread throughout the region (Drahokoupil 2009). In his book, Jan Drahokoupil describes in detail the structural advantages that multinational corporations have gained over local businesses in Central Europe. These include privileges, tax exemptions (also total ones), influence over legislation, and much more. Jacek Tittenbrun points out that foreign capital began to obtain those privileges as early as in the mid-1980s (Tittenbrun 1992). As suggested earlier, servicing the interests of international capital is carried out by a well-paid layer of specialists which can be called the elite of the contemporary intelligentsia. Drahokoupil refers to that part of the intelligentsia engaged in servicing and legitimizing global capital in their countries as the "comprador service sector" (Drahokoupil 2008).

As suggested above, the transition of a considerable part of property in Central European economies into the hands of Western capital can be interpreted in David Harvey's analytical frame in which it would correspond to the processes he refers to as dispossession. For clarity, in purely legal terms, the notion would not be adequate to describe specific changes in ownership as these typically include legal transfers of property, usually formalized as a cheap sale, contribution, or repayment of debts. Be that as it may, such a spectacular process of transferring ownership from the hands of public or private national entities to global owners on such a scale has always needed good legitimacy (ideology), which is provided by the intelligentsia's interpretations of the transition period. This perspective can be linked to the vision of ownership transformation in the region outlined by József Böröcz as early as in 1992. The author proposes to speak of a "property vacuum" that was created when the Soviet Union withdrew from Central Europe (Böröcz 1992). According to him, a large part of the assets of Central European countries were doomed to be taken over by Western corporations because previous property relations were based on the political control of the region by the Soviet empire. After its withdrawal, the postsocialist states and their elites did not have sufficient resources to "create institutional frameworks of responding to the challenge of stimulating an original accumulation of capital" (Böröcz 1992: 99). It can be noted in this context that an important weakness of the economic elites in Poland and other peripheral and semi-peripheral countries turns out to be the weak legitimization of their ownership. The very notion of oligarchy, which is often applied to these elites, including in the academic discourse, contains an aspect of their delegitimization. Unlike the Western economic elites, the peripheral ones are usually unable to convince their societies that their wealth is part of the national wealth and thus serves the good of the country as a whole.

It is also worth noting that the waves of dispossession of Polish economic elites after 1918 and after 1989 both include an aspect of foreign takeover. After 1918, the authorities of the nascent Soviet Union were the main beneficiaries of the expropriation of Polish elites, with the Treaty of Riga signed in 1921 constituting the key act transferring the former Polish assets to them. After 1989, the assets were mainly taken over by Western entities. The dispossessions after 1945 were primarily expropriations of private property by the state treasury. The land assets in the western regions were in turn lost by German owners, although the financial capitals of the previous inhabitants of these lands had typically been evacuated earlier to the West, and much of the infrastructure and movable property from these lands was seized by the Red Army. At the same time, the western lands were informally considered compensation for the lost areas in the east which had passed to the Soviet treasury. Recent reprivatization scandals in Poland have also reminded the public that the Polish People's Republic concluded indemnity agreements with more than a dozen Western countries after the war. On the basis of those agreements, communist Poland paid compensation for the nationalized property of those countries' citizens.

However, if one adopts the perspective on communism as a transitory period, that is, look at it as a multi-stage cycle of transformation, including property transformation, then the expropriations after 1945 and the dispossessions after 1989 can be interpreted as two phases of a single process. The latter can be seen as transfer of private property, mostly owned by Poles, which, after a period of several decades of public administration, would be privatized again, this time with a significant element of redistribution toward small and medium-sized owners and foreign capital. It is possible, in such a view, to consider the black image of the communist period, which can be easily demonized because of its political and symbolic defeat, as a useful legitimization for the acquisition of property rights by new owners. That image of the evil and irrational communist administration of property is used to justify the transfer of wealth from the hands of the previous Polish owners – mostly public but previously largely controlled by the bourgeoisie and landed gentry – to

Western corporations. A direct transfer would be more difficult to legitimize, but after a period of several decades of public administration by "bad communists," culminating in a spectacular economic crisis, the estates in question had largely acquired a status of "nobody's" property and had been devalued, making it easier to change their owners.

This is, of course, a subjective perspective on the interpretation of these processes, and it only becomes coherent when considering their dynamics and geo-economic changes throughout the century, especially from a post-1989 perspective, owing to which one knows that the communist project in the Soviet bloc ended in a total failure. Indeed, it can be pointed out that one deeper implication of the victory of the Bolshevik Revolution in Russia was that it permanently destabilized property relations throughout what became the Soviet bloc over extended periods of time. In many countries, these relations have not been fully settled to this day. In Poland, for example, the issue of reprivatization remains systemically unresolved, while in many countries of the former Soviet Union deoligarchization, that is, the expropriation of a large part of the national bourgeoisie, forms a constantly recurring political demand. Thus, on the one hand, the victory of the Bolshevik Revolution deprived Western investors in the Russian Empire of their property, while on the other hand, in the long run, by destabilizing property relations over a vast area of CEE, it opened the door to their capital expansion as soon as the Soviet Union began to decline. In view of this, the revolutionary movements in the global periphery, even if they are able to overthrow capitalist relations in individual countries for a while, ultimately prove contrary to their own intentions. Due to their impermanence, they may inscribe themselves into the logic of the world system operation. In particular, they serve the interest of its core and undermine the possibility of long-term capital accumulation in the periphery.

5   Conclusion: the Inevitability of Dispossession in the Periphery

The interpretation of the intelligentsia's visions of Poland's history proposed in this text can be characterized as exaggerated. The main goal of this chapter, however, is to point out the naturalized assumptions of discourses that can be considered as legitimizations of the postcommunist transformation. In particular, they serve the naturalization of the intelligentsia's dominant position in the contemporary Polish field of power. Thus, the narratives in question naturalize processes that can be interpreted from a broader historical perspective as the dispossession of Polish economic elites and the expropriation of Polish society as such. This is because the intelligentsia's interpretations often more or less explicitly present the assumption that those expropriations and the seizure of a large part of property by foreign capital were overall beneficial to the nation. They allegedly allowed it to relieve itself of its backward feudal elites and to democratize itself both in political and economic dimensions, that is, to become more modern and more Western. Thus, the interpretations in question ignore or naturalize the issue of Poland's capital dependence on the Western core, legitimizing its semi-peripheral status in the world system in cultural terms. From such an intelligentsia-centric perspective, the Polish economic elite which emerged in the second part of the nineteenth century is seen as an anomaly, the importance of which in the history of Poland should be minimized.

Moreover, the aforementioned processes of loss of economic capital and property are seen from such a perspective as inevitable by virtue of Poland's permanent position in the world system. The basis for those interpretations is a deeply naturalized conviction in the dominant intelligentsia discourses about the inability of Poles to develop their own economic elite and, more broadly, the inability to accumulate financial capital on a large scale. This inability is mostly presented in the form of an implicit assumption and understood not as a structural limitation, but as an intrinsic cultural weakness of Polishness as such. Such weakness that can even be considered a condition in which it is dangerous for Poles to attempt to create their own economic elite or accumulate large capital surpluses. Therefore, for their own sake, they must cyclically be freed from the accumulated economic resources in order to modernize, emancipate themselves, and attempt to move closer to the Western culture understood as a source of civilization, morality, and progress (Böröcz 2006). Within the dependency theory, the superiority of the Western core over the periphery, including CEE, would be understood mainly in economic terms, especially defined as the capacity for multi-generational capital accumulation. In the intelligentsia perspective, however, it is defined primarily in cultural terms. Thus, to sum up, one can speak of the contemporary Polish society as dominated by intelligentsia elites which largely replace the classical bourgeoisie. The aforementioned elites promote a vision of the country's history in which their own role is highly valued, as is the role of culture as a major factor in development. The role of the bourgeoisie, including the historical Polish bourgeoisie of the late nineteenth and early twentieth centuries, is usually depreciated, and the story of the loss of their capitals, which can also be seen as a process of dispossession, is overlooked or naturalized.

References

Agnblad, J., Berglöf, E., Högfeldt, P., & Svancar, H. (2001). Ownership and control in Sweden: Strong owners, weak minorities, and social control. In F. Barca & M. Becht (Eds.), *The control of corporate Europe* (pp. 228–258). Oxford University Press.

Böröcz, J. (1992). Dual dependency and property vacuum: Social change on the state socialist semiperiphery. *Theory and Society, 21*(1), 77–104.

Böröcz, J. (2006). Goodness is elsewhere: The rule of European difference. *Comparative Studies in Society and History, 48*(1), 110–138.

Charle, C. (1990). A la recherche des bourgeoisies européennes. *Le Mouvement Social, 153,* 91–97.

Credit Suisse Research Institute. (2022). *Global wealth report 2022.* Credit Suisse Group AG. https://www.credit-suisse.com/about-us/en/reports-research/global-wealth-report.html.

Deloitte. (2015). *Czy oszczędności krajowe będą w stanie finansować długoterminowy wzrost gospodarczy w Polsce?* Deloitte Polska. https://igte.pl/wp-content/uploads/2019/06/Czy-oszczednosci-krajowe-beda-w-stanie-finansowac-dlugoterminowy-wzrost-gospodarczy-w-Polsce.pdf.

Drahokoupil, J. (2008). The rise of the comprador service sector: The politics of state transformation in Central and Eastern Europe. *Polish Sociological Review, 162*(2), 175–189.

Drahokoupil, J. (2009). *Globalization and the state in Central and Eastern Europe: The politics of foreign direct investment.* Routledge.

Eyal, G., Szelényi, I., & Townsley, E. R. (1998). *Making capitalism without capitalists: Class formation and elite struggles in post-communist Central Europe.* Verso.

Gagyi, A., & Gerőcs, T. (2022). Reconfiguring regimes of capitalist integration: Hungary since the 1970s. In A. Gagyi & O. Slačálek (Eds.), *The political economy of Eastern Europe 30 years into the "transition": New left perspectives from the region* (pp. 115–131). Springer International Publishing.

Gál, Z., & Lux, G. (2022). FDI-based regional development in Central and Eastern Europe: A review and an agenda. *Tér és Társadalom, 36*(3), 68–98.

Gerőcs, T., & Pinkasz, A. (2018). Debt-ridden development on Europe's Eastern periphery. In M. Boatcă, A. Komlosy, & H.-H. Nolte (Eds.), *Global inequalities in world-systems perspective: Theoretical debates and methodological innovations* (pp. 131–153). Routledge.

Grabski, W. (2016). *Idea Polski: wybór pism.* Ośrodek Myśli Politycznej, Narodowe Centrum Kultury.

Grocholski, Z. Hr. (1929). *Kresowe ziemie ruskie Najjaśniejszej Rzeczypospolitej.* Koło Polaków Ziem Ruskich.

Guriev, S., & Rachinsky, A. (2005). The role of oligarchs in Russian capitalism. *Journal of Economic Perspectives*, *19*(1), 131–150.

Harvey, D. (2003). *The new imperialism*. Oxford University Press.

Hensel, J. (1979). *Burżuazja warszawska drugiej połowy XIX w. w świetle akt notarialnych*. PWN.

Jasiecki, K. (2010). O nieznanych, z reguły nie badanych kręgach bogactwa. In M. Jarosz (Ed.), *Polacy równi i równiejsi* (pp. 71–118). ISP PAN.

Jasiecki, K. (2013). *Kapitalizm po polsku. Między modernizacją a peryferiami polskimi*. Wydawnictwo IFiS PAN.

Kochanowicz, J. (2006, August 21–25). *Polish kingdom: Periphery as a leader* [Paper presentation]. 14th International Economic History Congress, Helsinki, Finland.

Kowalik, T. (2012). *From solidarity to sellout: The restoration of capitalism in Poland*. Monthly Review Press.

Kula, W. (1983). *Historia, zacofanie, rozwój*. Czytelnik.

Luxemburg, R. (1898). *Die Industrielle Entwicklung Polens*. Duncker and Humblot.

Meardi, G. (2014). Peripheral convergence in the crisis? Southern and Eastern European labor markets and industrial relations. *Warsaw Forum of Economic Sociology*, *5*(1(9)), 7–27.

Mich, W. (2000). *Ideologia polskiego ziemiaństwa 1918–1939*. Wydawnictwo UMSC.

Mousseau, F., & Devillers, E. (2023). *War and theft: The takeover of Ukraine's agricultural land*. The Oakland Institute.

Myant, M. (2018). Dependent capitalism and the middle-income trap in Europe and East Central Europe. *International Journal of Management and Economics*, *54*(4), 291–303.

Naczyk, M. (2021). Taking back control: Comprador bankers and managerial developmentalism in Poland. *Review of International Political Economy*, *29*(5), 1650–1674.

Nölke, A., & Vliegenthart, A. (2009). Enlarging the varieties of capitalism: The emergence of dependent market economies in East Central Europe. *World Politics*, *61*(4), 670–702.

Palma, J. G. (2008). Theories of dependency. In A. K. Dutt & J. Ros (Eds.), *International handbook of development economics. Volume One* (pp. 125–135). Edward Elgar.

Piatkowski, M. (2018). *Europe's growth champion: Insights from the economic rise of Poland*. Oxford University Press.

Piketty, T. (2020). *Capital and ideology*. The Belknap Press of Harvard University Press.

Sałach, K., & Brzeziński, M. (2020). Political connections and the super-rich in Poland. *Working Papers 553, ECINEQ, Society for the Study of Economic Inequality*.

Scheiring, G. (2022). The national-populist mutation of neoliberalism in dependent economies: The case of Viktor Orbán's Hungary. *Socio-Economic Review*, *20*(4), 1597–1623.

Slačálek, O., & Šitera, D. (2022). Czechia 30 years on: An imperfect oligarchy without emancipatory alternative. In A. Gagyi & O. Slačálek (Eds.), *The political economy of Eastern Europe 30 years into the "transition": New left perspectives from the region* (pp. 133–150). Springer International Publishing.

Smoczyński, R., & Zarycki, T. (2021). The extended family: Descendants of nobility in post-communist Poland. *Communist and Post-Communist Studies, 54*(4), 157–175.

Švihlíková, I. (2022). *How the Czech Republic became a colony*. Transform! European Network for Alternative Thinking and Political Dialogue.

Tittenbrun, J. (1992). *Upadek socjalizmu realnego w Polsce*. Dom Wydawniczy Rebis.

Tittenbrun, J. (1993). *The collapse of "real socialism" in Poland*. Janus Publishing Company.

Turkowski, A., & Zarycki, T. (2023). From Wallerstein to Rothschild: The sudden disappearance of the Polish school of dependency theory after 1989 as a manifestation of deeper trans-formations in the global field of social science. *Journal of World-Systems Research, 29*, 149–173.

Tyszka, F. (2019). *Foreign debt, crisis management, systemic transformation. Poland 1989–1994* [Unpublished doctoral dissertation]. European University Institute.

Zarycki, T. (2004). Uses of Russia: The role of Russia in the modern Polish national identity. *East European Politics and Societies, 18*(4), 595–627.

Zarycki, T. (2007). History and regional development: A controversy over the "right" interpretation of the role of history in the development of the Polish regions. *Geoforum, 38*, 485–493.

Zarycki, T., Smoczyński, R., & Warczok, T. (2017). The roots of Polish culture-centered politics: Toward a non–purely cultural model of cultural domination in Central and Eastern Europe. *East European Politics and Societies, 31*(2), 360–381.

PART 2

Staying Close to Social Experience

CHAPTER 6

Industry 4.0 as a Sociotechnical Imaginary Experienced from Below: the Case of Small and Medium Industrial Enterprises in Poland

Renata Włoch

1 Introduction

In the contemporary academic world, the fact that scientists are able to perform scoping or a systematic review of a given notion is a sure sign of its saturation in scholarly discourse. Such is the case with Industry 4.0. A review by Ghobakhloo et al. (2021) analyzes 745 articles from the many thousands published in recent years, highlighting that "the amount of hype surrounding Industry 4.0 has led to the excessive growth of academic publications during the past few years, from a handful of articles in 2014 and 2015 to thousands of academic contributions in 2020." Still, the popularity of this concept among scientists is but a spillover from its acclaim in the business sector. McKinsey, a global consultancy, reports that while Industry 4.0 was scarcely noted in Google searches prior to 2014, a survey five years later revealed nearly seventy percent of companies considered it a strategic priority, with many already adopting related technologies (McKinsey 2022).

What exactly is Industry 4.0? Perplexingly, while there is an abundance of research on Industry 4.0, defining it remains a challenge: multiple articles on the subject first emphasize the haziness and definitional ambiguity of the notion, before proceeding to enumerate the technologies integral to its development (Abdulnour et al. 2022; Alcácer and Cruz-Machado 2019; Chiarini, Belvedere, and Grando 2020; Yu and Schweisfurth 2020; Mittal et al. 2018). Broadly speaking, Industry 4.0 represents an industrial realm that harnesses new digital technologies throughout the value chain. The original idea of Industry 4.0, presented in 2011 by a group of German scientists and engineers, revolved around the possibility to merge real and virtual spaces within cyber-physical production systems (Kagermann and Wahlster 2022). The ideal Weberian type of a cyber-physical system means that there is a loop between the physical and digital worlds: sensor-equipped machines capture data from the digital world (physical to digital); they process, analyze, and share these data with other machines using cloud computing enhanced by algorithms of artificial intelligence (AI) (digital to digital); and then they convert the automatic decisions made in the digital realms into action, driving tangible outcomes and transformations in the physical world through machines equipped with actuators.

All of these data-generating devices can be connected within the industrial internet of things (IIoT); some of them will take the form of a new generation of mobile, flexible, and AI-enhanced robots. Industry 4.0 also encompasses novel manufacturing technologies such as 3D printing, although its implementation is very slow: in 2021 it comprised only 0.1 percent of the global manufacturing sector. Ghobakhloo et al. (2021) systematically pinpoint the following technological pillars of Industry 4.0: additive/advanced manufacturing; augmented and virtual reality; automation and industrial robots; blockchain; big data analytics; cloud data and computing; cybersecurity; cyber-physical production systems; Internet of services; Internet of people; industrial internet of things; and simulation and modeling, often referred to as the "digital twin." Collectively, these advancements drive the Fourth Industrial Revolution, marking a significant phase in the digitization of manufacturing (McKinsey 2022).

Recent understandings of Industry 4.0 emphasize its foundation on the efficient use of data and intelligent algorithms throughout the production process (Klingenberg, Borges, and Antunes Jr. 2019). As noted by Śledziewska and Włoch (2021), it entails the comprehensive integration of sensor data, connected devices, and system information, transforming linear value and supply chains into intricate networks. From design to maintenance, each stage of a product's lifecycle becomes a critical network node, linking suppliers, machinery, workers, and consumers. As products become increasingly data-driven, they are complemented by digital services enhancing their core functions. This evolution leads to the mass personalization of products tailored to individual consumer needs. Industry 4.0 culminates in the form of an intelligent factory: highly automated, employing hybrid teams of people and AI-enhanced machines, and integrated horizontally within company (from production to sales and distribution) and vertically within the product life-cycle by way of efficient datafication.

All in all, Industry 4.0 strives to encompass all the major technologies underpinning the emerging digital economy, from cloud computing through human–machine interfaces to AI algorithms I use the latter term as a shortcut though; in fact, these are predominantly machine learning or deep learning algorithms. The definitions often emphasize that Industry 4.0 is a kind of digital transformation, only in the manufacturing sector (Horváth and Szabó 2019), and this is an important feature to which I return below. However, the mere adoption of these technologies is not enough; it necessitates overarching organizational and processual shifts to truly realize a digital industrial era. In 2022, two people responsible for introducing the notion in 2011 observed that "a decade after its introduction, Industrie 4.0 has been established globally as the dominant paradigm for the digital transformation of the manufacturing industry" ((Kagermann and Wahlster 2022).

In this chapter I show that Industry 4.0 is a specimen of a significant and powerful sociotechnical imaginary that shapes economic policy and organizational choices of companies and influences societal expectations regarding economic development. At their core, as outlined by Jasanoff and Kim (2015), sociotechnical imaginaries are visions of desirable futures that are collectively endorsed and institutionally reinforced. But they are more than just visions; they are propelled by a communal belief that advancements in science and technology can foster a desirable societal order. What sets them apart from other imaginaries is their forward-facing nature – they tend to prescribe proper course of social action designed for achieving desirable future outcomes. They do not just envision the future; they lay out a roadmap for achieving it. As Pesch (2021 aptly puts it, "the future social order is not only conceived but also enacted in sociotechnical imaginaries." While Jasanoff and Kim pinpoint their creation and sustenance to state institutions, viewing them in a macrostructural light, recent research suggests a broader reach. Scholars like Gardner (2022), Hermann et al. (2022), and Sismondo (2020) argue for their tangible impact at the mesolevel – within organizations and societal groups. This perspective shines a light on a gap in Jasanoff and Kim's framework: they perhaps overlooked the burgeoning influence of other potent and persuasive social actors, notably large corporations and global consultancy firms, on shaping and disseminating these visions.

This chapter is divided into three main sections. In section 2, I trace the origins of the Industry 4.0 notion, highlighting its inception within initiatives taken by the German government and its development by one of the most influential nonprofit organizations and consultancy entities – the World Economic Forum (WEF). As a result, I present Industry 4.0 as a distinct political and business project, aligned with a particular developmental imperative. Next, drawing from a rich body of critical literature, I discuss the key elements of this specific imaginary upheld by various societal actors – ranging from governments to academia, consultancy firms, and technology providers.

In the final section, I briefly illustrate how the imaginary of Industry 4.0 exerts an impact at the level of small and medium-sized industrial enterprises in Poland. For this purpose, I rely on the qualitative research conducted between 2022 and 2023 among the CEOs of seventeen small technology vendors. The firms chosen for this study represent a diverse array in terms of size, production specifics, and geographical distribution. Care was also taken to include companies recognized within national rankings for innovation and advancement in Industry 4.0. During these interviews, participants elucidated the particularities of their solutions, described their collaborative interactions with industrial entities, and offered insights into the evolution of the Polish industrial landscape. The interview transcripts were anonymized, and unique codes were randomly attributed to each interview (D1–17). The collected data was subsequently encoded and scrutinized using qualitative data analysis software. This method allowed for the extraction of thematic patterns related to the contextual variables, incentives, barriers, challenges, and unique features of Industry 4.0 implementations within the scope of Polish industrial enterprises.

2 The Inventions of Industry 4.0

The introduction and popularization of the Industry 4.0 concept was the result of actions by a group of actors with clearly defined economic and political interests. The term "Industrie 4.0" was proposed in 2011 by a group of German scholars closely collaborating with the business sector and public institutions: Henning Kagermann, a physicist and one of the founders of SAP, a company specializing in providing digital systems for enterprises; Wolfgang Wahlster, an artificial intelligence researcher; and Wolf-Dieter Lukas, a physicist who at the time worked at the German Ministry of Education and Research. In an article detailing the successful proliferation of the "Industry 4.0 brand," Kagermann and Wahlster (2022) admit their initiative had strong political support from the start. This support was prominently demonstrated by the then Chancellor of Germany, Angela Merkel, who "spontaneously incorporated the new label 'Industrie 4.0' into her opening remarks at the Hanover Fair" (Kagermann, Wahlster 2022: 1).

The "spontaneous" behavior of the Chancellor was, in fact, a calculated move. The German government recognized that the concept of Industrie 4.0 could serve as a strategic vision, aiding the German economy in overcoming the aftermath of the 2008 global economic crisis. This was coupled with the belief that heavily industrialized economies could navigate the crisis more efficiently by adapting to the new demands of the digital economy. In reality, the concept of Industrie 4.0, adeptly marketed as an innovative idea by a group of scientists and businesspeople, was the result of several years of conceptual work by a consortium of governmental and business institutions, in which the nonprofit organization WEF played a substantial role (Hirsch-Kreinsen 2016).

Over time, Germany began to regard the Industrie 4.0 concept as an instrument of their soft power, bolstering their return to their rightful position in the global economic arena:

> The term "Industrie 4.0" has spread virally and is now associated with Germany all over the world, similarly to "kindergarten" and "autobahn." Industrie 4.0 is an export hit that has received attention and recognition in business, science, and politics around the globe. For the first time in the high-tech world, we have once again been able to establish an innovative concept from Germany internationally, after they had mostly come from North America or Asia for many years. Industrie 4.0 has made Europe the most innovative factory supplier of the world.
> KAGERMANN and WAHLSTER 2022: 2

According to Marxist theorist of digital economy Christian Fuchs (2018), at the heart of the "Industrie 4.0" initiative was the belief that infusing digital technologies into industrial companies would enhance their efficiency and profitability, mirroring the agile and successful ICT companies. Such a move was expected to spur the growth of the German economy, which is deeply rooted in its industrial foundations. However, Fuchs posits that the business elites might have had a more covert motivation: automation and robotization could potentially diminish the power of the German workforce, known for its education, unionization, and consequent costliness. In his opinion, "Industrie 4.0," viewed as the new German digital ideology, can be construed as an attempt to amplify capital gains. "Industry 4.0 is an ideological phantom formed in the contemporary bourgeoisie's collective brain. It aims at advancing new forms of accumulation, control and class struggle from above" (Fuchs 2018: 287).

Over the past decade, the Industry 4.0 concept has taken a prominent place in Germany's economic development strategy. In April 2015, the strategic evolution of the Industry 4.0 concept saw the establishment of Platform Industrie 4.0. This was a collaborative venture initiated by the German associations BITKOM (Federal Association for Information Technology), VDMA (Mechanical Engineering Industry Association), and ZVEI (Central Association of the Electrical Engineering and Electronics Industry), all with the backing of the German government. The objective of this initiative was to convene key stakeholders to jointly navigate the challenges and potential of the digital metamorphosis within the manufacturing sector. By 2019, experts from Platform Industrie 4.0 had updated the 2030 vision for Industry 4.0, from that moment on encapsulated under the title "Shaping digital ecosystems globally." The emphasis shifted from the digital transformation of individual enterprises to the transformation of entire value chains. This idea was adopted by several other countries, especially in Northern Europe. Polish government also undertook efforts to transplant it onto Polish soil by establishing the Future Industry Platform in 2019 (Future Industry Platform 2021). Nevertheless, its widespread popularity might not have been realized without the endorsement of the influential World Economic Forum.

The WEF is widely considered a pivotal organization in shaping global agendas in the area of economic development and political arrangements of economic order; it champions an openly neoliberal agenda and promotes the notion of multistakeholder capitalism (Rothkopf 2009). This perspective contends that global corporations bear a unique responsibility to address challenges like poverty and the climate crisis. Moreover, it asserts that such corporations should be actively involved in political processes, positioning them as significant entities alongside nation states. It is important to underscore that the worldview and specific ideas for reforming global politics and economics presented by the WEF are subjects of significant controversy. Advocacy for a "great reset" and endeavors to establish an economic and political order wherein major corporations assume a role commensurate with the state have notably attracted criticism from right-wing commentators. Conversely, left-wing activists accuse the WEF of Eurocentrism, latent racism, and the pursuit of a turbo-capitalistic vision of reality predicated on the exploitation of peripheral regions.

The WEF traces its roots to 1971, when the inaugural meeting of economic and political elites was convened in the Swiss resort of Davos by the German business professor, Klaus Schwab. In 2015 the WEF was officially established as an international nonprofit organization for public–private cooperation under Swiss law. Funding for the WEF's operations is sourced from its nearly 1,000 member companies – global entities boasting annual turnovers in excess of five billion USD – as well as public subsidies. Of note, the WEF's Board of Trustees boasts influential figures such as Kristalina Georgieva, Managing Director of the IMF; Christine Lagarde, President of the European Central Bank; and former Vice President of the United States, Al Gore. In 2023, the Davos meeting convened 2,700 participants, all focused on deliberating "global challenges." All in all, as Schiølin (2020) notes, due to its connections and global networking with the rich and the mighty, the WEF is particularly adept in spawning imaginaries that "fabricates, distributes and exercises power in ways that reach far beyond the economic consultancy that its name suggests."

The transformation of a local German economic vision into a global phenomenon can be attributed to the founder and executive chairman of the WEF himself, Klaus Schwab. In 2016, Schwab published a book titled *The Fourth*

Industrial Revolution (2016). In the work, he unfolds a vision of rapid and radical socio-economic change – nothing less than the "transformation of humankind" – spurred by the widespread adoption of innovative technologies. In his opinion, an unprecedented revolution is unfolding before our eyes, with the ensuing changes being "historic in terms of their size, speed, and scope." This is driven by the megatrends represented as technological drivers of the Fourth Industrial Revolution: physical, digital, and biological. The book's narrative is imbued with technological determinism and optimism: technologies are the driving force of development, so the emergence of new technologies "naturally" induces profound changes in the functioning of economic systems and social structures alike. Schwab believes that the disruptive influence of the Fourth Industrial Revolution on politics, economics, and society necessitates collaboration among various actors in a new international framework: "The disruption that the fourth industrial revolution will have on existing political, economic, and social models will therefore require that empowered actors recognize that they are part of a distributed power system that requires more collaborative forms of interaction to succeed" (Schwab 2016: 28). Such a perspective aligns seamlessly with his concept of multistakeholder capitalism, which he has been championing for nearly five decades.

The final element in the successful marketing trajectory for the Industry 4.0 concept was the involvement of major consulting firms such as McKinsey, Deloitte, and KPMG. These firms perceived the "Industry 4.0" concept as an excellent material for a new management fad that could aid them in selling their services by emphasizing that companies must introduce digital technologies if they want to survive. As Madsen (2019) notes, the concept of Industry 4.0 fits such usage exceptionally well. Its attractive and catchy name easily garners attention in the media and among corporations. Importantly, it automatically connotes progress and advancement: version 4.0 must be better than version 3.0. It also facilitates the easy creation of neologisms, like "Work 4.0" or "University 4.0." Additionally, it provides a nebulous and open field for interpretation – as I mentioned earlier, researchers still grapple with agreeing on a definitive meaning for Industry 4.0. Embedded in the essence of Industry 4.0 are enthusiastic promises regarding the revolutionary shift in economic activities, even suggesting a paradigm shift in the functioning of the entire economy. Management fads also have the characteristic of presenting themselves as context-independent: solutions related to Industry 4.0 are portrayed as universally beneficial for every country without exception and without considering its specificities. Above all, the rise of the Industry 4.0 concept was facilitated by the familiarity of the industrial production paradigm and its resonance with prior management trends such as lean production and agile. This sense of recognition was not solely rooted in the industrial context but was also influenced by the ubiquitous phenomenon of digitalization, which has made inroads into every economic sector and facet of life. By synergizing these familiar narratives, the Industry 4.0 concept effectively encapsulated the ongoing shifts, achieving rapid dissemination. This merging of the industrial and digital themes, both highly relevant and recognized, was pivotal to its success.

Returning to the chapter's introductory remarks, it is striking how swiftly and enthusiastically the academic community embraced the concept of Industry 4.0. Alongside terms like "sharing economy" and "network society," Industry 4.0 became a catch-all phrase, offering a coherent framework to understand the rapid socio-economic transformations underway. Traditional media, especially those focused on business, as well as social media platforms, constituted the "fashion-setting community" (Madsen 2019), fueling a distinct hype surrounding the digital economy. They indulged in reports about Amazon's automated warehouses or Volkswagen's smart robots. Furthermore, technology vendors had a vested interest in promoting the idea emphasizing the imperative of integrating new technologies. Under their financial patronage, numerous reports emerged, crafted by consulting firms, often in collaboration with academic professionals. These findings were grandiosely showcased at various industry conferences and seminars, attended by the representatives of industrial companies.

3 Industry 4.0's Ideology of Change

The discourse surrounding Industry 4.0, advanced by the WEF in collaboration with major consultancies and academic researchers, showcased certain distinguishing characteristics, predominantly concerning the aspects of societal evolution. The critical analyses conducted by Hirsch-Krausen (2016), Pfeiffer (2017), Avis (2018), Madsen (2019), Schiølin (2020), and Vicente and Dias-Trindade (2021), among others, allow one to identify the principal attributes of the transformation process associated with Industry 4.0: the inevitability of change and the imperative of change.

3.1 *The Inevitability of Change*

The discourse surrounding Industry 4.0 is rooted in the underlying belief in the inevitability of change. As Avis (2018) aptly puts it, the transition to the Fourth Industrial Revolution, or 4th IR, is seen as a continuation of a historical trajectory that appears almost preordained. In a similar vein, Hirsch-Kreinsen (2016: 12) argues that the "starting point of Industry 4.0 discourse is the advancement of digital technologies, seen as the driving force of the future economic and societal transformation." This perspective can be characterized as technodeterminism, where Industry 4.0 stands out as a testament to the belief in linear technological evolution. Such a progression is perceived as an unstoppable force, bound by the inexorable logic of history that evolves in distinct phases. Not only are social actors encouraged to align with this trajectory for their welfare, but this narrative also redefines their very role and *raison d'être* in the broader societal context.

Schiølin (2020 sharpens this argument by asserting that the sociotechnical imaginary of Industry 4.0 is marked by a pronounced future essentialism, which posits that there exists a singular correct trajectory of development: societies either adapt or face the prospect of decline. Additionally, as Pfeiffer (2017) elucidates, this envisaged future is devoid of a socially anchored essence and is not tethered to particular individuals or communities. Instead, it is contextually vacuous and bereft of substantial content, rendering it vulnerable to "exploration and exploitation, calculation, and control" by dominant economic players within the ambit of digital capitalism.

Interestingly, this buoyant deterministic and essentialist narrative contrasts sharply with the prevailing discourse in the social sciences, which heralds the emergence of a service-based economy rather than an industrial one. In many economic development analyses over the past half century, the industrial sector has been perceived as a still necessary, yet increasingly outdated, form of economic activity. An example of such an approach is the concept developed by Alvin and Heidi Toffler (1990), who nearly half a century ago prophesied the advent of the Information Age, where knowledge plays an increasingly significant role in the economy and society. The Tofflers conceive of societal change in terms of megatrends that shift the paradigm of how society operates. They believe that the rapidly approaching Third Wave, heralding an economy founded on knowledge and services, would induce a social shock of a magnitude comparable to the two initial waves: the Neolithic, which revolutionized agriculture, and the Industrial, rooted in inventions that facilitated mass production, consumption, education, and entertainment. In a similar vein, Daniel Bell and Alain Touraine predicted the marginalization of the industry's significance in the economy and its decreasing impact on societal welfare and prosperity (Granovetter 1979).

The postindustrial narrative intensified with the advent of the Internet economy, and subsequently, the digital economy. The nascent digital economy, grounded in the production and consumption of virtual digital goods, seemed to underscore the obsolescence of industrial activity. The presumption was that while automation and computerization enhanced production efficiency, they did not instigate a radical transformation in the mode of production itself. Furthermore, the industrial sector appeared to be the most resistant to digitization. As one American analyst astutely observed, "software has, to this point, been unable to devour the physical world. While data holds significance for tangible industries like manufacturing, construction, agriculture, and health care, it does not tell the entire story. Constructing a building demands substantial cranes, not merely a digital twin of a crane" (Mandel 2018).

Against this backdrop, the carefully marketed Industry 4.0 concept highlights the continued relevance of physical production. It resonates with arguments like those of, who assert that we are not transitioning to a postindustrial economy but rather evolving within the spectrum of industrial societies. Pfeiffer (2017) offers a nuanced perspective on this shift. She posits that Industry 4.0 might be an effort to meld the industrial sector with the digital revolution, using it not just as a technological pivot but also a strategic marketing tool. This implies a vision where the industrial sector, despite a broader focus on services and a shift in innovation hubs to ICT and service sectors, can still harness the advantages of the Fourth Industrial Revolution.

Industry 4.0 seeks to weave itself into narratives of progressive industrial evolution, positioning the digitized industry as the next logical phase of economic development and sequentially following the prior three stages. The first stage was ignited by the invention of the steam engine, the second was driven by the advent of electricity, and the third emerged from automation and computerization. Industry 4.0 heralds the Fourth Industrial Revolution, rooted in digital technologies. Thus, provided the industrial sector leverages the emerging, particularly digital, technologies, the significance of manufacturing will not wane.

3.2 *The Imperative of Change*

As discussed above, the notion of Industry 4.0 strives to craft an image of a predetermined, scripted future. This vision of the future is seen as both inevitable and attainable, promising rewards if approached correctly but threatening dire consequences if misunderstood or mishandled. While a sense of future essentialism is inherent in most sociotechnical imaginaries, Industry 4.0 uniquely amplifies this through an unyielding and dialectical interplay of pessimism and optimism, which establishes clear expectations for societal actors (Schiølin 2020). Those who align with the vision set forth by the proponents of this imaginary stand to reap the benefits of peace and prosperity. However, deviation or resistance carries stark implications. Such actors are perceived not just as negligent but, in extreme scenarios, courting potential ruin or even obliteration. The following quote from the website of Deloitte, one of the leading consulting firms engaged in promoting Industry 4.0, aptly illustrates this:

> The Fourth Industrial Revolution, commonly known as Industry 4.0, appears to be changing the way businesses function and, by extension, the stakes by which they are forced to compete. Organizations must decide how and where to invest in these new technologies and identify which ones might best meet their needs. Without a full understanding of the changes and opportunities Industry 4.0 brings, companies risk losing ground.
> COTTELEER and SNIDERMAN 2017

Transitioning to Industry 4.0 promises advantages for entire economies and societies, from job creation to sustainability, and even reshaping political landscapes. As Avis (2018) notices, "the 4th IR is almost presented in neutral terms as a societal development that has to be managed for the benefit of all." But the primary audience for this message concerning the benefits of Industry 4.0 and the risks associated with disregarding its historical trajectory are companies whose operations stand to be radically transformed by the technologies of Industry 4.0 (Hirsch-Kreinsen 2016). An essential component of the narrative surrounding the Fourth Industrial Revolution is the vision of a new enterprise that operates based on the effective use of digital technologies. Numerous consultancy reports extol the myriad benefits of adopting Industry 4.0 technologies, ranging from operational efficiency to customer engagement. Experts from McKinsey, another representative of the Big Four in consulting, argue as follows:

> Industry 4.0 refers to the "smart" and connected production systems that are designed to sense, predict, and interact with the physical world, so as to make decisions that support production in real-time. In manufacturing, it can increase productivity, energy efficiency, and sustainability. It increases productivity by reducing downtime and maintenance costs.
> MCKINSEY 2022

However, adopting these innovations is not a frictionless process. Companies grapple with issues such as data protection, cybersecurity, and managing organizational transformation. Implicitly, Industry 4.0 carries normative expectations, guiding companies on the technologies and changes essential for maintaining a competitive advantage. From this perspective, the concept of Industry 4.0 is no different from other management fads: it entices managers with the promise of productivity growth as a result of implementing new technologies (Madsen 2019). Empirical data further underscores these narratives. As per a 2018 McKinsey Global Institute analysis, leading adopters of Industry 4.0 could expect a staggering 122 percent positive shift in cash flow by 2025. On the other hand, late adopters might only see a modest ten percent increase, and nonadopters could experience a sharp twenty-three percent decline. Moreover, a Lighthouse survey highlighted productivity, sustainability, and resilience as top priorities for respondents, with the Fourth Industrial Revolution technologies deemed instrumental in achieving these goals (McKinsey 2022).

Importantly, the scale, scope, and particularly the pace of the change is so immense that it essentially does not afford societal actors the time to reflect on priorities. The trajectory is already delineated and determined – the sole option for a company is to jump on the bandwagon as swiftly as possible. In describing this characteristic of the discourse on Industry 4.0, Schiølin (2020) proposes the concept of "epochalism," which posits the unique nature of the current transformation. By portraying the present changes as epoch-defining, radical interventions gain legitimacy. The discourse becomes a tool to stifle critique and fast-track agendas, making resistance appear vain.

The assertions regarding the Fourth Industrial Revolution are often presented as self-evident truths. As such, the 4th IR emerges not just as a forecast future but one that has been actively constructed and, to some extent, predetermined. As Pfeiffer (2017) articulates, it is a future that has already been "traded."

To direct the evolution of Industry 4.0 toward the anticipated and desired trajectory, various tools and indices have been formulated. These instruments evaluate if companies demonstrate the appropriate level of engagement in the implementation of new technologies and whether they do so effectively and with adequate speed. Internationally recognized tools such as The Singapore Smart Industry Readiness Index, The Industrie 4.0 Maturity Index, and RAMI 4.0 (Reference Architectural Model Industrie 4.0) offer insights into how and at what pace a company integrates digital technologies, as well as how it adjusts its organizational structure and culture (Mittal et al. 2018). A notable aspect of these tools is their international recognition, ensuring that companies are aligning with global standards and that their strategies resonate with their international counterparts. A company that has achieved optimal maturity will have seamlessly integrated digital technologies into its production processes, modernized its products, and woven a digital thread throughout its value chain. Furthermore, it will harness technology to its fullest extent, driving data integration, optimizing business benefits, and steering its operation with data-driven insights. Indices developed under the commission of the European Union (EU), such as the Digital Intensity Index (DII) and the Digital Economy and Society Index (DESI), tend to be less normative in nature. These tools allow for a comparative analysis of the degree of digital technology implementation across various EU member states. Nevertheless, their visualizations clearly highlight which countries are lagging in digital transformation, potentially signaling concerns regarding their overall economic health.

Conversely, tools and indices developed by consulting firms are imbued with the almost sacrosanct presumption that companies which align with the digital maturity model will inevitably attain merited success. A case in point is the 2017 collaboration between the WEF and McKinsey, resulting in the "global lighthouses" initiative. Their consequent reports assume that these "lighthouses," ever since their recognition by the WEF and McKinsey in 2018, have illuminated the path for the Fourth Industrial Revolution. Lighthouses are companies that exhibit prowess in driving transformative changes leading to establishment of smart factory. This excellence is not just rhetorical; their track record boasts 139 cases that translate into tangible financial, operational, and environmental dividends. On the other hand, the reports are imbued with normative condemnation for firms that are unable to enact changes in a swift and efficient manner. Companies that falter in this transformative journey often find themselves ensnared in the "pilot purgatory."

4 Industry 4.0 from Below: the Perspective of the Polish Technology Vendors

As of 2023, there was not a single company operating in Poland among the lighthouses of Industry 4.0; this year, however, a branch of Danone has made its debut on this prestigious list. Additionally, Polish industrial companies did not fare well in the EU's DESI ranking. Poland takes the twenty-fourth place among EU countries regarding the incorporation of digital technology in business operations. Only 40 percent of Polish small and medium-sized enterprises (SMEs) achieve a basic level of digital intensity, falling short of the EU average of 55 percent. Only two percent of industrial enterprises are classified as having a very high Digital Intensity Index, and 10 percent are in the group with a high DII. This means that only 12 percent of Polish industrial enterprises have implemented at least seven out of the twelve digital solutions considered in the DII index; as a rule, these are large companies, employing more than 250 people. Simultaneously, over the past three decades, the Polish industry has become increasingly integrated with global value chains, primarily in the role of a subcontractor for technologically less-complex products.

In this section of the chapter, I propose to briefly examine how the ideology of change embedded in the assumptions of Industry 4.0 affects the functioning of industrial SMEs in Poland. To do so, I will view this through the lens of a group that has well-defined and entrenched interests in promoting this concept, namely the Polish vendors of technology. Nevertheless, they also have a deep understanding of the specific characteristics of these companies and often empathize with their situation. The surveyed entities are local digital technology suppliers for industrial companies; they themselves often meet the definition of SMEs. Generally, they act as solution integrators, searching for technological solutions offered by various corporations and then supporting companies in their implementation. Unlike large technology vendors, they focus on personalizing their services and building close relationships with individual clients. Thus, they often provide not only technological solutions but also consulting services. Their experience of cooperating with dozens of SMEs gives a bird's-eye view of the reception of the Industry 4.0 concept in Poland, especially the impact of the basic properties of this ideology, that is, the inevitability and imperative of change, on the functioning of small industry. Engaging the perspectives of this group allows for an overarching viewpoint on the reception of Industry 4.0 among Polish industrial SMEs.

First, from the statements of technology providers, there emerged a deeply internalized and unchallenged belief in the linear and inexorable progression of current technological changes: the Fourth Industrial Revolution is approaching and takes no prisoners. If Polish industrial firms do not implement digital technologies, they risk being eliminated from the market. Moreover, in the discourse of many technology suppliers, there was an undercurrent of a unique economic patriotism. These companies viewed their operations of providing bespoke devices and systems not merely as purely business-oriented endeavors, but also as vital support for the Polish industry and the Polish economy, which should keep pace with the revolutionary shifts. A daunting challenge, from their perspective, is the alarming technological backwardness of Polish firms. Not only do these companies lack understanding of how to implement more advanced systems that would optimize their production, but many also have not yet adopted technologies considered typical for previous industrial revolutions. Consequently, they remain inadequately computerized and automated, and continue to operate with an outdated machinery inventory:

> We have a significant technological gap in Polish industry that we need to catch up on. Companies are still lagging, with little real progress. While some are improving, most haven't reached that "Industry 4.0" standard. Many are described as being at levels like 3.5, 3.7, or 3.1. Some are even

seen as still being at 2.9, indicating they've not yet hit the third industrial revolution

D3

Second, technology vendors unanimously emphasized that the imperative for swift and effective implementation of new technologies stems from the need to integrate Polish industry more effectively with the European one, particularly the German manufacturing sector. Western companies are keen on automation for mass production, including through smart robotics. Conversely, small-scale production becomes increasingly unviable for them, primarily due to a shortage of labor willing to undertake tasks perceived as "difficult, dirty, and hazardous." The hesitance of Western, notably German, industrial companies to address the more arduous and less desirable elements of production provides a niche for Polish minor manufacturers to undertake these aspects of the production process. The strength of the Polish industrial sector is grounded in its adaptability to external demands, aptly encapsulated in the sentiment: "Our strength lies in our ability to change and adapt" (D12). Another salient merit of the Polish industrial milieu is its relatively subdued union presence, particularly when contrasted with sectors like the German counterpart, emphasized the vendors. This dynamic facilitates the implementation of substantial digital changes with reduced fear of labor resistance.

Countries such as Germany or France favor robotization and the production of repetitive series, whereas Poland specializes in the production of heavier batches, which are harder to automate. This resistance in production plants against introducing new technologies and robotization is not only due to a lack of knowledge among employees but also stems from the fact that Poland receives orders for less repetitive series, passed down by other countries that focus on mass and repetitive production. These countries recognize that repetitive production is easier, simpler, and cheaper, which ultimately allows them to pay higher salaries to their workers. Poland, on the other hand, is dubbed the "welding shop of Europe," signifying that we specialize in more complex and atypical productions (D11).

Simultaneously, there was a prevalent expression of doubt concerning the appropriateness of Industry 4.0 principles in meeting the requirements of Polish industrial enterprises. Polish industrial firms predominantly engage in short-run production, positioning themselves at intermediary levels within the value chain. Typically, both the design and sale of the final product are situated outside of Poland's jurisdiction. The nature of short-run production presents challenges in its automation and robotization; the process undergoes frequent modifications, and the associated costs and time constraints of altering equipment between distinct production batches diminish its efficiency.

Consequently, Polish firms rarely have the capacity to implement ambitious and comprehensive solutions such as smart factories or seamlessly integrated systems for production datafication.

As a result, and third, the representatives of technological solution providers emphasized that, from their perspective, the portrayal of the Industry 4.0 concept envisioned in the media by consulting firms and public institutions could indeed inhibit the inclination of Polish companies to undertake modernization efforts. To small entities in particular, the implementation of new digital technologies appears as a costly and time-consuming process demanding advanced digital skills from both production staff and management personnel. Companies often struggle to translate abstract terms like "digitalization," "datafication," "platformization," or "Industry 4.0" (or even "5.0"), and the application of AI into everyday production practices. They also lack an understanding of the necessity to radically restructure processes and organizations, which are essential components of the smart factory concept and the associated successful digital transformation.

Still, the narrative prevalent in industry conferences and reports conveys a certain sense of imperativeness about Industry 4.0 for many firms. The companies often feel that without adopting digital systems and delving into robotics and automation, they will be left behind. This prompts some to make hasty and inadequately thought-out decisions, such as purchasing sophisticated robots, the operation of which might necessitate the calibration of an entire production process built on machinery from several decades ago. Consequently, these implementations are often carried out in a non-systematic manner, misaligned with the company's overarching business strategy. This leads to their abandonment when quick and substantial returns on investment fail to follow. As noticed by one of the largest technology vendors, cooperating with dozens of industrial companies,

> many people get really excited about Industry 4.0 and try hard to bring these technologies into their companies, sometimes even forcing the employees to comply. But then there's disappointment when things don't work out as hoped. It's not a magic wand that guarantees success. These technologies are just tools. You need the right foundation and infrastructure for them to work effectively
>
> D5

He further elaborates that "in Poland, we want to build Industry 4.0 before we have built Industry 1.0, 2.0, or 3.0" (D5). In his view, industrial companies are deciding to implement technologies, following certain trends without considering the real possibilities of their use in their production cycle. Another issue is that Polish SMEs generally do not employ any methodologies that allow for assessing the profitability of investment in technology. A paradox of digital technology implementation is the often-occurring increase in product quality coupled with a simultaneous decline in efficiency, leading to customer disappointment due to the expectation of quick and measurable return on investment. As a representative of a company offering personalized digital management systems stated, "The slogan 'Industry 4.0' is a bit overhyped at this moment. Many companies have not reaped benefits from it, and it's hard to convince the boards" (D4).

In general terms, it can be posited that technology vendors, on the one hand, find it challenging to depart from the prevailing narrative surrounding Industry 4.0, viewing it as the archetypal model for digital transformation. On the other hand, their extensive experience suggests that companies operating within a complex economic reality, defined by product specificity and positioning within value chains, find it immensely challenging to conform to this model. Polish firms tend to robotize discrete segments of the production continuum, amalgamating contemporary robotic solutions with either automated production lines or manually executed tasks. Additionally, they adopt production management systems facilitating the convergence of legacy technological modalities with cutting-edge innovations. Concurrently, however, the distinct symbolic violence embedded within the foundational tenets of the Industry 4.0 ideology appears to constrict the strategic latitude available to industrial firms, which occasionally, under its influence, embark on irrational yet financially onerous technological deployments.

5 Conclusions

From a sociological perspective, the concept of Industry 4.0 is interesting regarding the instrumental use of conceptual–theoretical frameworks about the stages of industrial revolutions developed in social sciences to legitimize a specific political–economic agenda, backed by numerous interests of political and business actors. The remarkable surge of this concept in academic literature, especially in management and organization fields, indicates that this specific, constructed genesis of the concept is not obvious to the multitude of scientists producing hundreds of articles about the propriety technologies of Industry 4.0, its stages, ways of measuring progress, and impact on productivity. This can be seen as an extraordinary case of discursive seduction: Industry 4.0 is widely recognized as the next, logical stage of economic development.

Researchers who treat the concept of Industry 4.0 as a subject of critical reflection constitute a distinct and disciplinarily scattered minority. In this chapter, I presented the main threads of critical reflection on Industry 4.0 as a specific sociotechnical imaginary. The concept of Industry 4.0, propagated by major consultancies and institutionalized in the form of state industrial development strategies, shapes societal expectations surrounding economic advancement and influences company behavior at the micro-level. The buzz around Industry 4.0 creates a powerful marketing atmosphere, amplifying the perceived necessity of such solutions. By generating a sense of inevitability of change and the necessity to adapt, it prompts companies to make hasty, poorly thought-out, and ultimately less beneficial decisions about implementing new technologies, as is well illustrated by the case of Polish small and medium-sized industrial firms.

Reconstructing the pathway of the Polish government and business elites in introducing the Industry 4.0 concept, as well as examining the direct experiences of Polish entrepreneurs, presents itself as an important research responsibility. It can presently be said that, in their case, the concept of Industry 4.0 on Polish soil constitutes a specific case of center–periphery logic, where the center represents modernization, and the periphery signifies those lagging behind. This modernization discourse perpetuates and strengthens a dynamic based on subordination – it legitimizes dominance over those deemed "backward" or "outdated." Such discourse has been eagerly adopted by actors who find it beneficial, further perpetuating a narrative of comprehensive industrial revolution and transformation. This gives rise to the following question: while Industry 4.0 undoubtedly presents opportunities, how can we ensure a balanced discourse that does not alienate or stigmatize those in transition?

References

Abdulnour, S., Baril, C., Abdulnour, G., & Gamache, S. (2022). Implementation of Industry 4.0 principles and tools: Simulation and case study in a manufacturing SME. *Sustainability*, 14(10), 6336. https://doi.org/10.3390/su14106336.

Alcácer, V., & Cruz-Machado, V. (2019). Scanning the Industry 4.0: A literature review on technologies for manufacturing systems. *Engineering Science and Technology, an International Journal*, 22(3), 899–919. https://doi.org/10.1016/j.jestch.2019.01.006.

Avis, J. (2018). Socio-technical imaginary of the Fourth Industrial Revolution and its implications for vocational education and training: A literature review. *Journal of Vocational Education and Training*, 70(3), 1–27. https://doi.org/10.1080/13636820.2018.1498907.

Chiarini, A., Belvedere, V., & Grando, A. (2020). Industry 4.0 strategies and technological developments: An exploratory research from Italian manufacturing companies. *Production Planning and Control, 31*(16), 1385–1398. https://doi.org/10.1080/09537287.2019.1710304.

Cohen, S. S., & Zysman, J. (1987). *Manufacturing matters: The myth of the post-industrial economy*. Basic Books.

Cotteleer, M., & Sniderman, B. (2017). *Forces of change: Industry 4.0*. Deloitte. https://www2.deloitte.com/content/dam/insights/us/articles/4323_Forces-of-change/4323_Forces-of-change_Ind4-0.pdf.

Fuchs, C. (2018). Industry 4.0: The digital German ideology. *Triple C, 16*(1), 280–289.

Future Industry Platform. (2021). *Future Industry Platform – set up by the state, handed over to industry*. Retrieved Month 11, 2023, from https://przemyslprzyszlosci.gov.pl/future-industry-platform-the-mission-and-contact/.

Gardner, J. (2022). Imaginaries of the data-driven hospital in a time of crisis. *Sociology of Health and Illness, 45*(4), 754–771. https://doi.org/10.1111/1467-9566.13592.

Ghobakhloo, M., Fathi, M., Iranmanesh, M., Maroufkhani, P., & Morales, M. E. (2021). Industry 4.0 ten years on: A bibliometric and systematic review of concepts, sustainability value drivers, and success determinants. *Journal of Cleaner Production, 302*, 127052. https://doi.org/10.1016/j.jclepro.2021.127052.

Granovetter, M. (1979). The idea of "advancement" in theories of social evolution and development. *American Journal of Sociology, 85*(3), 489–515. https://doi.org/10.1086/227047.

Hermann, R. R., Pansera, M., Nogueira, L. A., & Monteiro, M. (2022). Socio-technical imaginaries of a circular economy in governmental discourse and among science, technology, and innovation actors: A Norwegian case study. *Technological Forecasting and Social Change, 183*, 121903. https://doi.org/10.1016/j.techfore.2022.121903.

Hirsch-Kreinsen, H. (2016). "Industry 4.0" as promising technology: Emergence, semantics and ambivalent character. *Soziologisches Arbeitspapier, 48*.

Horváth, D., & Szabó, R. Z. (2019). Driving forces and barriers of Industry 4.0: Do multinational and small and medium-sized companies have equal opportunities? *Technological Forecasting and Social Change, 146*, 119–132. https://doi.org/10.1016/j.techfore.2019.05.021.

Jasanoff, S., & Kim, S.-H. (Eds.). (2015). *Dreamscapes of modernity: Sociotechnical imaginaries and the fabrication of power*. The University of Chicago Press.

Kagermann, H., & Wahlster, W. (2022). Ten years of Industrie 4.0. *Sci, 4*(3), 26. https://doi.org/10.3390/sci4030026.

Klingenberg, C. O., Viana Borges, M. A., & Valle Antunes, J. A., Jr. (2019). Industry 4.0 as a data-driven paradigm: A systematic literature review on technologies. *Journal of Manufacturing Technology Management*, *32*(3), 570–592. https://doi.org/10.1108/JMTM-09-2018-0325.

Madsen, D. Ø. (2019). The emergence and rise of Industry 4.0 viewed through the lens of management fashion theory. *Administrative Sciences*, *9*(3), 71. https://doi.org/10.3390/admsci9030071.

Mandel, M. (2018). Digital manufacturing and the Internet of goods. *Forbes*. https://www.forbes.com/sites/michaelmandel1/2018/11/03/digital-manufacturing-and-the-internet-of-goods/?sh=1f27e7e17629.

McKinsey. (2022). *What is Industry 4.0 and the Fourth Industrial Revolution?* https://www.mckinsey.com/featured-insights/mckinsey-explainers/what-are-industry-4-0-the-fourth-industrial-revolution-and-4ir.

Mittal, S., Khan, M. A., Romero, D., & Wuest, T. (2018). A critical review of smart manufacturing and Industry 4.0 maturity models: Implications for small and medium-sized enterprises (SMEs). *Journal of Manufacturing Systems*, *49*, 194–214. https://doi.org/10.1016/j.jmsy.2018.10.005.

Pesch, U. (2021). Imaginaries of innovation: Turning technology development into a public issue. *Science and Public Policy*, *48*(2), 257–264. https://doi.org/10.1093/scipol/scab017.

Pfeiffer, S. (2017). The vision of "Industrie 4.0" in the making – A case of future told, tamed, and traded. *NanoEthics*, *11*(1), 107–121. https://doi.org/10.1007/s11569-016-0280-3.

Rothkopf, D. J. (2009). *Superclass: The global power elite and the world they are making*. Farrar, Straus and Giroux.

Schiølin, K. (2020). Revolutionary dreams: Future essentialism and the sociotechnical imaginary of the Fourth Industrial Revolution in Denmark. *Social Studies of Science*, *50*(4), 542–566. https://doi.org/10.1177/0306312719867768.

Schwab, K. (2016). *The Fourth Industrial Revolution* (1st U.S. edition). Crown Business.

Sismondo, S. (2020). Sociotechnical imaginaries: An accidental themed issue. *Social Studies of Science*, *50*(4), 505–507. https://doi.org/10.1177/0306312720944753.

Śledziewska, K., & Włoch, R. (2021). *The economics of digital transformation: The disruption of markets, production, consumption and work*. Routledge.

Toffler, A. (1990). *The third wave: The controversial new perspective on tomorrow from the author of Future Shock*. Pan Books.

Vicente, P. N., & Dias-Trindade, S. (2021). Reframing sociotechnical imaginaries: The case of the Fourth Industrial Revolution. *Public Understanding of Science*, *30*(6), 708–723. https://doi.org/10.1177/09636625211013513.

Yu, F., & Schweisfurth, T. (2020). Industry 4.0 technology implementation in SMEs – A survey in the Danish-German border region. *International Journal of Innovation Studies*, *4*(3), 76–84. https://doi.org/10.1016/j.ijis.2020.05.001.

CHAPTER 7

Multiculturalism and Multilingualism in Smaller 'Cities of Immigration and Emigration': Płock, Kalisz and Piła, 2019–2022

Anne White

This chapter discusses changes to Poland's emerging identity as a country of immigration. It employs, but also critiques, the term 'multiculturalism'. Shortly before the refugee influx following Putin's full-scale invasion of Ukraine in February 2022, Poland had achieved statistical net immigration (Okólski 2021). Over just a few years, it had undergone the process labelled by demographers 'migration transition', defined in its simplest sense by King and Gëdeshi (2022: 132) as 'passage from a country of net emigration to one of net immigration'. This chapter considers whether the migration transition also means that Poland is achieving a multicultural identity, focusing specifically on linguistic identities.

Given that immigration is different in scale and kind in different Polish locations, it is possible to address this question only with reference to individual places. Until recently, labour migrants have been concentrated in the biggest Polish cities and on farms in Mazowieckie region. However, they have now begun to spread in greater numbers to other regions and to smaller cities and towns (Górny and Śleszyński 2019; Kałuża-Kopias 2023). This chapter is based on qualitative research in three smaller cities, Płock, Kalisz and Piła, whose 2021 populations were 118,000, 98,000, and 72,000, respectively (GUS 2022a: 30). The chapter focuses mainly on Ukrainians' use of Polish and the reactions of local Poles, but also on how some Poles have responded to the presence of Ukrainians by reviving their Russian and in a few cases also learning Ukrainian. I argue that this apparently successful linguistic collaboration helps speed the migration transition in the three cities, making Ukrainians feel more at home and ready to settle.

Although Zelinsky's (1971) hypothesis of mobility transition presented the entire process of modernisation, contemporary migration scholars tend to use the term migration transition to denote the stage of development at which a country becomes sufficiently prosperous so that net emigration is replaced by net immigration. Considering that temporary migration is never adequately captured in statistics, it is impossible to pinpoint this moment. Okólski (2021) concludes that Poland achieved net immigration around 2018. However, exact figures and dates are not very significant to this chapter, which is based on qualitative research, and adopts a bottom-up approach. How does it feel to live in a society undergoing a migration transition? Poland's acquisition of a refugee destination identity in 2022 was impossible to miss, but what had been the impact of the perhaps less visible migration processes in the years 2014–2022? Unlike demographers and economists, I adopt a sociological approach to migration transition and investigate Poland's acquisition of a new identity as a 'receiving country'. The chapter uses the language of migration scholars, avoiding the term 'host' country, which is problematic in view of the often-unfriendly reception accorded to migrants when they are abroad.

Arango (2012: 46) observes that 'a receiving country is one in which the most socially significant phenomenon in terms of international mobility is immigration'. It seems that by 'socially significant' he is referring to identity; however, his article does not expand on what constitutes social significance. Later in the same publication (2012: 54), Arango explains that societies undergo a process of 'socialisation' into the receiving country identity. Berriane et al. (2015: 516), writing about Morocco, say that the country has to acquire a 'self-image as an immigration society'. Similarly, Fassmann and Reeger (2012: 65–66) argue that becoming a receiving society involves a process of 'social learning'. Alexander (2003) charted a parallel process of evolving policies towards migrants in 'new immigration cities' of Western Europe and Israel. Cities which had begun by treating migrants as strangers and guestworkers progressed through an 'assimilationist' phase and in some cases arrived finally at a policy of 'pluralism', i.e., multiculturalism.

As Castles and Miller (2014: 34) point out, immigration itself also passes through stages, which they label 'the migration process'. In the 1950s and 1960s migrants to countries such as Germany, the Netherlands and the United Kingdom were mostly temporary labour migrants. However, over time they began to bring over family members and settle in the receiving countries. White (2011) and Friberg (2012) have analysed how the same process of family reunification and settlement occurred rapidly after Poland's European Union (EU) accession as families reunified in the United Kingdom (UK) and Norway. Since the English word 'immigration' implies migration for settlement, it is at this stage of settling that one can accurately refer to the country as a 'country of immigration'. The process of settlement involves the arrival of more women and children and people from different walks of life, as well as the ageing of the migrant pioneers, so over time the ethnic minorities – as the migrants eventually are often regarded – adopt a demographic profile akin to that of the majority population.

This process of socio-demographic diversification within the migrant population is well-illustrated in the case of the wave of labour migration from Ukraine which is the chief cause of Poland's change to the country of immigration status. Initially mostly short-term and circular, with a preponderance of men, and mostly from west Ukraine, it became increasingly differentiated linguistically and in other respects. Many Ukrainians began to migrate for the first time, but, in addition, Russian-speaking Ukrainians who previously migrated to Russia diverted to Poland and other EU countries (Grzymała-Kazłowska and Brzozowska 2017: 105; Górny and Jaźwińska 2019). The number of Ukrainian students rose to 36,000 by 2021 (GUS 2022b). Despite obstacles to family reunification created by the temporary status of many migrants, more and more children joined their parents; in 2021, twelve per cent of temporary residence permits to Ukrainians were granted for family reasons (Urząd do Spraw Cudzoziemców 2021). Researchers agree that, overall, the trend is towards settlement (Musiyezdov 2019). Settlement among new migrant populations is often accompanied by increasing intermarriage with the majority population. This is also true for Ukrainians, with the number of Ukrainian–Polish marriages registered in Poland rising from 346 in 2011 to 1972 in 2019 (Szukalski 2020: 30).

New receiving countries are often also typified by the sudden arrival of migrants of various different nationalities, as for example in Italy in the 1970s (King et al. 1997: 2). Migrants of other nationalities are also becoming more numerous in Poland. Whereas previously they had mostly originated from former Soviet countries such as Belarus and Georgia, countries of origin have been becoming increasingly diverse. For example, in July 2021 the top six countries for migrants holding seasonal work permits in Poland – with at least 10,000 permit holders per nationality – were Ukraine, Belarus, India, Nepal, Uzbekistan and the Philippines (Ministerstwo Rodziny i Polityki Społecznej 2021: 9). However, Ukrainians constitute the vast majority of foreigners in Poland, particularly since February 2022.

This new ethnic diversity could be conceptualised as 'multiculturalism', although it has to be remembered that Ukrainians are the only sizeable minority, so there are just two predominant 'cultures' rather than many. In Polish the term multiculturalism (*wielokulturowość*) is often employed to describe a state of ethnic diversity. However, as highlighted for example by Wessendorf and Vertovec in *The Multicultural Backlash* (2010), 'multiculturalism' is not a neutral term. It is often misunderstood and misrepresented by right-wing media and politicians. Another hazard of using it as a scholarly analytical tool is that it also refers to a range of government and local government policies, varying between countries and even cities. At the core of such policies is an attitude of respect towards migrants and minorities, and an acceptance that the best outcome for both minority and majority populations is to avoid migrant assimilation (where migrants become culturally merged into the receiving society) and promote integration. Integration in this context is usually understood in the sense used by social psychologist Berry (1997): a 'halfway house', where migrants feel connected to cultural aspects of both their country of origin and the receiving society. Multiculturalism is therefore a policy based on the premise that everyone's culture possesses equal merit, and that the receiving society is, like the EU, 'united in diversity'. Ideally, multicultural policy removes distinctions in terms of power and opportunity between majority and minority populations.

Although multicultural policies share these features in common, the different varieties of multiculturalism also reflect the specifics of the country involved. In the UK, with its large non-white population, multicultural policies – in the 2020s more often labelled 'equality and diversity' – form part of the struggle to tackle endemic racism. In Poland, multicultural policies, usually pursued on a city level, have until recently focused largely on history. Unlike the sequence described by Alexander (2003) in Western Europe, multiculturalism largely predated the arrival of migrants. Policies are cultural in the sense that they centre on museums, architecture and different cultural memory events. Celebration of Poland's pre-Second World War ethnic diversity has been linked – in some of the largest cities – to a policy of welcoming foreign investors, tourists and (in time) also increasing numbers of migrants. Social justice towards contemporary migrants is seen through the lens of the Holocaust, expulsions of Germans, Ukrainians and other nationalities at the end of the Second World War, and the communist regime's ideology of ethnic homogeneity. Becoming a city with a kaleidoscope of different nationalities is viewed as recovering normality for these historically multiethnic locations. In *The Multiculturalism of Monocultural Wrocław*, Dolińska and Makaro argue (2013: 53) that although Wrocław's Polish residents in 2011 believed their city to have a multiethnic population, multiculturalism in reality was fundamentally a memory project. Nonetheless, over just a few years the city truly did become multiethnic, in the sense of housing a large Ukrainian minority. Ukrainians may have constituted one in ten residents by 2017 (Wrotniak-Chałada 2017).

It is difficult to find neutral labels for policies promoting social equality, and 'multiculturalism' is no exception. One danger with labelling policies 'multicultural' is that the term highlights 'culture' at the expense of other aspects of integration. For migrants, these other aspects are also essential domains of integration (Ager and Strang 2008). Migrants are, for example, people who need access to decent housing, education, and regular jobs, where they will not be exploited. It often seems irrelevant to use ethno-national labels, or to think about the history and religion of people whose predominant social identities in such situations are as tenants, school pupils or employees. It can even be unhelpful to remember history and culture. For example, a Ukrainian refugee struggling to pass a Polish school exam in 2022 had nothing to do with the Wołyń massacres of 1943 – even though for some Poles 'Ukrainian' has precisely this connotation. In fact, as this example suggests, to use ethnic labels is often potentially xenophobic. Politicians and right-wing media like to present migrants as cultural threats, but majority populations should not overculturalise or overethnicise migrants by seeing them through the lens of culture only.

However, there do exist other situations where culture is highly relevant to migrants' experiences. The most significant of these is language competence, recognised by Ager and Strang (2008: 170) as underpinning other core domains of integration. In my own research over the years (see e.g., White 2011, 2018) many Polish migrants have expressed the idea that language is 'fundamental'. Janicki (2015: 244) identified poor language knowledge as the most basic barrier for Ukrainians in Lublin region, denying access to all other areas of potential integration. Integration is conceptualised by liberal politicians and scholars as a 'two-way street', in which both migrants and the receiving society and state should make steps towards coming together (Ager and Strang 2008). However, this is at odds with the nationalist stance, widespread in receiving societies, that only migrants need to adapt their behaviour. According to this monolingual language ideology,

> reducing the observable evidence of otherness (as an irritant or affront to the singularity of the dominant monolingual majority) and re-asserting the authority of the majority through the sole legitimacy of 'its' language are more important than enabling or empowering the multilingual minority and fostering social integration based on reciprocal accommodation of indigenous and immigrant populations.
> STEVENSON 2006: 158

Stevenson was writing about how Germans and Austrians adapted to the new immigration country status, and his comments on the persistence of monolingual ideologies in transitioning societies suggest that overcoming monolingualist prejudices may be one of those aspects of social learning (Fassmann and Reeger 2012) on which societies in migration transition need to focus. A multicultural approach to migrant linguistic integration would entail promoting bi- or multilingualism for everyone, so that (a) the migrants' right to use their own language is respected, but they are offered opportunities to learn the majority language and (b) wherever possible, the majority population should be helped to learn migrant languages.

1 The Research Project

Italy or Spain underwent protracted migration transitions with clear-cut stages: emigration, return migration, and immigration (Arango 2012: 3). By contrast, Poland is a sending and receiving country simultaneously. Only the biggest cities – roughly speaking, the metropolises of over 500,000 population – have already shed the 'emigration' identities which were significant in the years following Poland's 2004 EU accession. The research puzzle in my project 'Polish Cities of Immigration and Emigration' was to discover how immigration and emigration identities intersected in smaller cities. In particular, I wanted to discover whether people of various nationalities living in smaller cities had a special experience thanks to the fact that many local Poles have either lived in foreign countries, are circular migrants, or have friends and family abroad. The project was partly funded by the Narodowa Agencja Wymiany Akademickiej (Polish National Agency for Academic Exchange). It was approved by University College London Research Ethics Committee.

In 2019–2022 I conducted 124 semi-structured interviews in Płock, Kalisz and Piła, as well as interviews with key informants such as priests and teachers, and observation both on the spot and on Facebook. All three cities forfeited their positions as regional capitals in 1998, losing out as a result on investment opportunities, but they occupy fairly high, though different, positions in Polish city rankings (Wałachowski and Król 2019). They are located in the wealthiest regions of Poland, Mazowieckie and Wielkopolskie. It turned out that smaller cities were interesting places to study the migration transition, since they are favoured by many parents as good places to bring up children. Migration for settlement is perhaps particularly likely to occur in locations which are considered to be safe and child-friendly.

It is impossible to generalise on the basis of just three cities; indeed, every city is experienced by migrants in unique ways, as Cichocka (2021) illustrates for example with reference to Poles living in Amsterdam and Berlin. Nor was it possible to engage in strict comparisons, given the different historical circumstances in which I did the fieldwork: just before the COVID-19 pandemic; during its later stages; and after Russia's full-scale invasion of Ukraine. The situation has changed radically since February 2022, when Ukrainian women and children found refuge across Poland, including its smaller cities (Pawłowska 2022), and an estimated 100,000–400,000 male labour migrants returned to

Ukraine (Pacewicz 2023). However, Ukrainians' developing sense of belonging, networks and experiences of engaging with Poles in the smaller cities before the full-scale invasion remain relevant to their lives today. Hence the findings constitute more than just a snapshot of a historical period which is now completely 'in the past'.

Interviewees included 70 Ukrainians; 37 Polish return or circular migrants; one Italian; and 16 non-EU citizens from around the globe, including Australia, Taiwan, Uruguay, Venezuela, Nigeria, Turkey and Bangladesh, as well as post-Soviet countries. The main focus of my project was on Ukrainians, and it was not part of the research to count or interview representatives of all the different nationalities located in each city. The remaining foreign population was highly diverse in terms of nationality, consisting of very small groups from a few countries as well as a scattering of individuals. Some factories – particularly in and around Kalisz – employed temporary workers from outside the Former Soviet Union. Ukrainians in Kalisz mentioned working with Nepalese, Thai, Indonesian, Filipino, Venezuelan and Nepalese people as well as Georgians, Belarusians and Russians. Very small clusters of nationalities such as Turks and Bangladeshis worked in a few restaurants and cafes. Only a handful of international students were enrolled on degree programmes in these cities; I interviewed five (Belarusian, Ukrainian and Kazakh). Most non-Ukrainian interviewees were economic migrants or married to Poles. The marriage migrants were often, as far as they knew, the only representatives of their own nationalities in the city. They generally spoke Polish or English at home.

Since Ukrainians were the only population of foreigners to constitute a language community in the three cities, and because of the word limit, this chapter focuses mostly on the 69 Ukrainian labour migrants among my research participants. I recruited them via Facebook; courtesy of the warden of a migrant hostel; through Polish acquaintances; and by snowballing. Hence, they could not be strictly representative of the Ukrainian population in Poland. Nonetheless, they were typical in that most had first arrived in Poland recently – 64 of them since 2015 – and because they came from almost every corner of Ukraine. In this group, 18 were Ukrainian speakers from western Ukraine, and 51 were from other regions, mostly Russian speakers. We usually conversed in Russian – which I speak fluently, unlike Ukrainian – or a mixture of Russian with Ukrainian. A handful of interviewees were confident enough to want to give an interview in Polish. Since Ukrainian- and Russian-speakers lived and worked together in Poland, they were used to translanguaging – switching between Russian and Ukrainian, or mixing the two (*Surzhik*). The local Facebook groups communicated mostly in Russian, with some Ukrainian; after February 2022 the position was reversed.

The interviewees were aged nineteen to sixty, with an average age of thirty-eight. In terms of gender, 43 were women and 26 were men, a disparity which arose partly because I stopped interviewing Ukrainians after the 2022 invasion and was unable to complete my interview plan in Piła. Forty out of 69 were living with family members, including two women whose partners were Polish. The educational and occupational profile was similar to that of Bydgoszcz respondents surveyed by Górny et al. (2019). Only 26 out of 69 had higher education, and 41 worked in factories. Other workplaces included construction sites, hairdressing and beauty salons and restaurant kitchens. A handful were doing low-status white-collar jobs. The interviewees possessed a diverse range of personalities, outlooks and strategies, although there were certain sub-groups, such as middle-aged migrants who had come to Poland to finance their children's higher education in Ukraine, and skilled male manual workers, particularly welders and drivers, who were satisfied by their earning power in Poland. Overall, the sample illustrated well the socio-demographic diversity of the Ukrainian (labour migrant) population in Poland, as noted by other researchers, and they had a diverse range of contact with local Poles. Hence it is impossible to generalise, for example, about 'Ukrainians in Kalisz'.

2 Ukrainians' Polish Language and Linguistic Encounters

In general, the Ukrainian interviewees were pleased to be living in the cities, where they considered the quality of life to be better than in the metropolises. They sometimes commented that a bigger city would offer a greater range of employment, but – apart from a handful of ambitious women with higher education – most were ready to put up with the smaller-city labour market in exchange for a more relaxed and healthy way of life and the company of their family and friends. For example, Kvitka, aged twenty-one and childless, remarked:

> I've visited other cities in Poland, my husband and I have travelled around, looking for better work. We did want some better jobs. But I realised that I like it here. It's peaceful. I have lots of friends, lots of Polish friends who could help me out in any situation, that's a big plus. And it's not so noisy. It's good for living.

My interviews with Polish return migrants and foreigners of different non-Ukrainian nationalities suggested that these smaller-city residents often made the same compromise. Moreover, parents with children in Polish schools were impressed by the helpfulness of the Polish teachers, and, in general, local people were considered to be friendly, patient and not prejudiced against Ukrainians.

Just a few people complained that Poles were impatient with their attempts to speak Polish. In Piła, Vera, a fairly recent arrival, mentioned 'When you go up and talk to them, in broken Polish of course, they start pretending they don't understand what you're saying. And they begin speaking aggressively, not that they shout, but you can feel the aggression'. Lev and Taras, also fairly recent arrivals, but hoping to move to Warsaw, contrasted prejudice in Kalisz with their impressions of more open attitudes in the capital. Lev said, 'You can tell by their behaviour that they seem displeased; when we start talking Ukrainian or Russian, they begin behaving like that'. He and his Ukrainian co-worker Taras blamed a prevailing monolingual language ideology: they 'had the feeling' that Poles 'think since we came to Poland we should speak Polish'.

However, the balance of opinion among my interviewees was that Poles were friendlier in the smaller city. This was unsurprising, given that this was a group of people who by and large had chosen to live outside the biggest cities and were making themselves at home. Ostap, in Poland for seven years and planning to settle, said he liked Piła because of the 'good attitudes to newcomers, to foreigners. I've heard about problems in other cities'. Inna, explaining why they had not moved to a metropolis, commented that 'the people we met in Kalisz, Poles, welcomed us very warmly, they treated us like their own. We didn't feel like foreigners, that there was any hostility. They made us feel at home and that was an important reason why we stayed'. Marina had only one Polish friend, but had achieved a feeling of belonging in Płock based on friendly conversations with Polish children and women as she walked and shopped in the city:

> I can chat with hardly any problems. ... I went into Kaufland and a Polish woman was telling me that she had bought a particular saucepan and didn't like the quality, so I suggested where she could buy a different one. It's that communication about trivial things with strangers in shops that I enjoy. It makes me feel very nice and secure.

Such urban sociabilities (Glick Schiller and Çağlar 2016) can help migrants' integration, despite their apparently superficial quality. Some Ukrainians attributed friendliness to the fact that local Poles had their own migration experiences. For instance, Irina (Kalisz) suggested that former migrants were 'more communicative, somehow more supportive. Nicer and more understanding, perhaps that's how to put it. They've experienced it for themselves'.

Some interviewees associated communication problems and micro-aggressions with brusque big-city residents. Nina, for instance, had previously worked in Warsaw and reported 'It happened in Warsaw – they'd say, "I don't understand!" and turn away and walk off. But here people are kinder. They try to find out what you want, they repeat your question if necessary'. Migrants are sometimes wary of speaking their mother tongue in public, in certain societies and circumstances, such as the UK after the Brexit referendum, where Poles sensed increasing negativity towards migrant languages (Guma and Jones 2019; Kozminska and Hua 2021: 15). However, none of my interviewees seemed to feel that this was necessary in the smaller cities. One person did avoid speaking Russian in public, but this was because her husband, after his experiences in a larger Polish city, told her it would be wise.

The only interviewee who recalled being told explicitly that she 'ought' to speak Polish was Zlata, whose encounter had taken place not in the smaller city, but with a ticket inspector on a train:

> He completely lost his temper. I knew I had a problem, but I couldn't formulate the answers to his questions as precisely as I wanted to. And he said 'If you want to travel in the EU you absolutely have to know the language. If you've come to Poland you ought to speak Polish'. And that was very unpleasant.

Such linguistic intolerance presumably indicated a deeper racism. However, the language dimension was important in its own right. Being told that Ukrainians 'ought' to speak Polish was particularly galling given that Zlata had been held back in this situation by her linguistic self-consciousness and perfectionism. Like many of my interviewees, she fully subscribed to the language ideology that it was important for migrants to learn the majority language. This made it all the more offensive when Polish people seemed to accuse them of not bothering to speak Polish. Comments included: 'I try to speak Polish. After all, it's a foreign country, and they have their own language' (Viktor) and 'When you come to a different country, like Poland, you need to study the language so you can speak it' (Oleksiy). Young university-educated female interviewees, like Zlata, were also adamant that they needed to perfect their knowledge in order to shape their career and get on in life. For instance, Yuliya, interviewed in Polish, suggested that 'If you want to be somebody you have to make a big effort and language is the first thing you have to master. The better you know it, the better job you'll get'.

As already suggested, a multicultural policy should include official support for learning the majority language, as long as minority languages are also respected. Given that migrants are empowered by being able to operate in the majority language, it is an essential component of integration policy. Moreover, gaining the State Certificate in Polish as a Foreign Language is a requirement for a permanent residence permit. The influx of refugees in 2022 considerably improved opportunities for Ukrainians to learn Polish in Poland (Jarosz and Klaus 2023). Nonetheless, some of my interviewees even before 2022 had studied Polish in further education colleges (*szkoły policealne*) and found these courses useful. More often, however, they relied on private lessons of differing quality, often taught by Ukrainians. This was partly because, like migrants in many countries, they lacked time for formal study. Anzhela, for example, confessed that her written Polish 'could be better, let's put it like that. I did understand that I would need it, if I wanted to stay in Poland and get a proper job. I went to classes for a year, but somehow it happened that I had lots of overtime, it got quite hard, I was doing two shifts a day'.

My findings entirely supported Brzozowska's (2022: 15) observation that 'Ukrainian migrants' language difficulties challenge the common view that Ukrainians do not encounter communication barriers and learn Polish easily and quickly due to cultural and language proximity and do not need much support in this area'. It may be that this assumption is partly based on the media stereotype – before February 2022 – of a Ukrainian migrant as a deskilled university graduate (Bielecka-Prus 2020). A more intersectional approach, as adopted in this chapter, indicates the actual diversity among Ukrainian labour migrants. In particular, as already mentioned, 43 out of 69 interviewees were not university graduates.

Ukrainians themselves sometimes partly choose Poland because of the perception that the language will be easy, compared to other potential destinations. In a 2022 survey, language similarity was named by 30 per cent of migrants and 40 per cent of refugees as an important reason for choosing Poland (Jarosz and Klaus 2023: 19). My interviewees made comments like: 'It's a bit easier in Poland, because the culture is somehow similar, and the language, there are lots of similar words, and you can learn it faster and understand it more quickly' (Ludmila). However, some then revised their opinions about Polish being easy after they arrived and began to encounter problems. Ihor, for example, said 'I'd thought it was very similar to Ukrainian. It's not that similar. There aren't that many identical words. Personally I find it hard – there is a language barrier. I understand, more or less, but it depends on the Pole'.

Ukrainians who had lived in Poland for several years could speak Polish to some extent, but they could also become stuck and stop progressing linguistically, partly because many had little close contact with Poles. Yeva, a Ukrainian philology graduate committed to staying in Poland, who had been living in

Poland for five years and would seem on these different counts to have a linguistic headstart, complained: 'I did have a close Polish friend but she emigrated to Germany to be with her sister. I mix with Poles at work but there is a language barrier and I can't express everything. I speak, but not much. I don't feel very free when I speak. I worry about saying the wrong thing'. Interviewees worried about pronunciation and grammar, but the main obstacle for many was not speaking, but writing grammatically and orthographically correct Polish. Varvara, for example, who had lived in Piła more than three years with her teenage son and spoke Polish confidently to her co-workers, confessed 'I still can't write … It is a problem for me because wherever you go you need to write … My son can write of course so he writes stuff for me and I copy it'.

3 Poles' Linguistic Practices

While perfectionists like Zlata or Yeva were inhibited from speaking Polish by their fear of making mistakes, for everyday interactions around the neighbourhood, social relations are often eased if neither the migrants nor the majority population feel inhibited about mixing languages (Hua and Wei 2018). Such relaxed practices seem to happen spontaneously in truly superdiverse locations such as parts of London where English native speakers constitute less than half the local population, as Wessendorf (2015) shows in her article '"All the People Speak Bad English": Coping with Language Differences in a Super-Diverse Context'. Even Polish cities such as Warsaw and Poznań are clearly not nearly as diverse as London. However, some workplaces are already multilingual, and this can lead to linguistic freedom and mixing, as long as the Polish workers are prepared to make overtures to the Ukrainians and try to understand Ukrainian and/or Russian. Oleksandra, for example, explained how, as a team leader in her factory, she managed fifteen people. This involved talking quickly, and she did not have time to worry about linguistic accuracy: 'All sorts of words fly out of my mouth: Polish, Ukrainian, and Russian. The Polish girls understand me – I've been with them for two years and they seem happy … When I speak fast I speak any old how'. Similarly, Olha, who lived in a hostel and socialised with Polish co-workers, mentioned 'Everyone speaks the best way they know how. You speak some sort of language and I think everyone else understands'. Svitlana, from the same hostel, reported 'They understand us very well, because they're constantly hearing Ukrainian language'.

Social relations are also considerably easier when members of receiving societies try to use the migrants' language. Written Ukrainian was hardly visible in Polish public places before the 2022 invasion: it was almost absent from the linguistic landscape (Levchuk 2021). Lublin was the only city to have online information in Ukrainian (Jarosz and Klaus 2023: 30). The situation changed impressively as part of the Polish welcome for Ukrainian refugees in 2022. Nonetheless, as my research showed, some ordinary Poles from different social backgrounds were learning Ukrainian even before the refugee crisis. Several Płock interviewees, who formed the majority of residents in their hostel, and also the majority of workers in some sections of their factory, mentioned that Polish co-workers and managers had learned some Ukrainian. Larysa reported, 'We do know some people who live here all the time, they work at our factory, and sometimes we socialise together ... They listen and learn our language. If we gather on the street, we're having a chat outside, we start laughing and telling stories, they ask us to repeat what we said, they're drawn into the conversation'. Other interviewees mentioned having Polish friends married to Ukrainians: in Piła, for example, Emma had arrived quite recently but already had a Polish friend with whom she communicated in Ukrainian. In Kalisz, Nina knew a Polish student of Ukrainian (studying at a big city university) whom she had met at Greek Catholic church services in Kalisz cathedral.

Russian also functioned as a *lingua franca* between Ukrainians and Poles. I was surprised by this, given that, teaching at a Polish university in the 1980s, I had formed the strong impression that most Poles resisted learning Russian at school. This impression was confirmed by one of my Polish interviewees in Płock, who laughed, 'I'm a relic of communist days, when Russian language was compulsory, so I don't know Russian. Obviously, if you're forced, you don't learn it'. Nonetheless, in all three cities, Ukrainian interviewees reported that Poles who had learned Russian under the communist regime and in the 1990s tried to communicate with them in Russian. For instance, Vadym, a Ukrainian speaker, mentioned that 'Poles used to learn Russian at school, they understand Russian better than Ukrainian. So you can interact with them in Russian'. Some Ukrainians would deliberately look out for older Polish employees in places like banks where they might find it challenging to speak Polish, and Russian seemed the safer option. Often, however, Poles took the initiative. This was usually interpreted as a friendly gesture. Varvara said that in Piła 'as soon as they hear you are Ukrainian, they start bringing out some words in Russian'. Boris, who had been the first Ukrainian in his workplace, mentioned:

> The men I work with, the people who are aged thirty-eight and upwards, that was when they still learned Russian at school. And when I began working there they started recalling their Russian. They liked reminiscing about schooldays and they try to converse with me in Russian.

One Polish return migrant I interviewed, a metal worker turned agricultural labourer, also mentioned 'I know Russian too, I had it in school. I don't know everything, but if I meet a Ukrainian, then I can have a normal conversation with them in Russian'. This ability to tap into schoolchild Russian helps explain how local Poles (as in other Polish cities) reached out to Ukrainian refugees in Russian immediately after the full-scale invasion. During my fieldwork in spring 2022, I was able to note the (initial) proliferation of written Russian around the cities, for example when I visited a school where the canteen, library and other common areas had been labelled by teachers in Russian for the benefit of Ukrainian refugee children.

English hardly seemed to function as a common language between Poles and Ukrainians – perhaps surprisingly, given that English is the most commonly taught language in Polish schools. Some Ukrainian interviewees had English classes at school but they usually said this was not to a high standard. Three interviewees who did try to speak English to Poles had not been able to make themselves understood. Only one person, a young West Ukrainian who did not speak any Russian, had persistently and apparently successfully used English after she first arrived, for simple interactions such as buying a ticket or asking directions. One Ukrainian mentioned trying to speak English to a Filipino resident in his migrant hostel, although he found Polish words coming out by mistake. The Venezuelan interviewee, a confident English speaker, worked alongside Ukrainians and was sometimes able to communicate with them in English. He had also picked up some Ukrainian, and commented 'Polish people sometimes listen me speak Ukraine and they say "You don't stayed in Ukraine. You stayed in Poland". And I say 'Yes, but I work with Ukraine people. Not with Polish people'.

4 Conclusions

Multiculturalism is an ambiguous term, to be used with care. In particular, it is important not to focus exclusively on cultural identities, 'overethnicising' migrant populations, since this can link to ethnic nationalism as well as false assumptions about cultural proximity, such as that Ukrainians need no support to learn Polish. Thinking in cultural terms also risks overshadowing migrants' other social identities such as their refugee status, gender or occupation. However, language is a key part of the migrant experience and when cities transition to 'immigration' status a part of this process involves learning to accommodate new language communities. Since ideologies of monolingualism are strong in receiving societies, a significant aspect of social learning during the migration transition process is for the receiving society to discard such assumptions, and be accommodating towards foreigners struggling to learn the majority language. Some of my informants believed that the fact that some of their Polish workmates and hostel acquaintances had their own migration experience contributed to their patience with and friendliness towards Ukrainians.

To some extent in Poland multilingualism is a spontaneous process, occurring as a result of everyday interactions. In superdiverse locations such as London or certain factories and migrant hostels in Kalisz, Piła and Płock a jumble of languages is used for communication between Poles and Ukrainians. It was encouraging to find that some Poles had learned a bit of Ukrainian and/or were using their school Russian to communicate with migrants. On the other hand, many Ukrainians were struggling to achieve a level of Polish commensurate with their aspirations, particularly written Polish, for which they needed formal instruction. A multiethnic society can only work well if governments invest in language teaching for migrants, at the appropriate level and at convenient times of day, and, even better, if there is support for the majority population to learn migrant languages.

References

Ager, A., & Strang, A. (2008). Understanding integration: A conceptual framework. *Journal of Refugee Studies, 21*(2), 166–191.

Alexander, M. (2003). Local policies toward migrants as an expression of Host-Stranger relations: A proposed typology. *Journal of Ethnic and Migration Studies, 29*(3), 411–430.

Arango, J. (2012). Early starters and latecomers: Comparing countries of immigration and immigration regimes in Europe. In M. Okólski (Ed.), *European immigrations: Trends, structures and policy implications* (pp. 45–64). Amsterdam University Press.

Berriane, M., de Haas, H., & Natter, K. (2015). Introduction: Revisiting Moroccan migrations. *The Journal of North African Studies, 20*(4), 503–521.

Berry, J. (1997). Immigration, acculturation and adaptation. *Applied Psychology: An International Review, 46*, 1–30.

Bielecka-Prus, J. (2020). Obraz imigrantek z Ukrainy w polskim dyskursie prasowym. *Studia Migracyjne – Przegląd Polonijny, 2*(176), 177–200.

Brzozowska, A. (2022). "All is not yet lost here": The role of aspirations and capabilities in migration projects of Ukrainian migrants in Poland. *Journal of Ethnic and Migration Studies, 49*(9), 2373–2390. https://doi.org/10.1080/1369183X.2022.2157804.

Castles, S., & Miller, M. (2014). *The age of migration: International population movements in the modern world* (5th ed.). Palgrave Macmillan.

Cichocka, E. (2021). Safe, accepted and charmed by the city: Why do migrants feel better in Berlin than in Amsterdam? *Journal of Ethnic and Migration Studies, 47*(9), 1940–1956.

Dolińska K., & Makaro, J. (2013). *O wielokulturowości monokulturowego Wrocławia.* Wydawnictwo Uniwersytetu Wrocławskiego.

Fassmann, H., & Reeger, U. (2012). "Old" immigration countries in Europe: The concept and empirical examples. In M. Okólski (Ed.), *European immigrations: Trends, structures and policy implications* (pp. 65–90). Amsterdam University Press.

Friberg, J.-H. (2012). The stages of migration. From going abroad to settling down: Post-accession Polish migrant workers in Norway. *Journal of Ethnic and Migration Studies, 38*(10), 1589–1605.

Glick Schiller, N., & Çağlar, A. (2016). Displacement, emplacement and migrant newcomers: Rethinking urban sociabilities within multiscalar power. *Identities, 23*(1), 17–34.

Górny, A., & Jaźwińska, E. (2019). *Ukraińskie migrantki i migranci w aglomeracji warszawskiej: cechy społeczno-demograficzne i relacje społeczne. Raport z badań.* University of Warsaw Center of Migration Research Working Paper 115/173.

Górny, A., Kołodziejczyk, Madej, K., & Kaczmarczyk, P. (2019). *Nowe obszary docelowe w migracji z Ukrainy do Polski. Przypadek Bydgoszczy i Wrocławia na tle innych miast. Raport z badań.* University of Warsaw Centre of Migration Research Working Paper 118/176.

Górny, A., & Śleszyński, P. (2019). Exploring the spatial concentration of foreign employment in Poland under the simplified procedure. *Geographia Polonica, 92*(3), 331–345.

Grzymała-Kazłowska, A., & Brzozowska, A. (2017). From drifting to anchoring: Capturing the experience of Ukrainian migrants in Poland. *Central and Eastern European Migration Review, 6*(2), 103–122.

Guma, T., & Dafydd Jones, R. (2019). "Where are we going to go now?" European Union migrants' experiences of hostility, anxiety, and (non-)belonging during Brexit. *Population, Space and Place, 25*(1), 1–10.

GUS. (2022a). *Polski rocznik demograficzny 2022.* Główny Urząd Statystyczny.

GUS. (2022b). *Szkolnictwo wyższe i jego finanse 2021, Tablice.* Główny Urząd Statystyczny.

Hua, Z., & Wei, L. (2018). Translanguaging and diasporic imagination. In R. Cohen & C. Fischer (Eds.), *Routledge handbook of diaspora studies* (pp. 106–112). Routledge.

Janicki, W. (2015). *Migracje kompensacyjne jako czynnik wzrostu obszarów peryferyjnych. Rola ukrytego kapitału ludzkiego.* Wydawnictwo UMCS.

Jarosz, S., & Klaus, W. (Eds.). (2023). *Polska szkoła pomagania. Przyjęcie osób uchodźczych z Ukrainy w Polsce w 2022 roku.* Migration Consortium, OBMF, and CeBaM.

Kałuża-Kopias, D. (2023). The spatial distribution of economic immigrants from Ukraine and Belarus and the socio-economic development of Polish counties. *SMPP, 1*(187), 163–186.

King, R., Fielding, A., & Black, R. (1997). The international migration turnaround in Southern Europe. In R. King & R. Black (Eds.), *Southern Europe and the new immigrations* (pp. 1–25). Sussex Academic Press.

King, R., & Gëdeshi, I. (2022). New trends in potential migration from Albania: The migration transition postponed? *Migration and Development, 9*(2), 131–151.

Kozminska, K., & Hua, Z. (2021). The promise and resilience of multilingualism: Language ideologies and practices of Polish-speaking migrants in the UK post the Brexit vote. *Journal of Multilingual and Multicultural Development, 42*(5), 444–461.

Levchuk, P. (2021). Ukrainian language in Polish public space. *Cognitive Studies/Études Cognitives, 21*, 2476.

Ministerstwo Rodziny i Polityki Społecznej (2021). *Informacja o zatrudnieniu cudzoziemców w Polsce (stan na 1 lipca 2021 r)*. Ministry of Family and Social Policy. https://shorturl.at/aENTV.

Musiyezdov, O. (2019). Ukrainian emigration in Poland: From "earners" to highly qualified specialists. *Ukrainskyi Sotsiologichnyi Zhurnal, 21*, 7–49.

Okólski, M. (2021). The migration transition in Poland. *Central and Eastern European Migration Review, 10*(2), 51–69.

Pacewicz, P. (2023, February 28). *Gdzie jest milion uchodźców z Ukrainy? W danych SG widać też lęk przed rocznicą 24 lutego*. Oko.press. https://oko.press/ilu-jest-uchodzcow-z-ukrainy.

Pawłowska, D. (2022, May 27). Uchodźcy z Ukrainy – zobacz, w których powiatach się zarejestrowali. *Gazeta Wyborcza*.

Stevenson, P. (2006). "National" languages in transnational contexts: Language, migration and citizenship in Europe. In C. Mar-Molinero & P. Stevenson (Eds.), *Language ideologies, policies and practices* (pp. 147–161). Palgrave Macmillan.

Szukalski, P. (2020). Małżeństwa polsko-ukraińskie zawierane w Polsce. Przyczynek do badania integracji imigrantów ukraińskich z ostatnich lat. *Polityka Społeczna, 8*, 28–36.

Urząd do Spraw Cudzoziemców. (2021, October 28). *Obywatele Ukrainy w Polsce – raport*. https://www.gov.pl/web/udsc/obywatele-ukrainy-w-polsce--raport.

Vertovec, S., & Wessendorf, S. (2010). *The multiculturalism backlash: European discourses, policies and practices*. Routledge.

Wałachowski, K., & Król, S. (2019). *Uciekające metropolie. Ranking 100 polskich miast*. Klub Jagielloński.

Wessendorf, S. (2015). *"All the people speak bad English": Coping with language differences in a super-diverse context*. Institute for Research into Superdiversity Working Paper 9.

White, A. (2011). *Polish families and migration since EU accession*. Policy Press.

White, A. (2018). Culture and Identity. In A. White, I. Grabowska, P. Kaczmarczyk, & K. Slany, *The impact of migration on Poland: EU mobility and social change* (pp. 160–185). UCL Press.

Wrotniak-Chałada, M. (2017, June 8). *Wrocław: 10 proc. mieszkańców miasta to obywatele Ukrainy*. Bankier. http://www.bankier.pl/wiadomosc/Wroclaw-10-proc-mieszkancow-miasta-to-obywatele-Ukrainy-7524488.html.

Zelinsky, W. (1971). The hypothesis of the mobility transition. *The Geographical Review*, *61*(2), 219–249.

CHAPTER 8

The COVID-19 Pandemic as a Source of Workplace Innovation: the Worker Perspective

Adam Mrozowicki and Jacek Burski

1   Introduction[1]

In the first months of the COVID-19 pandemic there were voices that it would be an event fundamentally changing various aspects of social life, including workplace (Kane et al. 2021). This was related, for example, to the expected wide spreading of remote and hybrid work (Felstead 2022), accelerated digitalization, automation, and artificial intelligence (Śledziewska and Włoch 2021), to the appearance of a new dimension of social inequality at the workplace frequently associated with the "essential work" category, often impossible to be provided remotely, or to the division into "teleworkable" and "non-teleworkable" jobs (Eurofound and European Commission 2021; McCallum 2022). The common denominator of various analyses was the conviction that the external shock, such as the pandemic, would initiate various adjustments at different levels of reality, which would encourage the acceleration and deepening of social changes, often observed already prior to the crisis (Delanty 2020).

In this chapter we attempt to answer the question how the COVID-19 pandemic translated to workplace innovation within public services, such as education, health care, and social care in Poland, in the first months of the health crisis. We define workplace innovations as the introduction of new solutions in the scope of work organization, technology, and social relations (Strumińska-Kutra and Rok 2016). In the conducted analyses we focus in particular on social innovations understood as "new ideas that work to meet pressing unmet needs and improve peoples' lives" (Mulgan et al. 2007: 8).

---

1   This chapter was prepared within the project NCN OPUS 19 "COV-WORK: Socio-economic consciousness, work experiences and coping strategies of Poles in the context of the post-pandemic crisis" funded by the National Science Center in Poland, NCN project number UMO-2020/37/B/HS6/00479.

This chapter contributes to the ongoing discussion on the conditions and specificity of collective innovations in public services during the pandemic (Drozdowski et al. 2022; Wiedner et al. 2020). We focus on the ways the workers[2] dealt with the crisis at such workplaces in Poland as the education, health care, and social care sectors, sometimes called "essential" due to their role in the maintenance of social reproduction during crisis (McCallum 2022). The empirical basis for the analysis consists of 11 focus interviews and 55 narrative biographical interviews with the persons employed in the three sectors which were conducted in the years 2021–2023. The choice of Poland makes it possible to analyze the meaning of workplace innovations in a country in which chronic underfunding of public services and staff shortages related thereto – for example, due to the introduction of a neoliberal model (Kozek 2011) – exacerbated the challenges of the global health crisis. Limited human, organizational, and material resources amplified the need – observed also in other countries – for the "improvised innovation" in order to secure basic services (Wiedner et al. 2020).

The chapter starts with a review of literature on the relation between workplace innovations and socio-economic crises and accompanying organizational challenges. Special attention is paid to the discussion of the results of studies on worker innovations during the COVID-19 pandemic. After the presentation of own research methodology, the next discussion centers around three cases that show different mechanisms of shaping the work organization changes (Kane et al. 2021). We look at the ways of dealing with the challenges in the first months of the pandemic, focusing on three cases: (1) online teaching in primary schools; (2) creation of COVID wards in hospitals; and (3) reorganization of work of nursing homes during lockdowns. We argue that some of the analyzed ways of coping with organizational problems may be considered grassroots social innovations that made it possible to fulfil the organization's goals (provision of key public services) and improve certain aspects of job quality. The chapter ends with a reflection on the meaning of improvised workplace micro-innovations in crisis situations.

---

2   For stylistic reasons, we use the words "worker" and "employee" interchangeably in the chapter. In the literature, "essential workers" is a much more common term, although in the case of public services one is more often dealing with "salaried employees."

2 Workplace Innovation and the Pandemic Crisis: a Review of Research and Concepts[3]

The starting point for the discussion on workplace innovations is the review of literature dedicated to workplace crises and innovations with special focus on the period of the COVID-19 pandemic. The workplace crisis is defined as a "low-probability, high-impact event that threatens the viability of the organization and is characterized by ambiguity of cause, effect, and means of resolution, as well as by a belief that decisions must be made swiftly" (Pearson and Clair 1998: 60). In reflection on crisis management there is also a thesis that crises may both threaten the existence of an organization and encourage its development (Milburn et al. 2016). Moreover, it is emphasized that crises create space for innovative actions in the organization, in particular when there were premises for them in the precrisis period, for example, in the form of organizational culture encouraging worker participation (Totterdill et al. 2016; Wiedner et al. 2020).

One of the conclusions of the discussion on the consequences of social order breakdown caused by crises, such as natural disasters or pandemics, points to the crucial significance of the new forms of "crisis solidarity" (Radzińska 2022), community, and mutual help (Illner 2021). It is easy to romanticize the co-responsibility of workers and citizens for crisis management, as noted by Illner (2021), while in fact it reveals institutional problems and shortcomings, including the withdrawal of the state (and sometimes also of the employers) from shaping effective anti-crisis strategies and lack of effective support in crisis. In the situation of a breakdown (or temporary suspension) of formal rules and structures in an organization, improvisation aimed at ensuring the continuity of provided services steps to the forefront.

One of the most influential concepts of innovation to date, which refers mainly to the macro-social level, even though it may also be applied to organization studies, is the theory of Joseph Schumpeter (2003). He sees crises as the months of "creative destruction" thanks to the activity of entrepreneur-innovators whose function is

> to reform or revolutionize the pattern of production by exploiting an invention or, more generally, an untried technological possibility for producing a new commodity or producing an old one in a new way, by

---

[3] We write extensively about the workplace innovations also in a previous article (Mrozowicki 2023) that is developed in this chapter.

opening up a new source of supply of materials or a new outlet for products, by reorganizing an industry and so on.
SCHUMPETER 2003: 132

As noted by Ziegler (2017), innovations are not just ideas, but ideas put into practice. What is more, their implementation is usually associated with the need for cooperation between people which adds the character of a participative social process to the innovations and opens discussion on the social character of innovations. Their relational nature is also emphasized by the fact that putting them into practice requires overcoming social resistance from individuals and groups that protect the *status quo*.

From the neoinstitutional theory perspective, innovation may be considered one of the manifestations of "institutional work" which is understood as "the purposive action of individuals and organizations aimed at creating, maintaining and disrupting institutions" (Lawrence et al. 2009: 215). This notion points to the possibility of institutionalization of innovations introduced in crisis conditions interpreted as "the routinization of practices of different kinds in everyday social life" (May and Finch 2009: 536). According to the "normalization process theory," innovation normalization includes "the work that actors do as they engage with some ensemble of activities (that may include new or changed ways of thinking, acting, and organizing) and by which means it becomes routinely embedded in the matrices of already existing, socially patterned, knowledge and practices" (May and Finch 2009: 540). The concepts of "institutional work" and "normalization" lead to the question to what extent the models developed during the COVID-19 pandemic became integrated in workplaces in the form of routine actions in a situation of a global public health crisis coming to an end.

Insofar as in Schumpeter's theory the emphasis is on new technologies, products, and ways of production, the studies on work organization focus on the concept of social innovations. Following Strumińska-Kutra and Rok, we assume that social innovations refer to "organizational changes in order to meet important social needs and create new social relations" (Strumińska-Kutra and Rok 2016: 9). Social innovations, as noted by Portes (2021), may also include the rearrangement of social roles and tasks within work organization. Social innovations include the increase of worker participation. As noted by Totterdill et al. (2016: 25), they strengthen the position of workers at the workplace and "entitle them to make everyday decisions, question the existing practices, share ideas and contact senior management." An important observation is the relation between the organizational culture that encourages innovations and better job quality, as noted in numerous studies (Gallie 2013; Totterdill et al. 2016).

It seems that the perspective dominating in management sciences that associates social innovations with a specific organizational culture and structure encouraging worker participation in the changes does not fully correspond to the reality of pandemic crisis in public services such as education, health care, social care, or public administration. Existing research states that the first months of the pandemic crisis were a period of intensive workplace innovations. However, they did not stem from the participative management culture but from the sense of duty and ethos of care which were often juxtaposed with fears, stress, and significant work intensification (Palęcka 2023; Vermeerbergen et al. 2021). The innovations also resulted from the need to ensure key services, such as care for the COVID patients, in the state of organizational chaos, time pressure, and shortage of resources (Wiedner et al. 2020). Drozdowski et al. (2022) point to "micro-innovations" in public institutions during the pandemic in Poland which manifested themselves, for example, in "de-bureaucratization" of decision making, change of the scope of duties, and peculiar ad-hocracy. What is important, the authors confirm the thesis that such innovations were in the first place of a conservative character since their main role was to fulfil basic organizational tasks in the situation of restrictions and challenges posed by the public health crisis.

The concept of "improvised innovations" (Wiedner et al. 2020) perfectly fits the description of the way of dealing with shortage of resources in a crisis situation by the frontline workers during the pandemic (McCallum 2022). Importantly, it complies with Merton's (1968) classical approach in which innovators accept culturally shaped goals – here: the provision of public services necessary for the everyday functioning of society – using unconventional methods to achieve them. Even though worker innovations were observed in different countries, it seems that "frugal innovation" (Nölke 2022: 97) in a crisis based on the mobilization of limited resources in order to satisfy important social needs is particularly present in countries such as Poland, in which expenditure on public services was among the lowest in the European Union even before the pandemic. Years of underfunding of education, health care, and social care produced, among other things, chronic staff shortages. Moreover the state's unpreparedness for the pandemic necessitated improvisations and ad-hocracy in many areas as proven, for example, by the reports of the Supreme Audit Office (NIK) on the functioning of schools and hospitals during the pandemic (NIK 2022a, 2022b). The latter laid bare the limitations of liberalization, commercialization, and partial privatization of public services introduced during their reforming in Poland near the end of the 1990s (Kozek

2011). In subsequent parts of the chapter we look closer at the collective ways of coping with the crisis which were introduced by the employees.

3 Methods and Research Data

An important element of the methodological approach in the study was the focus on the grassroots employee perspective of individuals and professional groups who – particularly in the initial period of the pandemic – experienced a change in their work process organization as well as intensification of their duties, and were exposed to extreme emotions with the source both in the workplace and outside (anxiety, panic, chaos, media information noise). The research centered around three areas of education, health care, and social care that, albeit in a different way, meet the "essentiality" criteria for the reproduction of social life (Mezzadri 2022): primary education – preparation for life in a society and caring for the children when parents are at work; hospital service – offering care to persons with health problems during the pandemic; and nursing homes – supporting persons who require constant care and are unable to function in a society on their own, often due to health problems and age.

In order to grasp the ways of coping with the pandemic and the subjective meanings ascribed to the crisis in an organization, we decided to use two empirical data collection techniques. First, we conducted biographical narrative interviews (BNI) with workers (Schütze 1983). Those enabled the analysis of the methods for dealing with the public health crisis from the perspective of their biographical experiences. Each interview included an answer to the question about one's life story followed by detailed questions focused on the problems at work during the COVID-19 pandemic and during its fading. Second, we conducted focus group interviews (FGI) which made it possible to understand different perspectives on the selected dimensions of job quality during the pandemic.

The empirical material included in total 55 biographical narrative interviews – 26 with teachers, 17 with doctors and nurses at hospitals, and 12 with persons working at nursing homes – gathered in the years 2021–2023. These were supplemented by 11 focus group interviews with the same professional groups (4 with teachers, 3 with doctors, 2 with nurses and 2 with nursing home staff). The interviews varied in terms of the informants' sex, age, and place of residence (big cities vs. medium and small cities), and were completed mostly in the Lower Silesia and Mazovia regions. All interviews were transcribed and anonymized. The gathered material is much more extensive than the topic of this chapter and only a part of the conducted analyses was used. These included theme coding, in the Atlas.ti software, of the ways in which the employees dealt with the challenges of the COVID-19 pandemic in their workplaces (Gibbs 2007). Workplace innovations were one of the first codes to emerge, and further analyses encompassed their technological, organizational, and social dimensions, as well as conditions and consequences, including association with other categories not discussed in the text in detail. Those categories described dealing with crisis, such as control over the labor process, resistance, and normalization (Mrozowicki 2023).

4 Employee Innovations in the First Months of the Pandemic: Conclusions from Studies

In this section of the chapter we focus on the analysis of three innovation dimensions present in the interviews with persons employed in primary schools, hospitals, and nursing homes. First, we were interested in how the pandemic had affected the introduction of new technological solutions which significantly changed the way the tasks entrusted to the frontline workers were fulfilled. This aspect was analyzed by studying the experiences of primary school teachers who were forced to switch to online teaching practically overnight in the conditions of limited support from central and local authorities and the management at their workplaces. Second, we investigated the organizational dimension of pandemic innovations by focusing on the cases of COVID wards which were opened in Polish hospitals at the beginning of the pandemic in March 2020. In this context we wished to learn about the ways in which – given the limited resources, the time pressure, and the increasing number of infected and sick persons – the doctors, nurses, and other medical and nonmedical staff tried to organize completely new units within the existing structure; how they organized their labor process; what resources they used; and to what extent these actions were autonomous in relation to the management. The last theme that we analyzed was innovation at the level of social relations (relational innovations) in which we included mutual help in the completion of atypical tasks as well as employees organizing themselves in trade unions during the pandemic. These issues are presented using the example of nursing homes.

5   Technological Innovations: the Case of Online Teaching in Primary Schools

In Poland, the first change to online teaching at educational institutions took place pursuant to the regulation of the Minister of Science and Higher Education of March 20, 2020. Closure of stationary schools and introduction of online teaching occurred also in the subsequent school year, 2020/2021. However, it was organized differently for kindergartens, primary schools, and secondary schools; moreover, primary schools had to observe differences in the introduction of online teaching for various educational stages, that is, grade one to three and grade four to eight. Also, in the school year 2021/2022 online teaching was temporarily introduced. The decisions regarding online teaching depended on the pandemic fluctuations: whenever the infection rate rose, various forms of lockdown for different levels of education were introduced. In other words, primary schools, secondary schools, and higher education institutions were subject to lockdowns to a different extent. As noted in NIK's report, "the Minister of Education and Science issued recommendations and guidelines on an ad hoc basis and often changed legal provisions, adapting them to the situation" (NIK 2022a: 10), and the obligation to secure the continuity of teaching rested on school principals who, according to NIK, fulfilled their duties well but for a few exceptions. What is important, the Ministry did not change the curriculum, which led to searching for innovative ways of its fulfilment in the changed conditions.

In this section of the chapter, we are interested mainly in the perspective of frontline workers – in this case, primary school teachers who offered online education in a situation of closed educational facilities. Within the gathered biographical narrative interviews and focus group interviews, they spoke about the change to online teaching, that is, how the classes were actually being conducted, for example, with the use of previously absent technological solutions. That change had to be introduced without earlier legal, organizational, or technical preparation.[4] What is more, it affected not only the teachers themselves but also school management, pupils, and their families. The teachers received small financial support of PLN 500.00 (EUR 125.00) from the central authorities to purchase computer equipment. At the same time there were no systemic solutions that would support the frontline workers in the sudden change of the labor process organization, for example, in the scope of

---

4   The national regulations on remote work have been consulted with social partners since spring 2020, but no labor law amendments were introduced until January 2023 except for ad hoc solutions included in anti-crisis regulations.

training, technological support, or methodological advice. This led to a situation where technological innovation (introduction of new digital solutions) was of a mandatory character, but its effectiveness mostly depended on the adaptation skills of frontline workers.

An important factor affecting how the change occurred was the organizational and material conditions of schools, teachers, and the pupils themselves. Also significant was the size of the city in which the school was located. In the case of the interviewees who lived in very large cities online teaching was usually introduced immediately. In smaller cities, due to lack of access to the Internet and appropriate computer equipment, pupils relatively often completed the tasks allocated by the teachers under their parents' supervision at home. Only after a few weeks and the preparation of solutions aimed at reducing the risk of pupil – and teacher – exclusion was online teaching introduced. It occurred, for example, by adapting classrooms to sanitary requirements or lending computer equipment.

A separate dimension of the technological innovation occurring on a mass scale in the Polish education system was the acquisition of skills to conduct lessons, communicate, and manage materials in the computer programs used. Once again referring to NIK's report, the support from the Ministry in the scope of online teaching training for teachers was insufficient (NIK 2022a: 17). We were in particular interested in the extent to which the introduction of technological changes affected the way of fulfillment of entrusted tasks and duties. We wanted to learn how the teachers of various profiles, professional positions, and experience levels approached the need to switch to online teaching and whether it was an impulse to build the feeling of agency at one's workplace. We analyzed the gathered material also in terms of the biographical and collective resources used by our interlocutors when adapting to new work conditions.

The main problem for the interviewed teachers was the issue of crossing the digital barrier, consisting first in learning how to use new applications and second in finding ways of conducting online lessons. In the former case, more problems were reported by older teachers, less computer savvy. However, younger employees also found it problematic to learn how to use remote communication applications. Sometimes the difficulties stemmed from the lack of Polish language versions of the applications used; in such cases, translations of specific functions were prepared and shared in peer groups. Support from other teachers or family members was used as well; here, children often came to the rescue: being forced to participate in online learning themselves, they showed their parents how to use the devices and programs.

The second problem – conducting lessons – was associated with the combination of technological innovations and new, often creative, educational solutions. Some teachers undertook innovative attempts to record their own films, prepared special spaces in their homes to conduct classes, and taught in a creative and less officially imposed way than at school. Nonetheless, the teachers emphasized difficulties in adapting to the new situation, a significant workload increase caused by the need to prepare materials, and intensified communication with parents and pupils with the use of computer applications and increased level of stress related thereto:

> Grażyna (teacher): Initially it is a discomfort at home that, in general, I have to face these people, and this is not a problem since I have been teaching for more than 20 years, but I have to use a computer where I do not know what the feedback is, whether anybody is listening, or, pardon me, whether somebody is picking their nose or lying down, and whether anybody is practicing with me, what the reception is, and how am I to conduct two difficult subjects, in the sense that physical education and music are specific subjects? It is not that I can open a white board and write; I have to practice and this has to be safe, or I have to sing and I need feedback, that is, either I need to hear or they have to be able to hear. This has to work together, be synchronized. So it was a totally different reception.

In the above quotation the interviewee highlights the stress related to the change of the setting from the one well-known to her and one she was used to (classroom) to the one she had to get used to – paradoxically, it was the space of her own home. An additional problem was posed by the specificity of the subjects taught when they required a more creative approach to lessons. The problem, however, appeared also in the case of more "standard" lessons such as mathematics or the Polish language.

An element of online teaching controlled by the teachers to a different extent was the issue of relations with pupils. Traditional classroom lessons required different interactive skills than did teaching the same (or similar) material with the use of a computer. Moreover, during the classes the teachers were sometimes assessed not only by the pupils but also by their parents or actual guardians, such as grandfathers or grandmothers taking care of the children. Certainly, this relation worked in the opposite direction too: the teachers had a chance to see how their charges lived and studied. Thus, the technological change – the introduction of online teaching – demanded social and organizational innovations (e.g. creative ways of conducting lessons) leading to changes in social relations at schools and relations between the schools and their surroundings.

At the same time, it has to be emphasized that the scale of problems related to the introduction of remote work in education was definitely the highest in its initial phases. Subsequent moves to online teaching generated significantly fewer problems, both material and organizational. Regarding the material aspect, during the first months of the pandemic, that is, around the beginning of the school year 2020/2021, the equipment shortages were supplemented via private or public effort. In the organizational terms, the methods worked out in the first phase of the pandemic were used, which proving their certain institutionalization. However, it did not mean the end of the problems caused by this form of teaching. Another challenge – mostly of a social character – proved to be the return of children to studying at schools. The period of lockdown affected the processes of building relations between pupils and, upon return, made the building of relations between the teachers and their charges more difficult. This once again required innovative solutions and "additional educational work" (Miecia, teacher).

Finally, it is worth adding that the pandemic-related problems as of the end of February 2022 were exacerbated by the inflow of refugee children from Ukraine due to the full-scale Russian attack on this country. As emphasized by our interlocutors, the key role in the organization of the didactic process in ethnically and culturally diverse classes in which some pupils did not speak Polish rested in the first place on the teachers and the management. This points to a recurring pattern of transferring the responsibility for crisis management to the lower levels of the organizational hierarchy.

6 Organizational Innovations: the Creation of COVID Wards in Hospitals

The Polish health care system in the context of fighting the COVID-19 pandemic was concentrated mainly around dedicated hospital units (COVID hospitals)[5] and COVID wards organized within standard hospitals (ad hoc organized organizational units which took care of the COVID patients requiring hospital treatment in the changed space and with dedicated medical and nonmedical staff teams). The main goal of creating these dedicated units was limiting the spread of pandemic and avoiding a paralysis of medical services in Poland. From the organizational perspective, these actions were aimed at

---

5   COVID hospitals were ad hoc-organized facilities to which COVID-19 patients were sent. In some cases, these were temporarily transformed regular hospitals, and in other cases – new facilities organized completely from scratch, for example, in the National Stadium in Warsaw.

enabling better use of material resources, transfer of knowledge, and concentration of medical staff efforts in the most pandemic-burdened areas of the health care system. In this section of the chapter we focus in the first place on the creation of COVID wards based on the BNI and FGI interviews conducted with doctors and nurses who have worked in such organizational units.

First, we have to emphasize that, like the introduction of online teaching, the organization of COVID wards was carried out without any prior material, organizational, or competence-related preparation by the central administration. This is interesting as the first information about the serious risk of a new virus pandemic appeared at least three months prior to the announcement of a state of epidemiological emergency in Poland in mid-March 2020. Despite that all, our interlocutors emphasized that the task consisting in the organization of a COVID ward was fulfilled in the conditions of organizational chaos and without support from hospital or ministry authorities, as confirmed by the findings in NIK follow-up reports (2022b).

The doctors and nurses pointed, for example, to shortages in personal protection equipment such as masks, gloves, and suits; the procedural chaos regarding rules for the admission and discharge of patients as well as rules for testing themselves and the patients; lack of possibility to actually separate the COVID patients from other patients due to space limitations; insufficient information flow regarding the virus characteristics and possible treatments; and attempts to avoid work in COVID wards both by the medical and nonmedical staff. On the other hand, the gathered material features accounts of the requirement to report in detail the work with coronavirus patients after COVID allowances were introduced, thus increasing the salaries of doctors and nurses in contact with the infected patients.[6] The intensified procedural control was in contradiction to the ad-hocratic organizational order necessitated by the crisis situation, increasing the stress related to potential mistakes subject to criminal liability. Many problems were associated with extensive workload, in particular during the peak waves of the pandemic, increased level of stress, and constant risk of illness for oneself and one's relatives.

The organization of each COVID ward required the staff and the management to form a team that would work in the ward as well as to prepare appropriate space, specially sectioned off from the rest of the hospital in order to avoid infection. The latter issue was solved, for example, by express renovations, room adjustment, creation of sluices, and dividing the space into clean and contaminated areas. Furthermore, due to the lack of

---

6 In April 2020 the government introduced financial compensation for the medical staff having direct contact with patients with a COVID-19 infection – a COVID allowance of 100 percent of a person's salary, up to a maximum of PLN 15,000 (approximately EUR 3,000).

effective pharmacological treatments – even though various possibilities were searched for by testing promising drugs in summary procedures – the only effective way of reducing the negative consequences of the disease was oxygen therapy.

> Kuba (doctor): It was a kind of economic espionage, that is, if something worked in another hospital and we did not have it, we tried it also; for example, we tried to buy it or make a change. For instance, in the emergency oxygen therapy ward, there is the opening for oxygen. It appears that these are simple devices, that when you branch it, you can obtain two access points.
> Interviewer: Two entry points.
> Kuba: Two entry points. It was in another hospital, and we did not have it yet, but then we got it. So somebody said that they had worked there and seen something like that and maybe we should also do it.

This quote from an interview with Kuba shows how they tried to increase the possibility of offering treatment to the largest number of patients possible using simple technical solutions unavailable within the original version of the device and, what may be more important, using informal contacts and information flow. This is significant also because the interviews with persons from the medical staff management emphasized the role of individual initiative of doctors and nurses, who tried to acquire the necessary knowledge about the virus, tests, vaccines, available therapies, and innovative technological or organizational solutions (e.g. on websites and Internet forums). The key role was played there by the recommendations of the Polish Association of Epidemiologists and Infectiologists, however, in practice the knowledge was often exchanged via informal channels between doctors.

On the one hand, the organization of a COVID ward required innovative spatial solutions and establishment of local procedures taking into account the regulations regarding the desired and undesired behaviors in a situation of epidemiological threat. On the other hand, it posed a challenge related to the formation of teams of doctors and nurses who were to work within the newly created units. Here, two aspects of COVID ward creation are worth mentioning. First, the risk of infection and serious illness caused fear due to which, according to some of our interlocutors, certain doctors and nurses did not want to work in such wards. This in turn led to tensions in employee relations. Interestingly, several interviews indicated that the tensions run in line with the division into professional groups: the nurses reported unwillingness to work in COVID wards among the doctors, whereas the doctors pointed to the resistance on the part of the nurses. In the first months of the pandemic, the transfer to a COVID ward was usually voluntary despite the frequent problem with staff shortage due to sick leaves and quarantine measures. In subsequent stages, the staff were increasingly often delegated based on regulations allowing to send employees to another hospital in order to fight the pandemic.

Second, the teams working in COVID wards had to face restrictive procedures regarding work under the risk of infection, which increased the physical and mental effort to be made. Moreover, work time was reorganized within such teams: they were divided into shifts so as to avoid ward work stoppage in case of infection and to reduce physical work in special suits. It is worth adding here that organizational innovations also had consequences of individual character. The doctors reported that they undertook special measures to protect their relatives against infection, for example, they rented separate apartments, divided private space in order to limit their contact with their partners or children, or avoided family meetings. The gathered accounts also mentioned increased alcohol consumption or psychological problems which stemmed from work in wards with high rates of patient death.

Thus, the pattern observed in the education sector occurred also in the health care sector: pandemic fluctuation translated directly into the scale of problems and, at the same time, the occurrence of grassroots employee innovations. The beginning of the pandemic, characterized, for example, by organizational chaos – including temporary reduction of hierarchical management due to limited resources and the need to rely on the involvement of staff – was a period of greater agency of frontline workers. In the case of health care, the situation was controlled to a greater extent but the above process of COVID ward creation still depended mainly on the creativity, willingness, and motivation of the doctors and nurses who worked there. Especially the latter pointed to the fact that, for some of them, the pandemic was a period when they became much more independent from the doctors as compared to the time before the pandemic.

7 Relational Innovations: Mutual Help and Organization of Trade Unions in Nursing Homes

Workplace innovations are necessarily based on communication with other persons and reconfiguration of interpersonal relations (Ziegler 2017), since every type of change requires overcoming the resistance and cooperation with colleagues and management. We suggest defining the special type of innovation aimed at interpersonal relations and creation of new groups and employee organizations as "relational innovations." Even though relational innovations took place in all the examined sectors, we analyze them based on nursing homes, in which they reached the fullest form. The gathered empirical material documents both the activities of mutual support within the organization of nursing homes and grassroots mobilization by the employees of this sector through unionization and organization of protests in order to improve their working conditions.

In the pandemic crisis, nursing homes were places distinguished by a heightened risk of a severe course of COVID-19 due to the characteristics of their residents, namely the concentration of older and chronically ill persons. Work in nursing homes during the pandemic was subject to various processes, from the intensification caused by increased burden on the employees taking care of dependent persons to the inability to fulfill everyday tasks (e.g. by physiotherapists). The employees functioned under a constant threat of full closure of the facilities in case of infection. This meant they had to be ready to remain with their charges for more than a dozen days without the possibility to return home and visit their close ones. This has to be seen in the light of the underfunding typical of the Polish public services sector and its staff shortages, which, upon the commencement of pandemic crisis, increased tensions within the teams. The above matter strengthened our interest in two situations: the cases in which employees spoke about the pandemic as a test they managed to pass despite difficulties, and the cases in which the pandemic crisis clearly affected the occurrence of collective interests in an organization, such as trade unions.

In the first example of relational innovations, the key element emphasized both by the employees and the managers of the nursing homes was the ties formed between those two groups in the pre-pandemic period, which translated into greater readiness for sacrifice and at the same time mitigated possible tensions at the time of the pandemic:

> Jola (orderly at a nursing home): And imagine that there was a man ... Osa [wasp] was his surname. He weighed 150 kilos. Our lift is 1.20 per 1.20 meters. He died on the fourth floor and we had to carry him to the lift on a blanket. This is nurses' work, but all of us orderlies worked at this. During this COVID, the few of us that remained were one big team. It was not like you have to do this, you have to do that.

In the above quote the interlocutor speaks about being a team and sharing duties, which was also confirmed in other narratives of nursing home staff. Some professional groups (e.g. physiotherapists) undertook other duties since it was impossible to fulfil their own everyday tasks. On the one hand, it was aimed at maintaining the labor process, and on the other hand, they tried to support others who were exposed to the risk or intensification of their tasks. Mutual emotional support was especially significant in the case of shortage of institutional support for employees, for example, in the form of psychological help, as mentioned by Ula:

> Ula (carer at a nursing home): There was no psychological support – no counsellor, therapist, or anybody who, I don't know, would come or anything. Between ourselves, so to speak, when we sat in the staff room with coffee or tea, then we simply spoke about it. And in fact we were therapists and psychologists for each other.

The social care sector proved to be a space in which relational innovations translated also into the development of employee interest representation in the form of trade union creation.[7] The organization of trade unions stemmed from the problems formulated bottom-up at workplaces. They were supported by the Central European Organizing Center (COZZ) foundation, cofinanced by the UNI Global Union federation, and working with Polish trade unions such as the Confederation of Labor. The processes of social care employee mobilization were continued in the period when the health crisis was coming to an end and the workload increased due to the inflow of refugees from Ukraine. Salary-related protests of social workers were organized in 2022, for example, in Łódź and Wroclaw, and new radical trade unions such as the Workers' Initiative were created in nursing homes in Wroclaw and other places.

One possible explanation of the increased mobilization in nursing homes compared to other sectors was the association of the experience of mutual support and social care with the creation of potential for employees organizing themselves. Bożena, a cook at one of the facilities and a trade union activist, says:

> Bożena (cook at a nursing home): This pandemic gave us this feeling that, despite everything, in extreme situations we are stronger together. If we started speaking each on our own, I suspect that we would achieve

---

7   This does not mean that there were no employee protests in other sectors; however, in the case of education they were much weaker, and in health care they took place mostly outside workplaces, in the form of demonstrations and a sit-in protest of seventy-five days in the fall of 2021 by medical and nonmedical staff in front of the Prime Minister's office, called the "White Village 2.0."

nothing. And when we started asking in one voice, this was a situation that not only persons in the trade unions but also from outside the unions joined us.

The difficult work conditions during the pandemic proved, according to the above-quoted interviewee, an important factor strengthening interpersonal relations, which translated into greater solidarity at a workplace. It has to be added that the persons working in nursing homes were relatively longer deprived of adequate personal protection equipment, which increased their fear and dissatisfaction. The interviews gathered within the project described cases where a protest was organized within one unit and situations in which employees from various nursing homes organized themselves in order to improve work conditions in a more systemic way. Moreover, thanks to the organized efforts and pressure on the government, they managed to obtain partial support on the government level in June 2023, when an agreement was signed providing for the increase of salaries for social care employees. However, it was not until July 2024 that the agreement was implemented in the form promised by the government.

8   Conclusions

This chapter was aimed at discussing the role of the COVID-19 pandemic as a specific, exogenous – in relation to work organization – and difficult-to-predict social crisis in the development of workplace innovation. We focused our analyses on the public services necessary for the functioning of society, such as primary education, hospital services, or nursing homes. The COVID-19 pandemic deepened the organizational, staffing, and material problems already existing in schools, hospitals, and nursing homes. Based on the conducted analyses we conclude that in the first phases of the pandemic, grassroots innovations made it possible to maintain the continuity of provided education, health care, and social care. Such thesis confirms and extends to other sectors the conclusions stemming from studies conducted within the health care sector in other countries which emphasized the significance of "improvisation" (Wiedner et al. 2020) and "emergent creativity" (Cohen and Cromwel 2021) in solving new problems and providing key services in the state of limited resources.

Pointing to the significance of "frugal innovation" (Nölke 2022) supplements the discussion on the "essential work" with a significant dimension of collective ways of dealing with a crisis at the workplace. It appears that, in the light of a global pandemic crisis, the creativity of frontline workers and lower management made the continued operation of primary schools, hospitals, and nursing homes possible. It is easy to "heroize" their attitude, but it is also difficult to avoid the conclusion – as formulated in the report of the Supreme Audit Office (NIK 2023) – about the bad preparation of state bodies and institutions to fight the epidemic and the inadequacy of the anti-crisis actions undertaken by them.

The transfer of responsibility for dealing with the crisis to the management and employees of schools, hospitals, and nursing homes may be interpreted in two ways. First, it points to the consequences of neoliberal austerity policies which accompany the liberalization and privatization of public services. Similarly to the case described by Illner (2021: 155), in the USA, in the light of the state's withdrawal, "responsibility for social reproduction was outsourced to the market and to civil society, completing the triangulation of social reproduction under austerity." Second, the state's weakness in the pandemic may be related to the specificity of "patchwork capitalism" typical for Poland and other Central and Eastern European countries (Gardawski and Rapacki 2021). It is characterized by the inconsistency of institutional order within which there coexist various, often contradictory, "rules of the game." This weakens such areas of the state's activity as coordination of anti-crisis policies, encouraging situational, reactive, and ad-hocratic solutions. It seems that these explanations do not have to be contradictory but are complimentary instead. In the Polish conditions, the neoliberal decentralization of responsibility and the austerity policies overlap with the patchwork institutional order, forcing grassroots adjustments of innovative character.

It is worth adding that the most of worker-driven organizational and relational innovations were not subject to "normalization." Except for new union organizations created during the pandemic, worker innovations did not lead to more permanent institutional solutions, for example, in the form of increased employee autonomy and participation in the workplaces. The situation is a bit different in the case of technological innovations related to remote or hybrid work. Even though it did not become the norm at schools, the digital competences developed during the pandemic – including the use of applications such as Teams, WhatsApp, or Messenger for communication – as well as the finally introduced legal regulations make its use easier. However, it seems that the grassroots potential for creativity and agency of workers was not sufficiently appreciated in any material or symbolic way, and its translation into changes in work organization in the postpandemic period is limited.

Translated by Amalia Woźna

References

Cohen, A. K., & Cromwell, J. R. (2021). How to respond to the COVID-19 pandemic with more creativity and innovation. *Population Health Management, 24*(2), 153–155. https://doi.org/10.1089/pop.2020.0119.

Delanty, G. (Ed.). (2020). *Pandemics, politics, and society: Critical perspectives on the COVID-19 crisis*. De Gruyter.

Drozdowski, R., Krajewski, M., Luczys, P., & Kubacka, M. (2022). In between: On the defensive reactivity of public institutions in Poland to the COVID-19 pandemic. *Ruch Prawniczy, Ekonomiczny i Socjologiczny, 84*(1), 229–246. https://doi.org/10.14746/rpeis.2022.84.1.17.

Eurofound and European Commission. (2021). *What just happened? COVID-19 lockdowns and change in the labour market*. Eurofound and European Commission Joint Research Center. Publications Office of the European Union. https://www.eurofound.europa.eu/system/files/2021-10/ef21040en.pdf.

Felstead, A. (2022). *Remote working: A research overview*. Routledge.

Gallie, D. (2013). *Economic crisis, quality of work, and social integration: The European experience*. Oxford University Press.

Gardawski, J., & Rapacki, R. (2021). Patchwork capitalism in Central and Eastern Europe – A new conceptualization. *Warsaw Forum of Economic Sociology, 2*(23).

Gibbs, G. (2007). *Analyzing qualitative data*. SAGE Publications.

Illner, P. (2021). *Disasters and social reproduction: Crisis response between the state and community*. Pluto Press.

Kane, G. C., Nanda, R., Phillips, A., & Copulsky, J. (2021). Redesigning the post-pandemic workplace. *MIT Sloan Management Review, Spring*, 12–14.

Kozek, W. (2011). *Gra o jutro usług publicznych w Polsce*. Wydawnictwa Uniwersytetu Warszawskiego.

Lawrence, T. B., Suddaby, R., & Leca, B. (2009). Introduction: Theorizing and studying institutional work. In T. B. Lawrence, R. Suddaby, & B. Leca (Eds.), *Institutional work: Actors and agency in institutional studies of organizations* (pp. 1–28). Cambridge University Press. https://doi.org/10.1017/CBO9780511596605.001.

May, C., & Finch, T. (2009). Implementing, embedding, and integrating practices: An outline of normalization process theory. *Sociology, 43*(3), 535–554. https://doi.org/10.1177/0038038509103208.

McCallum, J. M. (2022). *Essential: How the pandemic transformed the long fight for worker justice*. Basic Books.

Merton, R. K. (1968). *Social theory and social structure*. The Free Press.

Mezzadri, A. (2022). Social reproduction and pandemic neoliberalism: Planetary crises and the reorganisation of life, work and death. *Organization, 29*(3), 379–400. https://doi.org/10.1177/13505084221074042.

Milburn, T. W., Schuler, R. S., & Watman, K. H. (2016). Organizational crisis. Part I: Definition and conceptualization. *Human Relations*, *36*(12), 1141–1160. https://doi.org/10.1177/001872678303601205.

Mrozowicki, A. (2023). Innowacja, kontrola, opór, normalizacja: pracownicze sposoby radzenia sobie z pandemicznym kryzysem w miejscu pracy. *Przegląd Socjologiczny*, *72*(3), 9–38. https://doi.org/10.26485/PS/2023/72.3/1.

Mulgan, G., Tucker, S., Ali, R., & Sanders, B. (2007). *Social innovation: What it is, why it matters and how it can be accelerated*. Skoll Center for Social Entrepreneurship Working Paper. https://www.youngfoundation.org/our-work/publications/social-innovation-what-it-is-why-it-matters-how-it-can-be-accelerated/.

NIK. (2022a). *Funkcjonowanie szkół w sytuacji zagrożenia COVID-19*. Supreme Audit Office. https://www.nik.gov.pl/plik/id,25380,vp,28141.pdf.

NIK. (2022b). *Funkcjonowanie szpitali w warunkach pandemii COVID-19*. Supreme Audit Office. https://www.nik.gov.pl/plik/id,26701,vp,29499.pdf.

NIK. (2023). *Przygotowanie i działanie odpowiedzialnych organów państwa, instytucji i służb w sytuacji zagrożenia i wystąpienia chorób szczególnie niebezpiecznych i wysoce zakaźnych. Tworzenie i funkcjonowanie szpitali tymczasowych powstałych w związku z epidemią COVID-19*. Supreme Audit Office. https://www.nik.gov.pl/plik/id,28131,vp,30955.pdf.

Nölke, A. (2022). *Post-corona capitalism: The alternatives ahead*. Bristol University Press.

Pałęcka, A. (2023). Who cares for carers? Responsibilization and the discourse of self-care in health and social care literature during the COVID-19 pandemic. A critical review. *Qualitative Social Work*. https://doi.org/10.1177/14733250231204628.

Pearson, C. M., & Clair, J. (1998). Reframing crisis management. *The Academy of Management Review*, *23*(1), 59–76.

Portes, A. (2021). Innovation as social change: An institutional analysis. *International Review of Sociology*, *31*(3), 356–372. https://doi.org/10.1080/03906701.2021.2015983.

Radzińska, J. (2022). Zmiana postrzegania i doświadczania solidarności w pandemii COVID-19. *Studia Socjologiczne*, *2022*(3), 111–136.

Schumpeter, J. (2003). *Capitalism, socialism, and democracy*. Routledge.

Schütze, F. (1983). Biographieforschung und narratives Interview. *Neue Praxis*, *3*, 283–293.

Śledziewska, K., & Włoch, R. (2021). *The economics of digital transformation: The disruption of markets, production, consumption, and work*. Routledge.

Strumińska-Kutra, M., & Rok, B. (2016). Innowacje na rzecz jakości życia zawodowego: wstępne uwagi na temat społecznego charakteru innowacji. In M. Strumińska-Kutra and B. Rok (Eds.), *Innowacje w miejscu pracy. Pomiędzy efektywnością a jakością życia zawodowego* (pp. 7–23). Poltext.

Totterdill, P., Pot, F., & Dhondt, S. (2016). Definiowanie innowacji w miejscu pracy. In M. Strumińska-Kutra and B. Rok (Eds.), *Innowacje w miejscu pracy. Pomiędzy efektywnością a jakością życia zawodowego* (pp. 25–50). Poltext.

Vermeerbergen, L., Pulignano, V., Domecka, M., & Jansens, M. (2021). Working hard for the ones you love and care for under COVID-19 physical distancing. *Work, Employment and Society*, *35*(6), 1144–1154. https://doi.org/10.1177/09500170211021568.

Wiedner, R., Croft, C., & McGivern, G. (2020). Improvisation during a crisis: Hidden innovation in healthcare systems. *BMJ Leader*, *4*(4), 185–188. https://doi.org/10.1136/leader-2020-000259.

Ziegler, R. (2017). Social innovation as a collaborative concept. *Innovation: The European Journal of Social Science Research*, *30*(4), 388–405. https://doi.org/10.1080/13511610.2017.1348935.

CHAPTER 9

Social Life in an Era of Growing Uncertainty

Mirosława Marody

Uncertainty is an immanent feature of human life, which is due to the fact that the boundary conditions of our actions are determined, on the one hand, by the behavior of other people that cannot be fully predicted, and on the other hand, by processes occurring in the external, institutional, and natural environment. The drive to reduce this uncertainty lies at the foundation of the processes of socializing human behavior, that is, the production of roles, norms, rules, and procedures that channel individual actions into repetitive, and thus also more predictable, patterns. The social order that emerges from these patterns has at its core a specific vision of reality, a value-saturated picture of the world that reflexively directs individual actions. This is what Max Weber had in mind when he wrote that "culture is a finite section of the meaningless infinity of events in the world, endowed with meaning and significance from a *human* perspective" (Weber 2012: 119; emphasis preserved).

Making sense of reality does not, of course, give us certainty about how individual people with whom we interact will behave or what the next day will bring, but it significantly reduces the sense of ontological insecurity. Although the last term is generally used to describe psychological phenomena, those involved in the construction of individual identity,[1] its content refers to a much broader and strictly social context. The currently experienced increase in ontological insecurity (see Marody 2021) can be seen as a consequence of the transformation and disintegration of those structures and images of reality which were formed in the period of modernity and which have determined the goals of social actors, given meaning and sense to the lives of individuals, and consequently legitimized the system as well as contributed to its reproduction. A detailed analysis of the factors entangled in these processes goes beyond the scope of this chapter; it is enough to say that the consequence of their impact was not only the multiplication of socially accepted patterns of lifestyles but also the loss of systemic coherence, that is, the growing discrepancy between

---

1   The term was introduced by Ronald D. Laing (1960) to describe symptoms accompanying temporary or permanent identity crisis. See also Giddens (1991).

the principles that regulate the functioning of systemic institutions and those that guide the actions of social actors (Touraine 2014).

As a result of all these changes, the reality around us ceased to be "obvious." It is no longer "naturalized" by individual actions consistent with the culturally produced and institutionally supported image of the world. In other words, the world we live in today is falling apart in all directions, additionally shaken by recurring economic crises joined in recent years by a series of catastrophic events such as the pandemic, the war in Ukraine, and the climate crisis. With the disintegration of this relatively tame world and the acceleration of its transformations, a sense of uncertainty grows in people, including not only the answer to the question "Who am I?" but also the more fundamental question of how to behave and what actions to take in order to survive in this whirlwind of change.

The answer to the first question is seemingly very simple: I am what I want to be. And although it sounds almost grotesque or like a distasteful joke in the world in which we currently operate, it is the only answer that modern culture provides us with – or at least the dominant part of it, in which a feature of the system is that it creates innumerable choices, and how these choices will be used is the individual's problem and responsibility. Similarly, it remains the individual's problem to tackle the uncertainty of whether, out of the multitude of available options, they have chosen the most appropriate one that will expand their possibilities for self-realization (cf. Giddens 1991).

The emergence of such a cultural perspective was driven by the processes of disintegration of social structures that have been taking place since the second half of the last century. They liberated individuals from the bonds of class membership and family obligations and the control of organizations, institutions, and neighbors (Beck 1992). Having gained the freedom to choose, to freely set the goals of their actions, their views, and their relationships, individuals were thus also given the opportunity to shape their biographies and lives. The aspiration to lead "a life of one's own," a life that is an expression of one's most personal desires and needs, an authorial biography not subject to social censorship (Beck and Beck-Gernsheim 1996), began to spread not only in the highly developed Western societies that gave birth to it, but also in those that entered the path of modernization later. It was patronized by the conviction that individual self-realization is the supreme value, a conviction sustained both by the content circulating on various levels of culture (cf. Bauman 2008; Illouz 1997) and by the results of sociological research (Ester, Halman, and de Moor 1993; Inglehart 1990).

In the case of Polish society, traces of such transformations are easily found in data collected since the 1990s as part of European Value Systems (Marody

2019; Jasińska-Kania and Marody 2004). They show a systematic increase in freedom aspirations – which include the freedom to proclaim one's own views and the possibility to influence the decisions of authorities – as well as a slow increase in tolerance toward diversity and a decline in the importance attributed to work, accompanied by a significant increase in the importance attached to leisure time and friends. Another evident feature is a spectacular decline in support for all opinions describing the traditional division of female and male roles, and – especially in the younger generation – a clear secularization trend. In 2017, when the latest EVS survey was conducted, we also noted a significant increase in the sense of control over one's own life.

The sense of control over one's own life, or sense of agency, is an inherent correlate of the vision of an individualized, reflective, and autonomous individual that has been developed in modern culture. However, the conviction instilled in individuals that they can be who they want to be encountered systemic limitations at the very beginning of this process, and thus triggered efforts to introduce corrections to the institutional order. This was reflected in significant shifts in the political agenda – since the second half of the last century, in Western societies, issues of economic divisions began to be replaced therein by cultural and social issues, dealing with transformations in the areas of morality, individual rights, quality of life, labor autonomy, as well as attitudes toward political elites and the state (Touraine 2014; Flanagan and Lee 2003).

The institutional changes resulting from the implementation of at least some of the postulates of this political agenda can be interpreted as Ronald Inglehart did (Inglehart and Welzel 2005). According to him, the shifts in hierarchies of values recorded in the research led to the transformation of the institutional order toward its democratization, respect for civil and political freedoms, and the extension of the empowerment of individuals to act in accordance with their individual choices, thus transforming the process of modernization into a process of human development.

A specific test for Inglehart's theory was the growing power of populist movements and the election of Donald Trump as President of the United States. Especially the latter event had a particularly significant symbolic meaning, since it took place in a society that was one of the first to discover the charms of self-realization and that for the past half century has set the course of the modernization processes described by Inglehart. In an attempt to explain this, he formulated the "cultural backlash thesis," according to which "the surge in votes for populist parties can be explained not as a purely economic phenomenon but in large part as a reaction against progressive cultural change" (Inglehart and Norris 2016: 2–3). In this light, support for Trump would be rooted in "a counterrevolutionary retro backlash, especially among the older generation, white men, and less educated people, who sense decline and actively reject the rising tide of progressive values, [and] resent the displacement of familiar traditional norms" (Inglehart and Norris 2016: 3). Therefore, it would constitute a "leftover" of modernization processes, without significantly changing their direction.

Slightly different interpretations of the recently registered changes are proposed by researchers working in the shadow of Inglehart's theory of social development (Hochschild 2016; Flanagan and Lee 2003; Stein 2001). First of all, they point out that the changes in values that have been taking place since the middle of the last century result from the breakdown of the overall picture of reality produced by modernity, and sticking to traditionalist values is not just a "residue" of the modernization processes, but an important element of the culture wars waged in modern societies. These researchers also emphasize the role that public opinion leaders and politicians play in the articulation of traditionalist values. Finally, their studies indicate that the production of competing images of reality grows out of the need to comprehend it, and that values are a part of these images rather than the result of axiological choices that the individual consciously makes in isolation from them.

Such findings help to better understand the importance for contemporary individuals of answering the question of identity, especially one formulated in terms of belonging to one of the sides of the ongoing cultural war. Manuel Castells wrote about this in the 1990s, pointing out that

> identity is becoming the main, and sometimes the only, source of meaning in a historical period characterized by widespread destruction of organizations, delegitimization of institutions, fading away of major social movements, and ephemeral cultural expressions. People increasingly organize their meaning not around what they do but on the basis of what they are, or believe they are.
> CASTELLS 2001: 3

Let us note, however, that these are flawed meanings, since they have no support in the institutional order, the evolution of which has been and still is determined by the interests of large corporations and temporary alliances of political forces. Of course, it can be assumed that our individual choices are made within the framework set by the existing institutional order, and thus will contribute to the reproduction of the entire system. And in fact, this is the general message found when one analyzes the more specific content of contemporary culture, as Eva Illouz (1997), for example, did. They boil down to a slogan that, to paraphrase the title of a well-known film, could be summarized in the recommendation "consume, work, love." The only problem is that the implementation of this recommendation encounters increasing difficulties in a world shaken by successive crises and a growing sense of uncertainty about how to maintain agency in a changing reality.

According to Geert Hofstede (1991), the response to this type of everyday uncertainty is largely dependent on the more general cultural patterns developed in a given society. This researcher assumes that all societies face similar problems but are characterized by different approaches to solving them. In the middle of the last century, Hofstede analyzed the attitudes and values of IBM employees from more than seventy countries, and on this basis he distinguished four universal dimensions that differentiate the cultures of the societies he studied. One of these dimensions turned out to be uncertainty avoidance, describing how members of a given society deal with new, unfamiliar situations.

According to Hofstede, in societies with high rates of uncertainty avoidance, change is perceived as a threat and causes strong anxiety and high levels of stress. At the institutional level, uncertainty is combated by the proliferation of regulations and detailed rules,[2] innovation and creativity of employees are curtailed, and conflicts are seen as a threat to the smooth functioning of organizations. On the other hand, at the level of individual actions and interpersonal relations, societies with high rates of uncertainty avoidance are characterized by a low level of tolerance for people who differ, and this includes ethnic as well as political, ideological, cultural, and religious differences. There is, however, a connivance to displays of aggression and other negative feelings, as this type of emotional disinhibition is seen as a way to release the tension accumulated through constant stress.

In Hofstede's study, Poland, with a score of 93 points, was included in a group of countries with a high uncertainty avoidance index. This group also contained Russia (95), Bolivia (94), Belgium (94), Japan (92), and France (86). By contrast, the lowest ratings on the uncertainty avoidance dimension were gained by countries such as Singapore (8), Jamaica (13), and China (30), while

---

2   It is worthwhile emphasizing several points in this context. First, overregulation of social life through rules and detailed norms of behavior does not really guarantee that people will follow them. Multiplication of principles often has the opposite effect because individuals are incapable of memorizing and observing all rules. Second, the tendency to avoid uncertainty should not be confused with the tendency to avoid risk. According to Hofstede, "uncertainty is to risk as anxiety is to fear. Fear and risk are both focused on something specific. ... Anxiety and uncertainty are both diffuse feelings" (1991: 197). Uncertainty manifests as an aversion to ambiguous situations, while high-risk behavior can be more frequent when uncertainty is reducible to the specific probability of a given event.

among the European ones, Denmark (23), Sweden (29), and England (35). It is difficult to point to any factor responsible for such groupings – it is neither the level of economic development, nor the type of religious denomination, nor belonging to a specific cultural circle. It is usually assumed that the history of a given society is responsible for the formation of this indicator. And indeed, when one reads into the characteristics included in the high uncertainty avoidance index, it is hard to resist the conviction that, in the case of Poland, they resemble a description of the traits that form the syndrome of "feudal service culture," another concept often used to explain the behavior of the Poles in social situations (cf. Leder 2016).

A random comparison of place in Hofstede's classification with the level of sense of control over one's own life as indexed in the 2017 EVS survey shows that in societies with high levels of uncertainty avoidance index, the percentage of people choosing answers indicating a high sense of control over life is lower than in those with low uncertainty avoidance index. For example, in Poland such answers were given by 47 percent of respondents, while in Denmark – 65 percent.

The sense of agency, however, now seems to be determined not so much by general cultural characteristics as by current events that affect our ability to act. From this point of view, one would expect that events such as a pandemic, rising inflation, or the war in Ukraine, which have significantly increased the level of everyday uncertainty about experienced reality, should translate into changes in the sense of control over one's own life. Indeed, if one looks at the reactions of Poles to these events, it is clear that the pandemic initially aroused negative emotions in them. However, they were tamed quite quickly. For although in the first months of the pandemic Poles were extremely obedient in their complying with the lockdown rules – which, by the way, could be linked to the aforementioned characteristics of cultures with a high rate of uncertainty avoidance – by the summer months there was already a massive return to "normal" behaviors focused around consumption.

Research conducted during the pandemic period has also shown that confidence in the institutional order increases during periods of heightened uncertainty. At least during the initial period of the pandemic, the assessment of the government's actions was very positive. In a survey conducted on March 12–13, 2020 by IPSOS, 71 percent of respondents thought that the government was doing well in containing the spread of the pandemic. However, a year later, in a mid-April 2021 CBOS survey (2021), only 43 percent of respondents thought the government was doing a good job of containing the epidemic (including nine percent who said it was "definitely good"), while 49 percent rated the government's policy in this regard negatively (including 22 percent who said it was "definitely bad"). What could be even more important, the perception of the government's actions toward the epidemic was primarily differentiated by age. The government's efforts to curb the epidemic were appreciated by only 12 percent of those under twenty-four and as many as 65 percent of those surveyed who were sixty-five or older. In contrast, 28 percent of the oldest respondents and 79 percent of respondents up to twenty-four years of age assessed them negatively.

The differential impact of age on the assessments of the government's effectiveness persisted in 2022, when we were dealing with the cumulative effects of three events affecting the level of uncertainty in society, namely the pandemic, the war in Ukraine, and rising inflation. According to the Kantar agency's survey, conducted in the last days of August 2022, 68 percent of respondents in the entire sample viewed the government negatively, while 24 percent spoke positively about it. However, among those aged twenty to twenty-nine, there were 77 percent negative ratings and only 12 percent positive ratings, while among those aged sixty and over, the rates were 59 percent and 34 percent, respectively.

One could explain these disparities by the conservatism of older people and the tendency of younger people to reject institutional authority, but a more interesting clue for justifying these age differences is provided by the results of a study conducted by Sławomir Sierakowski and Przemysław Sadura from Krytyka Polityczna. Based on the fragmentary data revealed in an interview with *Newsweek* (Pawlicka 2022), it appears that young and older people perceive differently the two main threats posed by the war outside our country and inflation inside it. Sierakowski's proposed explanation for this dissimilarity refers to the differences in the experiences of the two groups:

> The elderly take inflation rather calmly because they have already lived through it, but they are terrified of war because they remember stories about it firsthand. The young are exactly the opposite. They have long-term loans, and for the first time in their lives they see that what they bought the day before is now several dozen percent more expensive. They are in shock. Meanwhile, they think as follows about the war: "I will run away." After all, this is a generation that travels all around the world.

However, if one looks at this dissimilarity from the perspective adopted in this text, one would have to conclude that the sense of danger that inflation arouses in young people is primarily due to the fact that it threatens the lifestyle they have already achieved or aspire to. After all, that lifestyle is the quintessence of identity and the primary source of senses and meanings in times of ontological uncertainty. This connection can be seen in all the reports on how people are coping with inflation, which, in addition to purely pragmatic accounts, contain such evaluations for the actions taken as "It's humiliating" or "It's degrading and exhausting."

These accounts also demonstrate that the sense of uncertainty we are currently experiencing is related not only, or even not so much, to the future, to the fact that we are unable to estimate what changes all those negative events we are witnessing and complicit in will bring, but also, and perhaps even primarily, to the present, to the fact that we do not know how to save within ourselves the sense of agency that attests to our autonomy and ability to shape our own lives. We deal with the first one, involving everyday uncertainty, as best as we can. Research by Katarzyna Pawlikowska, for example, shows a significant increase in the search for political and economic information in the media – among men from 51 percent in 2018 to 82 percent in 2022, and among women, from 12 to 44 percent, respectively. On the other hand, the research conducted by Barbara Jaruga and Barbara Zajączkowska on the market for psychics, tarot tellers, and clairvoyants shows that not long ago we spent two billion PLN a year on esoteric services and now the amount is PLN 3.5 billion. Fourteen million Poles are ready to use the services of psychics and clairvoyants (qtd. in Święchowicz 2022).

Regarding the latter, that is, the sense of ontological uncertainty, Poles are doing increasingly worse because, as I mentioned at the outset, it is the result of all the civilizational changes that have profoundly ploughed up the systems of meanings and senses established during modernity. The ways of mastering it, proposed by contemporary culture and centered around consumption, are crumbling today in collision with the crises we have recently entered. There is also an ongoing battle between the growing individual demands for greater autonomy in all aspects of individual life and the growing ability of the technostate to supervise, manipulate, and control. Its completion would require the production of a new axionormative order and a corresponding new image of reality.

In the current situation, this is impossible, since contemporary society is, as Luhmann writes, "a society without an *apex* or *center*" (1990: 31; emphasis preserved) or – to express this in different terms – a "multi-paradigmatic" society, that is, one in which the diversity of human actions not only does not contribute to a more coherent narrative but, by its very existence, increases the level of social entropy and contributes to undermining faith in the sense of what we do. Within it, individuals are constantly confronted with information that undermines the choices already made and reveals new possibilities for action. In this kind of society, reaching a consensus is situational rather than based on commonly recognized knowledge about what reality is like and what is important. It can be said that in the long run any kind of activity loses its justification in the absence of a metanarrative that would endow it with meaning.

This relationship between the axionormative view of the world and a sense of ontological uncertainty can be seen when one looks at the two basic types of social order that are usually distinguished in sociology – traditional and modern. For traditional societies, the overriding value was the continuance and reproduction of the order established by ancestors or gods, while for modern societies it was progress. In the first case, the reward for the individual was joining the ancestors or salvation, in the second – individual success. Salvation and success could be achieved, at least theoretically, by anyone, as long as they followed the principles that formed the axiological order. In both cases, the values adhered to by individuals legitimized the system and were involved in the processes of its reproduction.

Meanwhile, what characterizes contemporary societies is the lack of such complementarity between the institutional order and the axiological order. Thus, it can be said that the growing sense of uncertainty that we are experiencing today is related not so much to the speed, depth, or scope of the changes that are taking place in the reality around us, but to the inability to interpret them in terms that would not only be shared by the majority of society members, but also sustained by their daily actions. The result is a huge deficit of sense, which begins to be filled by a multiplicity of competing values produced in the course of social practices, around which more or less recognizable "communities of meaning" are formed.

The above "communities of meaning" are sustained and reproduced in the course of interactions by the individuals involved. They can breed social actors who, under the banners of specific values, will shape not only the axiological order but also the institutional order subordinated to it. Of course, it is presently impossible to answer the question of which one among the already existing communities of meaning has the greatest chance, if at all, of achieving such a position as to be able to effectively determine the shape of institutions and to eliminate competing ways of seeing reality. One can only presume that, to permanently exist, this new order would have to be built across the divisions marked by today's culture wars.

References

Bauman, Z. (2008). *The individualized society*. Polity.

Beck, U. (1992). *Risk society: Towards a new modernity* (M. Ritter, Trans.). SAGE Publications.

Beck, U., & Beck-Bruun, E. (1996). Individualization and "precarious freedom": Perspectives and controversies of a subject-oriented sociology. In P. Heelas, S. Lash, & P. Morris (Eds.), *Detraditionalization: Critical reflections on authority and identity* (pp. 23–48). Blackwell.

Castells, M. (2001). *The rise of the network society*. Blackwell.

CBOS. (2021). *Obawy przed zarażeniem się koronawirusem i ocena działań rządu w kwietniu. Komunikat z badań nr 48*. Centrum Badania Opinii Społecznej.

Ester, P., Halman, L., & de Moor, R. A. (Eds.). (1993). *Individualizing society: Value change in Europe and North America*. Tilburg University Press.

Flanagan, S. C., & Lee, A.-R. (2003). The new politics, culture wars, and the authoritarian-libertarian value change in advanced industrial democracies. *Comparative Political Studies, 36*(3), 235–270.

Giddens, A. (1991). *Modernity and self-identity: Self and society in the late modern age*. Stanford University Press.

Hochschild, A. (2016). *Strangers in their own land: Anger and mourning on the American right*. New Press.

Hofstede, G. (1991). *Cultures and organizations: Software of the mind*. McGraw-Hill.

Illouz, E. (1997). *Consuming the romantic utopia: Love and the cultural contradictions of capitalism*. University of California Press.

Inglehart, R. (1990). *Culture shift in advanced industrial society*. Princeton University Press.

Inglehart, R., & Norris, P. (2016). *Trump, Brexit, and the rise of populism: Economic have-nots and cultural backlash*. Harvard Kennedy School Faculty Research Working Paper RWP16-026. https://research.hks.harvard.edu/publications/getFile.aspx?Id=1401.

Inglehart, R., & Welzel, C. (2005). *Modernization, cultural change, and democracy: The human development sequence*. Cambridge University Press.

Jasińska-Kania, A., & Marody, M. (Eds.). (2004). *Poles among Europeans*. Wydawnictwo Naukowe Scholar.

Laing, R. D. (1960). *The divided self: An existential study in sanity and madness*. Tavistock.

Leder, A. (2016, December 24). Relacja folwarczna. *Krytyka Polityczna*. https://krytykapolityczna.pl/kraj/leder-relacja-folwarczna/.

Luhmann, N. (1990). *Political theory in the welfare state* (J. Bednarz Jr., Trans.). Walter de Gruyter.

Marody, M. (2019). Transformation of Polish society. *Social Research, 86*(1), 57–81.

Marody, M. (2021). *The individual after modernity: Sociological perspective* (G. Czemiel, Trans.). Routledge.

Pawlicka, A. (2022, September 3). Badania poglądów Polaków. Wiadomo, co jest największą siłą PiS. *Newsweek*. https://www.newsweek.pl/polska/polityka/raport-o-pogladach-polakow-wiadomoco-jest-najwieksza-sila-pis/22k4g6n.

Stein, A. (2001). *The stranger next door: The story of a small community's battle over sex, faith, and civil rights.* Beacon Press.

Święchowicz, M. (2022, August 7). Klątwy bez klątw. *Newsweek 32*.

Touraine, A. (2014). *After the Crisis.* (H. Morrison, Trans.). Cambridge: Polity.

Weber, M. (2012). The "objectivity" of knowledge in social science and social policy (H. H. Bruun, Trans.). In H. H. Bruun & S. Whimster, (Eds.), *Collected methodological writings* (pp. 100–138). Routledge.

PART 3

In Search of a New Perspective

CHAPTER 10

Law in the Anthropocene Era

Marek Zirk-Sadowski

Lawyers often identify the knowledge of the Anthropocene with ecology. However, the difference between the two is significant. Ecology is concerned with the environment – that is, our surroundings – and protecting it. The name ecology is derived from the Greek words *oikos* (house) and *logia* (study of). Ecology mainly deals with ecosystems and how they lose balance as a result of rapid development and increase in human activity. The Anthropocene is a much more dynamic category that touches upon the very ontology of our universe. The term was originally used to describe a geological era and is primarily attributed to the Nobel laureate, P. Crutzen. In 2000, he proposed that we should recognize that we have been living in a new geological epoch, the Anthropocene, for the last 200 years.[1] Since 1980, ecologist E. Stoermer has also been using the term. In joint publications, both scientists link the emergence of the Anthropocene to, above all, the rate of carbon dioxide emissions. This geological category, dating from the commencement of significant human impact on Earth, disrupting the Holocene, proved to be the starting point for noticing the fundamental flaws in human civilization.[2]

Importantly, at least from the point of view of other sciences, including sociology and jurisprudence, it is scholars of the empirical sciences, mainly geologists, who provided convincing evidence that the Earth has indeed entered a new epoch, or perhaps a new era, which is arguably a better term. So far, their observations of previous epochs in the Earth's history have shown that it was natural phenomena – for example, meteorite impacts or major changes in plate tectonics – that initiated geological changes. This time, natural and empirical sciences point to the emergence of a new geological era, which they call the Anthropocene. As the name suggests, *anthropos* refers to us, humans,

---

1 In 1995, Crutzen was awarded the Nobel Prize in Chemistry for his efforts in studying the formation and decomposition of atmospheric ozone. A long-term employee in the USA's National Oceanic and Atmospheric Administration, he was also Director of the Department of Atmospheric Chemistry at the Max Planck Institute for Chemistry in Mainz, Germany.
2 The Holocene, or the youngest contemporaneous geological epoch, was the final stretch of the older Quaternary Period, which began 2.5 million years ago with the end of the last Pleistocene glaciation.

and our activity. Therefore, this new era is the effect of human activity. Our species is pushing the planet into a new, perhaps somewhat frightening, geological and biological era. Analyses of this problem tend to focus on climate change, but the scale of these shifts is much broader.

Philosophers and humanities scholars, who observe the effects of human activity, did not sound the alarm – the source of the warning was empirical research in the field of natural sciences, which turned out impossible to ignore. While focusing on the study of human behavior within the structures of industrial societies, social sciences and humanities overlooked the impending doom faced by these societies in planetary terms because their analyses, at best, look at the effect of globalization. The awareness of this planetary dimension and the recognition of its importance for the survival of humanity came from natural sciences.

Although the modern human, *Homo sapiens*, evolved around 250,000 years ago, our species basically spent most of the time since then hunting, gathering, and living in small groups of up to 200–300 people. It was not until about 10,000 years ago that we saw the emergence of agriculture (New Guinea), and life in villages where there was no ice age. In Europe, agriculture appeared around 5,000 years ago, that is, after the last glaciation. What followed was the prospectively successful period of stabilized climate over a period of 30,000 years, a part of the Holocene (Steffen et al. 2006). The change occurred around 1750 or 1800, when a certain kind of domination of one species – humans – caused the transition to the Anthropocene. By then, we had certainly learned how to use fire, including to modify landscape, but we mostly relied on our own energy and the energy of working animals, and a little on wind and water.

The beginning of the changes in the environment dates back to 1750, when new types of energy releasing heat into the atmosphere were introduced (Ellis 2018). The year 1950 is considered to be the turning point in the intensification of this phenomenon. From then on, the mass use of new energy sources resulted in the gradual increase in the overall temperature of the Earth's atmosphere. Ultimately, the global warming and changes in the atmospheric composition became the central issue in discussions regarding the Anthropocene. Importantly, 2015 was the first year when the Earth's average temperature rose by one degree Celsius above the preindustrial average. Humanity has now approached the limit of a two-degree rise, which climate scientists believe equals a planetary crisis. Of course, there are other factors at play here. In *Anthropocene: A Very Short Introduction*, E. C. Ellis lists ten important phenomena that make up the Anthropocene, including the carbon dioxide rate – carbonization, violation of the nitrogen cycle, loss of biodiversity, disruption of the ozone layer, and consumption of fresh water (Ellis 2018).

There is an ongoing debate whether we should try to return to the Holocene, or whether we must remain in the Anthropocene and leave a *safe operating space* for humanity. Some, like S. Žižek, speak of a "new nature." Nature is no longer "natural"; it is no longer the reliable "dense" background of our lives. The notion of "second nature" is therefore more relevant today than ever before. It can be understood both literally, as an artificially generated new nature – such as anomalies or deformed cows and trees – and, more optimistically, as genetically modified "improved" organisms. A group of American scholars who published an article in *Nature* several years ago refer to the term "planetary boundaries" (Sterner at al. 2019)[3] This also differentiates the discourse on Anthropocene and ecology. Of course, everybody understands the idea of boundaries or limits: we teach them to our children in order to protect them from danger. Meanwhile, the Anthropocene is about planetary boundaries, thus putting forward a new challenge for science: to investigate how the environment functions in a planetary system. That is why we have not yet developed a sensitivity to planetary boundaries. We react strongly to insignificant noises that occur nearby, but we are not alarmed by the echo of a distant explosion that might herald the end of the world.

There are several feasible responses to the warning about the effects of the Anthropocene: a return to the Holocene, staying in the Anthropocene and setting appropriate boundaries, or "second nature." Empirical sciences thus communicate the following message: the Anthropocene has emerged, but we are unsure how we should respond. The choice remains largely in the emotional-volitional sphere of societies that recognize the serious warnings of impending doom and in which Anthropocene has been given a sensational character and allowed to occupy an important position in popular (mass) culture. The impact of this culture on attitudes toward the Anthropocene has, on the one hand, given rise to fears of annihilation. On the other hand, one sees emerging groups that manifest their disregard for it and see it as an artificial sensation, typical of the methods of gaining interest through the means of social communication. We saw similar processes during the COVID-19 pandemic.

The success of generating a social response to the Anthropocene and acceptance of costly social policies, mainly climate-related and aimed at decarbonizing industrial production, is linked to the prevailing faith in science. As an aside, it should be noted that in Poland only 44 percent of people believe that

---

3   The term "planetary boundaries" is used, among others, by D. French and L. J. Kotzé (2021).

science is a significant element of everyday life, while 88 percent of those surveyed trust science. In contrast, 35 percent of respondents say that if science did not exist, daily life would not change. Only 23 percent are skeptical about scientific data, compared to 34 percent in the USA (State of Science Index 2022).

Thus, it makes sense that the starting point of this discussion should be a scientific description of the Anthropocene. The clash between scientific descriptions and the myths of progress prevailing in the collective consciousness gave rise to *sociopolitical phenomena*, the second step toward assimilating the categories of the Anthropocene that led to the popularization of empirical, scientific data. The emergence of new political ideologies, such as the rise of strong "green" parties in many countries, proved to be too limited a response to the problems of the Anthropocene. The entanglement of these parties in the political games of liberal democracies has weakened the radical nature of their demands and measures proposed to remove the threat.

The Anthropocene started to play a pivotal role in the generational transfer of views and ideologies, giving birth to new social movements led by Gen Z – young people born around the year 2000, symbolized by Greta Thunberg's radical position. These movements comprise not only young adults, but also high school pupils who clearly recognize a threat to the planet and thus their future existence. The shift to the "planetary level" has become a characteristic feature of the Anthropocene discourse. These youth-led movements accuse the older generation, currently in power, of being oriented toward the economic condition of countries, reacting poorly to demands for slowing down or even halting progress, and adhering to the principle of "After us, the flood." They also attest to a sense of physical danger and demand intergenerational solidarity manifested through the renunciation of prosperity achieved through aggression and the conflict between economic action and the environment. Warnings of threat, coming from *hard sciences*, have become the signal for a political response.

There is also an additional sense of threat, triggered by new scientific discoveries in biogenetics, which for many herald the imminent end of nature, or at least a modification of natural processes. In weaker terms, this sense of threat – following Freud – is what S. Žižek calls "das Unbehagen in der Kultur," or the uneasiness in culture (Žižek 2019). It seems that the latter has propelled the response to the Anthropocene into a third dimension – namely that of *academic reflection*. Here, the news of the threat was not as important as in the sociopolitical phenomena discussed above.

Thus, we can observe a new phenomenon: a message from the empirical sciences emerges and is transformed into a sense of threat, which is the basis for a response in the form of a story (news) about the direction in which the world is heading. Then, culture becomes involved, but through a model of rationality. Anticipating the next stage, I will say that normativity – the law – is created at the end of this process.

Above all, a philosophical dimension was established as a *third type of response to the problem of the Anthropocene* against the backdrop of discussions about the model of the human–nature relationship. This response to the Anthropocene consists mainly in taking practical action proved to be insufficient. As Thomas noted in 2014, the concept of being "endangered" is not purely scientific – the Earth has already gone through multiple successive climatic transitions and has survived five major mass extinctions of species. "Threat" is a matter of scale and value (Thomas 2014).

It can be hypothesized that the Anthropocene prompts a critique of human-oriented philosophy, which was initiated by Socrates with his famous sentence about the greater benefit he derives from talking to humans than from communing with trees. For a number of scholars, including P. Sloterdijk or D. Chakrabarty, the maximization of this attitude emerged in Kant's philosophy, which introduced sharp distinctions between our "moral" and "animal" (i.e. biological) nature, assuming that the latter will always be taken care of by the natural order of things. Kant's philosophy is assigned the majority of blame for separating morality from responsibility for nature. Most environmental moralists, such as P. Singer (2011), Ch. Taylor (2010), and T. Regan (1980), argue that it is correct to accuse Kant of species-oriented chauvinism and anthropocentrism.

Kant believed that nature had a purpose of its own and was organized in a particular way in order to achieve it. According to him, the purpose of nature is inscribed in its essence and is inherent in how it operates. This is because nature is hierarchical and has its own laws that govern its actions. Moreover, the purpose of nature is immutable and independent of human will and actions. It constitutes an important element of moral theory because it provides us with insight on how we should act in our relationship with nature. In general, the purpose in question is a significant part of our knowledge of the world and we should seek to understand this purpose in order to better comprehend our place and role in the world.

Kant also wrote about animals but did not develop a specific theory on this subject. He emphasized the concept of moral treatment of human beings, yet he did not mention much about moral treatment of animals. In other words, he argued that humans should act morally and respect the rights of other human beings, but he did not extend this to animals. For this reason, his philosophy is often criticized. Nevertheless, many contemporary philosophers are developing ethical theories that take into account moral treatment of animals, based on Kant's assumptions about morality and responsibility for our actions. Paradoxically, in this way Kant's philosophy can inspire the development of ethical theories concerning animals.

In this context, people typically refer to Kant's statements formulated in a brief text from 1786 entitled "Speculative Beginning of Human History," where the central theme of the philosopher's inquiry is the opposition between two aspects of human life. D. Chakrabarty notes that according to Kant, a human only knows how to use their morality to order their own life as the life of one species among many others. To change this would mean to bring into their moral existence something that has always lain outside it: the history of natural life on our planet (Chakrabarty 2018).

In conclusion, Kant states that the human success is contained in being "satisfied with Providence" (Chakrabarty 2018). This is achievable in spite of the fact that Providence often operates based on misfortune: wars, which ultimately force "even the leaders of states" to respect human life; the shortness of life, which ensures that whole species, not individuals, can improve; and the absence of a golden age free of labor but full of leisure (Kant 1786 [1995]). Ultimately, what matters is precisely the contentment with Providence and with the course of all human affairs, which, however, does not move from good toward evil, but slowly develops from worse to better. We are called by nature itself to contribute to this progress to the best of our abilities (Kant 1786 [1995]).

In *Critique of Judgement*, Kant makes a distinction between the moral life of human beings and their natural development. He recognizes that the human:

> as the single being upon earth that possesses understanding, and, consequently, a capacity for setting before himself ends of his deliberate choice, he is certainly titular lord of nature, and, supposing we regard nature as a teleological system, he is born to be its ultimate end. But this is always on the terms that he has the intelligence and the will to give to it and to himself such a reference to ends as can be self-sufficing independently of nature, and, consequently, a final end. Such an end, however, must not be sought in nature.
> KANT (1791 [2014])

Kant's philosophy created the modern separation between the laws of nature, which are mechanical laws studied by theoretical reason, and the laws of liberty, which are moral principles and are therefore studied by practical reason (Kuśmierczyk 2003). For more than a century, this distinction reinforced the widely criticized separation of the humanities from physics and the natural sciences. The conceptual distinction between these two categories, theoretically valuable, led to their moral separation.

By rejecting the dominance of epistemology, the philosophy that emerged against the background of the Anthropocene encourages us to rebuild ontological reflection and thus to undermine the moral separation of nature and culture. The juxtaposition of these two categories is said to be rooted primarily in methodological problems. The separation of the humanities from physics and empirical sciences was essentially conceptual and signaled the methodological weaknesses of the humanities. Ultimately, however, it moved to the axiological level and led to a moral separation of nature and culture. Hence, the proposal to "rebuild" the ontology of the world, going back to the pre-Socratics and a new search for the *arche*. A spectacular attempt at this type of thinking is G. Harman's *Object-Oriented Ontology: A New Theory of Everything* (Harman 2018), where one can see a certain resemblance to T. Kotarbiński's concept of reism.

Sometimes the essential role is attributed to the reconstruction of the humanities and the breaking down of barriers separating them from the exact and empirical sciences, rather than to the need for a new philosophical vision of the world. This is also prompted by the current state of the technical sciences that construct devices on the threshold of technology and biology – sympoiesis, as D. Haraway calls them (Buchanan 2018). Examples include models of artificial intelligence or widely understood electronic prostheses interacting with the human body, in which the separation of natural and humanistic elements breaks down entirely.

J.A. Thomas notes that only humanities and social sciences are capable of exhaustively describing what we may lose by failing to recognize the Anthropocene, but on the condition of a self-transformation of these fields of knowledge (Thomas 2014: 1589). The most important demand is to reject the tendency to separate the categories of the humanities and the natural sciences by de-objectifying nature, failing to see its location in the normative dimension. Climate change science requires us to have an ability that only the humanities can develop: the ability to see things from the point of view of nature.

According to E. Bińczyk, transformation will only become possible as a result of a broad interdisciplinary debate, in which it is necessary to discuss at least six narratives constitutive for the discussion of the Anthropocene: the eschatological dimension; the pedagogical dimension – our last chance to correct the course of capitalism; the rhetorical effect – the shocking confrontation of the time scales of geology and history; the hyper agency of *Homo sapiens* that has planetary and cosmic dimensions; human narcissism; and the outrage at irreversible losses (Bińczyk 2017, 2018).[4] The humanities that emerge as a result strive to separate the problem of the methodological distinction between natural and cultural objects from the issue of the moral separation of nature. The restoration of morals to nature is a central task for the humanities in the Anthropocene era.

The foundations of the divisions revealed by Kant have also been shaken in the *religious sphere* and challenged by Pope Francis. In *Encyclical Letter Laudato Si'* (Pope Francis 2015), he describes the Anthropocene as one dimension of the profound spiritual crisis of the modern civilization, dissolute in its consumerism. According to the Pope, the inadequate representation of Christian anthropology has led to the promotion of an erroneous view of the human's relationship with the world. The biblical human – the "lord" of the universe – should be understood as the world's "responsible steward." The Pope emphasizes that "we are not God" and unequivocally opposes treating humanity as a species with divine powers. In the document, he uses nature mainly to build metaphors or as symbols such as the lamb or the good shepherd.

Protestant theology and philosophy also have gone to great lengths in order to highlight the need to change the human's relationship with nature. One of the earliest proponents of these ideas was the somewhat forgotten Albert Schweitzer, a theologian, philosopher, physician, musician, and humanitarian.[5] He studied theology and philosophy at the universities of Strasbourg, Berlin, and Paris, and obtained his doctorate in medicine in 1905, after which he worked as a doctor in a hospital in Lambaréné, Gabon, Central Africa. He was known for his humanism and efforts for peace and understanding between nations. In 1952, he was awarded the Nobel Prize in Literature for *The Philosophy of Civilization* and humanitarian work on behalf of Africa's people. He died in 1965 in Lambaréné.

In *The Philosophy of Civilization*, first published in 1923, Schweitzer analyzes the concept of civilization and its impact on human development. He argues that civilization is a threat to human life and the natural environment, and that the only way to survive is to return to ethics, solidarity, and respect for life ("reverence for life") (Schweitzer 1976). Consequently, he criticizes the Western model of civilization, which emphasizes materialism, competition, and the superiority of one culture over others. Then, he contrasts it with the idea of a spiritual civilization, based on love of life and respect for every life form. In his opinion, only through this approach can we secure the future of humanity.

---

4 A thorough philosophical and cultural study of the Anthropocene is contained in Bińczyk (2018).
5 Schweitzer was popularized in Poland by renowned ethicist (Lazari-Pawłowska 1965).

The Philosophy of Civilization is an important philosophical and social sciences work that has influenced a number of discussions on the role of civilization in human development and environmental issues.

It must be stressed, however, that the Pope's encyclical and the works of the Protestant theologian Schweitzer are not a call for a resacralization of nature. On the contrary, Christianity began by desacralizing nature and rejecting the spirituality attributed to it. Meanwhile, sacred groves were the main sacred places which one could compare to temples in our civilization. Scenes of cutting down of sacred groves in Slavic and Baltic countries are present in historical chronicles as examples of radical eradication of paganism. Despite the loss of this theme in Western cultures, according to B. Malinowski, it was the analysis of the phenomena of sacralization and magical nature carried out in J. Frazer's *The Golden Bough. A Study in Magic and Religion* (Frazer 2016) that became the first impetus for the study of social anthropology. It revealed for the first time the ontological basis of our normativity, different from the Enlightenment pattern.

The dispute over the place of nature vis-à-vis the needs of civilization is revealed in those areas of the world where civilization is only just beginning the destruction of nature. Undoubtedly one such area is the Amazon. The dispute there not only concerns the normative content of law, but it actually runs much deeper, reaching the very ontological assumptions of law based on the Enlightenment thought. These come into conflict with tribal ontologies that immerse these communities in nature and thus reject exploiting nature as a source of raw materials for industrial societies (Ngwenya 2022). The work of contemporary legal anthropologists reveals *the ontological basis of conflicts concerning the law*. In their course, the essence of the religious and ontological dispute is revealed, which makes it impossible to build a common normative layer or to reduce the essence of the discussion to the problem of cultural relativism (Kurczewski 1977).

Today, the lively dispute over Amazon involves a party formed by people who feel *they are* nature and defend this concept as a form of spirituality, refusing to be outside nature (Krysińska-Kałużna 2017). M. Krysińska-Kałużna describes how Amazonian natives discover and deny the ontological assumptions derived from the European positivist thought of the Enlightenment. The latter assumes that there is nothing in the world that actions based on scientific experimentation cannot prove. The dominance of nature as an object and technical rationality is evident here. Indigenous cultures, on the other hand, recognize entities and forces that do not exist in the world of the Enlightenment's rationality, although their action or existence cannot be scientifically proven. There is a widespread belief in the power of shamans and similar persons.

The problem lies in the choice of an ontological model as well as the degree of cultural distance that prevents the diffusion of ontology. The illocutionary power of legal argumentation, also on Enlightenment grounds, is based on an accepted worldview and form of life. Indicating the differences in ontological foundations should be considered one of the most interesting problems in the analysis concerning the effectiveness of performative statements by competing cultures (Krysińska-Kałużna 2017). The problem of *anthropos* arises at the level of ontology and the different bases for each culture's world view. Cutting down trees in the Amazon is a purely technical activity for some, while for the indigenous peoples it means a struggle for identity understood as *being nature*.

All institutional solutions, even those protecting these indigenous peoples from violence, are treated as a façade because they do not recognize the essence of their subjectivity. In this sense, human rights cannot be considered valid only within a certain civilizational and social order. The anthropology of law reveals the possibility for people to recognize their rights only within the natural order. Human rights and the rights of a particular fragment of nature are inseparable. Freedom is revealed not only in the pure relationship between human beings, but also in the relationship of subjects simultaneously living in nature and inseparable from the ontological order in their natural environment. Thus, it is possible to fulfill these rights solely by being an element of the natural order (nature). Consequently, this is not merely a communication problem. It leads to the pessimistic conclusion that the possibility of solving the ongoing crisis lies only in collective historical experiences.

When it comes to indigenous peoples, this is also a problem of spirituality, which can be altered by enlightenment. Beyond this dimension, however, there also appears the problem of mutual misunderstanding of the ontological basis for empowering nature. Statements of bystanders questioning environmental protests – such as "Should we change the plans for building a freeway to save some frogs?" – are notorious. This is essentially an issue identical to the case of two communities rejecting each other's worldview. One example in the Western civilization is veganism. Here, rational discourse can only serve as a compromise to enable coexistence, but it will not lead to a consensus in the form of a common ontology. Thus, the ontology of law is the main source of problems in the application of law when it comes to these kinds of conflict.

However, it is necessary to note *the fourth kind of response to the Anthropocene: positive laws*, the result of conscious human activity, usually in the form of lawmaking by the state. In our civilization, this is the main normative mechanism for granting subjectivity (Pietrzykowski 2016). As a rule, legal discourse only considers granting subjectivity to humans, juridical entities, and animals. Nevertheless, law has the best chance of empowering nature – as postulated in other areas of culture – even if only in the legal sense. The ability to do that depends on a number of factors.

First, many types of identities, such as national identities, cannot be lived and "experienced" without the institutions, laws, symbols, and forms of rhetoric that establish such abstract categories as observable and acceptable frameworks for the experience of shared social practices.

Second, it should be noted that jurisprudence, especially in analytical and positivist terms, functions without reference to political programs and philosophy. It sets goals by integrating legal norms and social normativity (Dworkin 2022). Linking law to power gives it the power to change. Therefore, a politician who proclaims the need for a change must first master the tools of law. In a liberal democracy, the source of power is the support of the majority, required to set out social goals in bills and enforce them within the limits of the constitution. In a state based on the rule of law, courts play an equally important role in this process, particularly through the philosophy of judicial activism, which allows the goals contained in legislation to be corrected and updated through interpretation.

Third, in the positive laws of individual states and international organizations, the development of environmental law – today, one of the most significant fields of law – has led to the creation of new legal categories, preparing lawyers to extend subjectivity to elements of nature. Environmental safety as an institution of environmental law, and in particular the principle of sustainable development, is a significant achievement of modern legislation (Korzeniowski 2010).

It is safe to say that today, when it comes to economic, social, and political institutions, it is the legal institutions that provide the most developed tools for environmental protection and thus join indirectly in the process of slowing down the Anthropocene. Positive law is the most powerful tool of the Global Environmental Governance, which is the sum of international organizations, policy instruments, financing mechanisms, rules, procedures, and norms governing the processes of global environmental protection (Najam, Papa, and Taiyab 2006; Chochowski 2021).

Nowadays, a response to phenomena resulting from the Anthropocene is evident in the domestic law of each country. Positive law in the Anthropocene era must adapt to meet the challenges of human-induced environmental change. This includes creating new laws and revising existing ones to better protect the environment and mitigate the effects of human activity. The main

areas of law affected by the growing knowledge of the Anthropocene, all using different legal methods, include:
- environmental law: the body of law dealing with the protection and preservation of the natural environment, expanded in recent years to meet the challenges posed by the Anthropocene. This includes the creation of new laws to reduce greenhouse gas emissions, protect endangered species, and preserve biodiversity;
- climate change law: climate change has become a major focus of legal action in recent years, with international treaties such as the Paris Agreement providing a framework for reducing global emissions and addressing the effects of climate change;
- tort law: the body of law dealing with cases of civil wrongdoing, such as environmental damage caused by individuals or corporations. The concept of the Anthropocene has been used in some cases to argue that corporations or governments are responsible for their contribution to climate change and other forms of environmental degradation;
- tax law: according to a number of researchers, tax policies are one of the key areas that can be used to reduce anthropogenic pressures on the Earth's ecosystems, and to identify and reinforce climate-beneficial patterns of civilization practices (Chochowski 2021);
- international law: the Anthropocene has also led to a strengthening of international environmental law, with new treaties and agreements aimed at protecting the planet on a global scale.

In conclusion, the positive law of the Anthropocene must continue to evolve to effectively meet the challenges of human-induced environmental change and ensure the protection and preservation of the natural world for future generations.

However, we must not overlook the role of the philosophy of law in this process. This field examines the basic concepts, theories, and norms that shape law. In the context of the Anthropocene, it analyzes what the goals of law should be in the face of the climate crisis, environmental degradation, and other human-related problems. Philosophy of law has an important role to play in the Anthropocene era – a period in which humanity has affected the natural environment in ways that have negative consequences for ecosystems and human health. One new and important issue is the problem of environmental migrants (Westra 2009). Philosophy of law must also be involved in determining legal responsibility for the damage caused by human activity. Here, it can help determine what legal norms should be put in place to increase the legal responsibility of businesses and other entities for negative environmental impacts (Westra 2018). Moreover, it may assist us in understanding the legal and moral consequences of human actions toward the environment, as well as identify ways to minimize these negative effects, especially in non-democratic or authoritarian states (Antal 2021). However, the main role of philosophy of law is to develop legal norms and values that will help humans live in harmony with nature and protect the environment for future generations. In particular, this field can help elaborate concepts that will allow the rights of the natural environment to be recognized as essential to human well-being and survival. As a result, the law will have to pay more attention to protecting the environment and human health to avoid serious consequences for future generations.[6]

When it comes to legal regulations and application of the law, the greatest achievements can be observed in the field of public international law.[7] However, the traditional understanding of this law is insufficient here. Today, it operates as a specific language game equipped with categories such as the general principles of international law, the optimization principle, the weighing of principles-values, and judicial activism. Providing this field with new theoretical categories does not condemn it to mere legal positivism or a textual approach to law. The conceptual categories used indicate that – from a theoretical point of view – it is possible to break with a purely object-oriented view of nature in its relation to the human.[8]

It is important to note the difference between the legal concepts of natural law and the rights of nature (RoN). Natural law assumes that there are certain fixed and immutable laws, the validity of which we recognize through the study of nature and the values contained in it, obtaining knowledge of which actions are morally good and which ones are evil. These rights have their origin in nature, not in human law. Rights of nature, on the other hand, are a concept which assumes that nature and all its components, such as rivers, forests, mountains, or animals, have their own rights which must be respected and protected by humans. According to this concept, nature is treated as a subject of law, not just as an object that can be exploited by people.

In recent years, the concept of rights of nature has gained popularity, with the growing interest in environmental protections and sustainable

---

6 This is described in depth by Amirante and Bagni (2022). Chapter 2, in particular, offers a new perspective on environmental law in the Anthropocene, exploring the implications of environmental change for legal systems and the role of law in shaping human interaction with the environment.
7 Chochowski (2021) describes the development of legal regulations from the concept of sustainable development to global environmental governance.
8 A chronological list of the main treaties and recommendations related to international environmental laws is provided by Amirante and Bagni (2022).

development. Many countries, such as Ecuador, New Zealand, or Colombia, have already introduced laws recognizing rights of nature. In 2008, Ecuador became the first country in the world to recognize rights of nature in its constitution. Article 72 of that constitution states that nature has the right to exist, persist, and maintain and regenerate its life cycles, structures, functions, and processes in evolution. This recognition of nature's rights has been influential in inspiring similar legal frameworks in other countries.

One example of such radical solutions is New Zealand's Te Awa Tupua (Whanganui River Claims Settlement) Act, enacted in 2017, which recognizes the Whanganui River as a legal entity with rights and interests. The Act establishes a legal framework for the management of the river, and the river itself is represented by two guardians who are responsible for protecting its interests. On the other side of the globe, the Colombian Supreme Court ruled in 2018 that the Amazon region has legal rights and ordered the government to take action to protect the region from deforestation and other environmental damage. The court recognized the Amazon as an entity with rights to life, integrity, and protection of its natural resources (Epstein 2022).

The cases described above mark the beginning of the process consisting in abandoning anthropocentrism and in the gradual recognition of the postulate to extend subjectivity to beings capable of subjectively living and feeling their lives and the experiences that comprise them. Human rights cannot equal the moral confinement of people to their species (Regan 1980). We are thus waiting for a new Grotius to transform the subjective rights of nature into positive law. Affording legal subjectivity to nature will give rise to the need for international institutions to protect these rights, such as the Ombudsman for the Rights of Nature. While ecology prompts the occupation of an external attitude (Hart 1961), anthropos involves the law in the construction of new meanings, that is, it forces us to adapt a critical-reflective attitude toward the existing environmental legislation. The latter ceases to be limited to the role of a controlling factor, giving an advantage to the reflective attitude.

Translated by Grupa Mowa

References

Amirante, D., & Bagni, S. (Eds.). (2022). *Environmental constitutionalism in the Anthropocene: Values, principles and actions*. Routledge.

Antal, A. (2021). Environmental justice and autocracy in Eastern Europe: The case of Hungary. In S. Ryder, K. Powlen, M. Laituri, S. A. Malin, J. Sbicca, & D. Stevis (Eds.),

Environmental justice in the Anthropocene: From (un)just presents to just futures (pp. 40–50). Routledge.

Bińczyk, E. (2018). *Epoka człowieka. Retoryka i marazm antropocenu*. PWN.

Bińczyk, E. (2017). Dyskursy antropocenu a marazm środowiskowy początków XXI wieku, *Zeszyty Naukowe Politechniki Śląskiej. Seria: Organizacja i Zarządzanie*, 112, 47–59.

Buchanan, I. (2018). *A dictionary of critical theory*. Oxford University Press.

Chakrabarty, D. (2018). Humanistyka w czasach antropocenu. Koniec mitycznej Kantowskiej opowieści. *Prace Kulturoznawcze*, 22(1–2), 243–263.

Chochowski, M. (2021). Prawo i polityka podatkowa w czasach antropocenu. Szanse i zagrożenia dla sektora energetycznego. In G. Materna & J. Król (Eds.), *Szanse i zagrożenia dla uczestników rynku energii* (pp. 149–178). INP PAN.

Dworkin, R. (2022). *Imperium prawa*. Wolters Kluwer.

Ellis, E. C. (2018). *Anthropocene: A very short introduction*. Oxford University Press.

Epstein, S. (2022). Rights of nature, human species identity, and political thought in the Anthropocene. *The Anthropocene Review*, 10(2), 1–19.

Frazer, J. (2016). *Złota gałąź. Studia z magii i religii* (H. Krzeczkowski, Trans.). Vis-a-Vis Etiuda.

French, D., & Kotzé, L. J. (2021). *Research handbook on law, governance and planetary boundaries*. Edward Elgar Publishing.

Harman, G. (2018). *Object-oriented ontology: A new theory of everything*. Penguin.

Hart, H. A. (1961). *The concept of law*. Oxford University Press.

Kant, I. (1786 [1995]) . *Przypuszczalny początek ludzkiej historii i inne pisma historiozoficzne* (I. Krońska, A. Landman, & M. Żelazny, Trans.). Comer.

Kant, I. (1791 [2014]). *Dzieła zebrane, t. IV: Krytyka władzy sądzenia* (M. Żelazny, Trans.). Wydawnictwo Naukowe UMK.

Korzeniowski, P. (2010). *Zasady prawne ochrony środowiska*. Wydawnictwo Uniwersytetu Łódzkiego.

Krysińska-Kałużna, M. (2017). *Prawo jako mit. Relacja między tubylczym prawem zwyczajowym a prawem stanowionym*. Nomos.

Kurczewski, J. (1977). *O badaniu prawa w naukach społecznych*. Wydawnictwa Uniwersytetu Warszawskiego.

Kuśmierczyk, B. (2003). Związek człowieka i przyrody w filozofii kantowskiej. *Humanistyka i Przyrodoznawstwo*, 9, 47–55.

Lazari-Pawłowska, I. (1965). *Schweitzer*. PWN.

Najam, A., Papa, M., & Taiyab, N. (2006). *Global environmental governance: A reform agenda*. International Institute for Sustainable Development.

Ngwenya, D. M. (2022). Healing nature and creation in the Anthropocene: A reflection on the role of religion. In J. Chrysostome, K. Kiyala, & G. T. Harris (Eds.), *Civil society and peacebuilding in Sub-Saharan Africa in the Anthropocene: An overview* (pp. 127–141). Springer Nature.

Pietrzykowski, T. (2016). *Ludzkie, niezbyt ludzkie. Esej o podmiotowości prawnej w wyzwaniach XXI wieku.* Wydawnictwo Uniwersytetu Śląskiego.

Pope Francis. (2015). *Encyclical letter Laudato Si' of the Holy Father Francis on care for our common home.* https://www.vatican.va/content/francesco/en/encyclicals/documents/papa-francesco_20150524_enciclica-laudato-si.html.

Regan, T. (1980). Prawa i krzywda zwierząt. *Etyka, 18*, 110–111.

Schweitzer, A. (1976). Filozofia kultury. In I. Lazari-Pawłowska (Ed.), *Schweitzer* (pp. 128–205). Wiedza Powszechna.

Singer, P. (2011). *Expanding the Circle: Ethics, Evolution and Moral Progess.* Princeton University Press.

State of Science Index. Global Report. (2022). 3m-state-of-science-index-sosi-2022-global-report.pdf.

Steffen, W., Sanderson, A., Tyson, P., Jäger, J., Matson, P., Moore, B., Oldfield, F., Richardson, K., Schellnhuber, H. J., Turner, B. L., & Wasson, R. J. (2006). *Global change and the Earth system: A planet under pressure.* Springer.

Sterner, T., Barbier, E. B., Bateman, I. et al. (2019). Policy design for the Anthropocene. *Nature Sustainability, 2*, 14–21. https://doi.org/10.1038/s41893-018-0194-x.

Taylor, Ch. (2010). *Źródła podmiotowości. Narodziny tożsamości nowoczesnej.* Wydawnictwo Naukowe PWN.

Thomas, J. A. (2014). History and biology in the Anthropocene: Problems of scale, problems of value. *American Historical Review, 5*, 1587–1607.

Westra, L. (2009). *Environmental justice and the rights of ecological refugees.* Routledge.

Westra, L. (2018). *The role of environmental ethics and justice in the Anthropocene: Reconceptualizing the future of nature.* Routledge.

Žižek, S. (2019, September 20). Yes, it is a climate crisis. And your tiny human efforts have never seemed so meagre. *The Independent.* https://www.independent.co.uk/voices/amazon-fires-rainforest-capitalism-bolsonaro-climate-crisis-zizek-a9091966.html.

CHAPTER 11

Knowledge in the Face of Populism

Michał Kaczmarczyk

1   Introduction

Representatives of the classic theory of modernization in the 1950s and 60s universally called attention to the fact that one of the conditions for an upward advancement of traditional societies is democratization. In turn, a prerequisite for democratization is an increase in both economic prosperity and the level of education (Lerner 1958; Lipset 1960). The impact that the latter exerts on the quality of decisions made by a collective has been a running motif with a long history (Waldron 1999).

In Aristotle's opinion, group decisions supersede individual ones because the former make use of the expert knowledge possessed by a larger pool of people. For instance, a decision to wage war should be the outcome of opinions from naval warship designers and builders, military strategists, meteorologists, martial arts trainers, and other similar groups. Centuries later, Nicolas de Condorcet (1785) demonstrated that – taking into consideration that the probability of an individual making the right decision is greater than 0.5 – the chance of a proper choice grows relative to the number of the decision-makers included. In a similar direction, American pragmatist John Dewey (1958) saw democracy as the ultimate social achievement, transforming human beings through a culture shock – an intersubjectivity shock. In a sense, Dewey returned to a theme present in Aristotle's thought, highlighting general education as a fundamental precondition for successful democratization.

In accordance with this line of thinking – which culminates in modernity – only people able to read and write, open to communication, familiar with the foundation of constitutional order, economically cognizant, and sharing the values in common can make wise decisions that allow a democratic system to fully display its benefits. However, the links between education and democracy, although well-defended theoretically and empirically, have come to be doubted in recent years. This is connected primarily with rising authoritarian and populistic tendencies in countries which have a long-standing tradition of democracy and boast of a high or increasing percentage of citizens with secondary and tertiary diplomas (Hadiz and Chryssogelos 2017). Some research also suggests the existence of a treacherous feedback: rising populism undermines the foundations of a mature democracy (Ruth-Lovell and Grahn 2023). The paradox which I am going to discuss lies in the fact that governments and political groups representing the "new authoritarianism" or "new populism" (Frankenberg 2020) are characterized, among other things, by the undermining of the value of expert knowledge, professionalism, and a scientific vision of the world associated with Enlightenment traditions or even the ideas behind the French Revolution (Revelli 2017). Rejecting or ridiculing those values, populism promises to hand power over to people who have been purportedly oppressed and manipulated by the establishment. Rejection of the intellectualism of broadly understood political–economic elites might therefore lead to full implementation of the people's sovereignty principle. Importantly, the new populism does not aim to return power to the people through the institutions of direct democracy, such as referenda or other forms of inclusion in decision-making processes. Instead, new populism is a specific restitution of Marx's concept of a universal class, restoring appropriate dignity to the people's interests and attempting to represent their will against that of the privileged.

Setting aside the issue of how the "will of the people" might be read, I only wish to point out that any representation of a considerably sized collective constitutes a highly complex and difficult challenge. Moreover, meeting that challenge might be impossible due such factors as the inherent diversity of contemporary societies and their limited ability to discern the citizenry's needs. Therefore, I will instead focus on the issue of ressentiment vis-à-vis specialized knowledge: the existence of the former stands in contradiction to the rising level of education and the amplified role of knowledge, both of which are crucial for the very existence of twenty-first century society.

The ressentiment in question makes itself known not only in the results of social science research, but also in the rhetoric of political parties, journalists, and even academic texts, wherein its advocates rail against the "tyranny" of experts or other forms of perceived intellectual hegemony (Easterly 2015). Here I propose a hypothesis according to which this seeming paradox could be explained by looking at the altered nature of social knowledge – that is, the entire body of knowledge spread among all members of a society. According to my conjecture, that erudition is ever more diversified and thus inclusive; it ceases to be the object of monopolization. Still, it creates an occasion for populism to exploit a general claim of inclusion in order to undercut the authority of specialists. Herein I underscore a need to redefine traditional professionalism in response to the ongoing changes.

2 Modern Society and Inclusion

In the era of globalization, it is hard to speak of the existence of multiple societies. Following in Niklas Luhmann's footsteps, I will present a few relevant premises with reference his thesis (Luhmann 1995) regarding the presence of a single, global society that constitutes an increasingly more complex system of communication. Sociological concepts speak of an array of society–states or society–nations which are clearly distinct from one another but internally connected. Be they connected politically, economically, or culturally, they are losing face as the numbers and meanings of the links between states and various groups – or organizations within a state – are increasing.

Postulating the idea of a single world society, Luhmann (1995) returns to a classic question about the basic building blocks of society: what was it that welded the whole, deciding about its perseverance and dynamics? With reference to the linguistic turn in philosophy and the social sciences – but, above all, to system theory – Luhmann identifies communication as such an elementary component. In accord with his ontology, society thus exists in the form of communicative events which are composed of three elements: information, transmission, and comprehension. This triadic structure creates something of a network because each communiqué gives cause to refer back to it – demanding, on the one hand, a playback of its components, and, on the other, leaving subjects a certain range of freedom in shaping the message.

In a system understood this way, that is, as one encompassing the entirety of all communications, a multitude of interactions takes place. Consequently, these interactions can transmute into an organization that ultimately forms functional, society-wide systems –communicative systems which distinguish themselves by a specific, prominent code and the particular function they fulfill in society. The very presence of such systems is a trait typical of modern societies which, in the sixteenth century, began to gradually replace the hierarchical structure with a functionally diversified one. Within that structure, the objective of functional systems is not only to operationally individualize themselves and maintain a mutual independence of each other; this stems from the incommensurability of their codes and their different functions. Functional diversification constitutes, above all, a response to a need to allay uncertainty in a complex world. Ironically, the diversifying systems themselves heighten the level of complexity, and, by the same token, instigate a trend toward further diversification. Inasmuch as one could imagine local processes of a system collapse, a long-term halt to functional diversification seems unthinkable. Likewise, from Luhmann's perspective again, it is becoming increasingly more difficult to gain a comprehensive view of, not to mention control over, the social reality of a multifarious society.

Although society is becoming ever less steerable and the inner secrets of its systems are harder for the uninitiated to pick out, there can be no doubt that each of the systems tries to observe the rest in order to synchronize operations. Each system must also improve its internal problem-solving in order to realize its functions in a world changing progressively faster. Politics must therefore consider the law, economics, education, and the needs of citizens. Education in turn must make provisions for situational factors in order to optimize its actions; it also needs to meet the desires of those who have formulated expectations of it. All the phenomena outlined here lead to a conclusion that a need arises to create, reproduce, and modify knowledge's wealth of resources pertaining to both the operation of a given system and its ever more complex milieu. An important consequence of this structural imperative is the proliferation of communications, whereby systems attain a level of redundancy sufficient for the selection and stabilization of effective operations. A focus on the multiplication of communications (system self-preservation) requires, in turn, the motivation of potential communicators – that is, systems increasingly engage people not only in communication, but also in dealing with the internal affairs of the systems themselves (Kaczmarczyk 2006).

I present here a vision of a society in which functional systems play a progressively larger role because precisely such a description of the contemporary world makes it possible, in my opinion, to explain the changes knowledge is undergoing. There are two fundamental determinants of those changes: (1) expansion of specialized erudition responding to the needs of each system; and (2) the participation of ever greater masses of people in the reproducing of communication, interest in the operation of each individual system, and motivation to participate in all of this. The first determinant is of fundamental meaning for the professionalization of systems – the evolution of a range of specific roles whose task is to bring the functions of the system to fruition by working on people. This is an attempt to transform human actions in such a way as to realize the positive side of the code (Kurtz 2011). Not all systems, however, require such professionalism; some systems sufficiently motivate people to use the system functions on their own. Nevertheless, various kinds of professional roles emerge which are necessary for the functioning of organizations inside the system – for example, the stock exchange or certain businesses.

To name the second determinant – the growing number of people involved in the functioning of the system – I use the term inclusion (Stichweh 2016). However, inclusion is naturally associated with various forms of exclusion. Even rather blameless social inclusion, such as belonging to a specific family, corresponds with the fact that any and all nonmembers of that family are excluded; citizenship, too, is accompanied by the exclusion of noncitizens, and so on. Every system elaborates a set of internal criteria for recruitment into various roles, or even thresholds for admissible communication. A case in point is the admissibility of legal communication within a family or among social contacts (Luhmann 1999).

Nonetheless, all these phenomena taken together should not obscure the fact that, over the course of the nineteenth and twentieth centuries, the world was dealing with unprecedented inclusion. Considering the scale of these processes, it is evident that the phenomenon is of an increasingly global nature. As Luhmann (1999: 630–631) notices, the universality of incorporating people into functional systems completely transforms the way that subjects function and self-reference in society: there is no hierarchy that would demarcate a permanent place in the social structure for each individual, and no clear criteria for identity have been elaborated either. It is important to note that increased inclusion entails a general rise in knowledge about the functioning of systems on the part of persons incorporated into society. To a certain extent, that knowledge begins to stand in contradiction to professionalization which is primarily of an exclusionary nature. This is due to the complementary roles/professions involve: a teacher needs a pupil, a judge needs a defendant, an attorney a client, a clerk an applicant, a therapist a patient, and a journalist a readership. It is assumed that a professional knows more and will, to a certain extent, treat others as objects. In the meantime, inclusion leads to fervent claims to knowledge and even its co-creation. Such a contradiction underlies the current crisis of authority and the populist tendencies. However, before moving to political considerations, it is worth looking at this phenomenon in its other versions.

The first example can be the economic system. In one sense or another, nearly everyone has always been part of the economy – that is, humans have gained resources for themselves and their families, worked, and consumed, demonstrating more or less of thriftiness in the process. These practices, however, were not always connected with the application of certain expertise. Today most people must possess more specialized know-how – how to pay with a credit card, how to calculate taxes, and how an investment market works – in order to deal with everyday matters. Even projecting grocery costs and covering other expenses now requires not only a keen awareness of one's own budget and plans, but also familiarity with the market in one's country and the world; beyond that, it is useful to have fair acquaintance with government regulations and forecasts as well as their consequences. To a small business in Poland, even information about the USA–China relations may prove valuable.

The exponential increase of economic knowledge accompanying present-day economic development might be invisible precisely because it is ubiquitous. At a time when critiques of capitalism are trendy, the invisible aspect might be the fact that this growth in knowledge is powered by an ever-deeper inclusion. Still, the phenomena aiming to incorporate people playing subjective roles into key economic processes are only nascent and thus not so evident. This pertains especially to the phenomena described collectively as the knowledge-based economy: de-standardization while maintaining a mass scale, widespread use of the human imagination in production, and decentralization of that production (Unger 2019). An important component of this type of economy is prosumption – the disestablishment of the asymmetry between producers and consumers. One of the most important problems of modernity is the fact that the knowledge-based economy is still of a more insular nature: it tends to remain the domain of geographical regions such as the Silicon Valley, whereas most of the world's laborers are internees rather than technology aces. The early capitalism described by Karl Marx also was of such a limited nature. Shifts toward this knowledge-based economy's takeover appear as inevitable as did capitalism expansion in the mid-nineteenth century; a vital indicator of such changes could be the evolution of a company's focus from production, through vending, to marketing – in other words, an orientation whose chief characteristic is that it is directed toward the satisfaction of consumer needs. Ultimately, social marketing aims to realize the common good through active involvement of consumers in collective actions.

Another example of a progressive inclusion could be science and research. Just like the economy, they not only fulfill a social function of providing "truth" but also shape their own audience: ever larger masses of people are drawn into the production and popularization of this type of knowledge as well. In contrast with traditional societies in which knowledge was reserved for a narrow group of wisemen or priests, nearly everyone today undergoes primary education and many subsequently continue to trace scientific advancements. There are, moreover, numerous people who participate in research even without working at a university. In such ventures as Zooniverse, one can discover one's personal planet or join any number of medical, psychological, or sociological projects. Scholarship is no longer a narrow circle of professionals of whom findings are expected, but, to an ever-greater degree, a generally societal endeavor. In the case of sociology, this is reflected in the rising popularity of qualitative research methods which transmute into a dialogue between the interviewer and the interviewee. The blurred lines between the academic elite and the general public do not mean, however, that the divide can be wholly erased. To a great extent, science and research continue to bear the vestiges of the classic, scholarly ivory tower consigning knowledge that is mostly inaccessible to laypeople and often obscure from the perspective of social practice.

A sound example is the discovery of anthropogenic global warming: from the beginning this has never been easily observed and certainly not visible to the naked eye. It could even be said that the fundamental function of purely scientific knowledge is moving toward the providing of knowledge to society – knowledge that would have remained hidden without a systematic and coordinated effort ensured by scholars with their instruments and the organization of their work. Suffice it to consider such fields of science as genetics, neuroscience, quantum physics, big data social research, or astronomical observation to comprehend the chasm separating the colloquial from the scientific. The organization and infrastructure are, however, merely the tip of the iceberg of science understood, above all, as an activity made possible by an inner, core rigor by which the accuracy of evaluations is appraised – a certain scholarly ethos once described by Robert Merton (1973) as a nexus of universalism, communality, disinterestedness, and organized skepticism. Science must therefore remain, in its own way, closed: it cannot allow just any codes or programs. In other words, science and research can realize their social function if they are operationally closed, if they have full control over their code. That closing off, however, means that scholarly knowledge can arouse suspicion: it is esoteric not only because its language is enigmatic and the objects of its study are inaccessible – examples include black holes, mitochondria, global financial flows, or long-term demographic trends. It is also hard for science and research to win the trust of the general public especially to the degree that they are abstruse, costly, and demanding of recognition for their sometimes-alarming prognoses.

In the case of academia, social inclusion is particularly difficult because it requires a certain amount of effort on the part of both the scholars and the public. It is also demanded of scholars that they separate the operationally closed system from a cognitively closed one. Still, the fact that science must sustain its codes and programs does not mean that it is to be cognitively closed, and refuse taking into account the interests and cognitive contributions made by the general public. Moreover, this does not mean that science should remain wholly separated organizationally from the educational system which upholds recruitment of an audience. On the one hand, the ability to partition a cognitive openness from an operational closedness continues to be a challenge for academia because these two aspects of science and research touch on the same thing, namely knowledge, although requiring a certain duality of attitudes. On the other hand, academia's audience might not be very willing to engage in the learning when that necessitates a long period of preparation as well as intellectual capabilities. Science requires trust – despite the fact that it often reaps no direct or profitable results. Although its inaccessibility might pique interest, the system of education often cools that down, directing a child on a different career track and thus also hindering the building of trust in science.

Added to these problems is a syndrome typical of the crisis of broadly understood professionalism. In other words, there is a lack of trust in science and knowledge exactly due to its operational closedness as well as the relevant thresholds that need to be surmounted before scholarly communication is disseminated – such as the system of reviews, editorial board decisions, or research grant sources. These very necessary guarantees of the professional nature of scholarly work can give rise to ressentiments among a public that feels that it does have effortless access to knowledge. People who can easily harvest "answers" from Internet queries might be led to pose a few questions: how is the esoteric and hermetic communication of academia better, why are the sciences not democratically controlled, or why is science and research not subordinated by the economy? This kind of question betrays a sense of being lost in the functionally diversified society and an antipathy toward a functional sequestering of science. This suggests the possibility of subjecting the sciences to a political or economic regime, but also lays bare the ressentiment of political and economic audiences alongside a desire for scientific, academic activity (Ziman 2000). Nevertheless, such a democratization could, in some forms, lead to an implosion of the system of science, research, and education.

One of the more spectacular cases of inclusion is sport, which at the beginning of the nineteenth century constituted entertainment for narrow circles of the aristocracy and bourgeoisie, an addition to a lengthy list of rituals of belonging to a particular group or club. It was only in the twentieth century that this evolved into mass entertainment with its core formed by professional sports competitions that draw huge audiences. Still, what is known as the sociology of sport takes the professional core and the mass audience insufficiently into account; it concentrates instead on organized groups of fans, for example, football fans, which are of little significance in the functioning of an entire society. Inclusion through sports – like the economic, legal, or political one – is primarily a communicative phenomenon: it refers to more or less active participation in a striving toward "achievements." Corporality is also engaged in this process, but that aspect is secondary to communicative inclusion and structurally coupled to the health care system.

Of great meaning on the local and global scales, though not so much on the national scale, is legal inclusion which manifests itself, among other things, in arbitrage and mediation which are on the rise as alternative forms of dispute resolution vis-à-vis court adjudication. The law – which in antiquity had long constituted sacred and secret knowledge – slowly became closer at hand for average citizens; in fact, legal knowledge began to be seen as a significant civic virtue. Currently, citizens wish to be involved in the creation of the law: they assess it, sometimes rectify it via cases presented for judicial review, and often resort to civil disobedience (Kaczmarczyk 2010). The movement toward inclusion here stands in certain contradiction to the emerging functional core of the legal system – the judiciary endowed with autonomy and independence. Unlike other persons on the periphery of the system, judges not only can but actually must make decisions which will be considered the "voice" of a law.

Still, the unique, constitutive position of justices in the legal system – that is, the premise at the heart of the system's functional inimitability – is occasionally undermined by populist movement specifically in the name of inclusion. This leads to a blurring of not only the division of roles, but also of the distinct operational features of the legal system. Its collapse would nonetheless mean that inclusion, in whose purported name the mainstay is attacked, would be rendered impossible. One can only include into something already constituted, and differentiation (*Ausdifferenzierung*) requires mechanisms that secure an operative closure or cohesion (*Geschlossenheit*) – for instance, constitutive roles, practices, organizations, or programs.

The paradox lies in the fact that inclusion does not guarantee widespread professionalization. It is perhaps most noticeable in a political system which, within the framework of democratic procedures, appears to assume that citizens are knowledgeable and aware of their increasingly complex society and uncertain future. Therefore, that system is concurrently obliged to set limits on majority rule in the name of minority interests, specialist expertise, responsibility for future generations, and many other rational reasons. Particularly crucial, it seems, is the diversity of contemporary societies and the existence of not one, but rather many majorities and minorities, differing in various ways – including social status, interests, sociopolitical views, and similar aspects (Preuss 1984). Even if the average level of education is on the rise, it thus appears that civic knowledge is ever more in deficit, ever more essential. Political demands and claims for inclusion are bourgeoning. A temporary solution might be a form of inclusion that is of a local or professional nature: citizens of Gdańsk would decide about Gdańsk and not Krakow, while farmers would decide about crop cultivation and animal husbandry and not about, for instance, match factories. That, however, would not forestall the questions that inevitably arise in an era of interdependencies: why should only farmers decide about agricultural affairs without green party activists and ecologists; why should only residents of Gdańsk decide about the city and not tourists or urbanists; and what about immigrants?

In pluralistic societies there is a broad spectrum of majorities and minorities and political divides might not be the most critical ones. Nevertheless, political parties do try to deal with this issue by aggregating interests; they express postulates in a form abstract enough to gain the favors of sufficient collectivities, targeting specific concerns and characteristics. At the same time, political movements with ambitions to govern cannot allow their programs to get too general as that would risk the loss of a group's perspicuity against the backdrop of better profiled parties. By the same token, solid comprehension of the nature of a diversified society and its dynamics is the best asset held by political professionals and their insight. However, their knowledge, which is instrumental in nature, stands in contradiction to the vested interest of both narrow and the most general social groups with universalistic values of environmental protection, working on behalf of future generations. A rebellion by the people as a universal class against the elite or the establishment likely has little chance of success in postmodernity. Nevertheless, the principle of inclusion constitutes a perfect tool to be utilized in political battles.

As is evident, simultaneous with the expansion of audiences that complement constitutive roles in society – such as the scholar or the entrepreneur – is the mounting significance of knowledge on both sides of the relationships thus formed. On the one hand, the experts need to know more and more about the expectations and needs of the public; on the other hand, the public acquires professional knowledge in order to play a part in the system. As mentioned earlier, this phenomenon itself confirms the enormous augmentation of the knowledge an average person today applies on a daily basis. It is, for instance, medical information independently obtained from the Internet, scholarly knowledge recalled from school or university days, financial information from the bank, anatomical knowledge drawn from practicing a sport, technical knowledge associated with using a computer or installing solar batteries, or legal knowledge.

That notwithstanding, the expansion of knowledge oftentimes undercuts not only certain traditional professions, but also the structure of the system. This is the case, for example, of religion. Lack of a clerical monopoly on theological knowledge, not to mention monopolies on psychological or historical knowledge, is all too perceptible and painfully affecting representatives of hierarchies now anachronistic. A believer today will usually know much about the sources of their religion, but also much about other religions, belief systems, and philosophies; a believer today can develop a critical attitude toward what they believe and how they practice that belief. There is an awareness of an unalienable right to choose.

In the face of this massive upsurge of knowledge many a social system is forced to transform its constitutive roles, form new channels of inclusion, and shape new mechanisms for the creation and sorting of information. Simultaneously, prevalent claims to inclusion often go hand in hand with the public's unjustified belief in its own wisdom – or lack of an awareness of its own ignorance. Nevertheless, it should be noted that an increase in a society's body of knowledge does not mean that the overall ratio of knowledge rises in comparison to ignorance. That is not the case because information is characteristically diversified, and ever more so due to the development of the virtual world. Consequently, when information reproduces, so does the level of complexity; much remains opaque for the society learning and acquiring knowledge (Nassehi 2019). In other words, societal self-reflection is running at an expanding deficit, although this fact appears to be weakly present in the general consciousness. The paradox elucidated here – the rise in both knowledge and ignorance – is but one of the characteristics currently emerging from a systematically generated body of social knowledge.

3   The Nature of Social Knowledge

Since, from a social perspective, knowledge is paired with ignorance, and ignorance is paired with opacity, then it is worth looking into the nature of the last of these. Opacity primarily lies in the fact that our knowledge is increasingly less shared by all. This is true even if the resources of the knowledge we do have in common are still relatively vast – including, among other things, language, cultural patterns, and (albeit to a smaller degree) cultural content. Our individual pools of knowledge resources overlap not as much. We participate in increasingly varied social circles, organizations, and systems; we use more individualized media platforms than the television and radio which once brought generations together – with children, parents, and grandparents listening to the same content synchronously.

The vast pluralization of individual pools of knowledge can go unseen since knowledge is usually associated with information. It is imagined that common information is circulating somehow, somewhere in a shared information space. In my understanding, however, knowledge is more than facts and data. According to predominant philosophical approaches, knowledge means justified convictions – that is, beliefs held by a specific person, in a specific context, and for specific reasons, and leading to specific attitudes and behaviors (Haddock and Macpherson 2011). Newer philosophical concepts, however, suggest that knowledge is not so much beliefs as specific attitudes and behavioral tendencies; the very phrase "to hold a belief" is rather vague (Hunter 2022).

Regardless of the quandaries raised by philosophers, it can be claimed that knowledge is highly individualized today. At the same time, it is changeable and flexible due to the high level of social mobility and quick changes of contexts: beliefs held are applied, but also tested practically. This dynamic knowledge is usually secondary. Born out of communication and transferred as such, it is thus not only contextual, but also strongly verbal and relatively detached from imaginator connotations. Moreover, this is primarily technical expertise which is in constant need of correction and intensification. Each individual addresses their claim to an expansion of knowledge to, above all, functional systems; offered in return is an individual contribution. Society thus functions increasingly according to a Google model: we seek knowledge and obtain it, but concurrently provide – usually unconsciously, and never cost-free – information about what we know or do not know to IT companies and partakers of their networks.

More information is always and everywhere of great importance for anyone, but it takes on greater social value today as it shapes the audiences of functional systems. An audience directs its claims to those systems, while observing and participating in them. In response, systems operate in such a way as to fulfill the imperative of creating and delivering new information, thus decreasing, at least superficially, their own opacity. A need for transparency is manifest in every system: the politician must openly present a program; the law must be widely known, hence the *vacatio legis* convention; today's economy must fully inform consumers about products, hence advertising; and scholars must publish their findings. Society as a whole wants to be more transparent for itself in the spectacle of sports, through social opinion surveys, essays by columnists, and articles by sociologists, and finally, through Internet platforms. As Armin Nassehi (2019) observes, the fundamental function of digital networks is to render everything visible: the aim is full transparency which, nonetheless, can never come to fruition. Ultimately, the communicative imperative leads to new forms of opacity. Even the chapter at hand will contribute to the murkiness: written due to the "publish or perish" requisites of academia, it will escalate the already astronomical number of similar publications, hampering a reader's ability to unearth the most useful content.

The reproduction of knowledge – which is of a processual and contextual nature, yet ever more specialized – leads to a crisis of organizations of all shapes and sizes. Businesses, associations, educational institutions, and political parties – like people themselves – know less about the environs in which they function and are incapable of redressing the deficit. As a consequence, these organizations become increasingly backward, if not anachronistic, vis-à-vis network forms of data exchange. All will respond to their crises by networking – forming conglomerates of schools, universities, or corporations, as well as new channels of information and new positions responsible for information policies.

The aforementioned issues associated with opacity lead to two subsequent ways of addressing an increasingly acute lack of information. The first is to simplify the material, and the second is to store it. On the one hand, these two reduce complexity, but, on the other hand, they generate their own problems. Simplification facilitates reduction of the intricacies in the world around us: elementary schemes are applied to explain or generalize. Furthermore, straightforward methods – for example, algorithms applied to big data – often turn out to be much more effective than multivariate analyses, interpretations, or, what we depend upon most often, intuition (Stephens-Davidowitz 2023). In the contemporary world, simplicity is becoming not only the main principle of the new knowledge economy, but also a cultural value: it makes life easier, improves interpersonal relations, demystifies the world, and seems to regain for us the lost harmony with nature. Simplicity fulfills positivism's dream and is, in a way, the essence of science which aims to encapsulate the complexity of the world in simple formulations. Yet, simultaneously, it is always an impoverishment of our subjective experience in which convolution means a fascinating richness in cognitive form and content. The objective of phenomenology in philosophy and the social sciences was to salvage or recoup that richness in the era of academia's triumphs. In a world in which measurements and algorithms dominate, the humanistic goals of the phenomenologists appear to be even more justified: the realization of those goals would mean, however, discord with one of the main principles governing knowledge's development.

The second response to the hunger for information is a tendency to warehouse data outside the human brain: not only in books, but also on hard drives, in computer clouds, and on a variety of portable, digital storage devices to which access is ever simpler and more intuitive. Our erudition is more than just what is stored on and processed through these objects, but they do, to a degree, embody our technical knowledge; that characteristic decides, to a great extent, about their economic value and the possibilities of growing user wealth. Knowledge itself – somewhat like those embodiments – is taking on an increasingly objective nature: it is treated as a commodity that can be sold and exchanged for other utilitarian and economic valuables. For instance, students pay for courses that provide access to specific types of employment or provide the know-how needed for a specific technological or business purpose.

Knowledge is therefore treated as a ready-made quantum of information about means of action; it is devoid of autotelic, humanistic, and contextual aspects. Thinkers like William James, Alfred North Whitehead, and Edmund Husserl have long railed against such non-holistic treatment of knowledge. Nowadays, however, this problem is especially severe, particularly since the recommended approach to knowledge contradicts its increasingly more dynamic nature and its links to communication systems. It is this aspect that seems to escape those who are merely users of information.

On the one hand, knowledge is fragmentizing, but on the other hand, it can be a finished product, treated simply as the result of an Internet search. Algorithmic thinking – reinforced by the way that search engines operate – is expressed in the very nature of keywords, instructiveness, and a detachment of erudition from its lines of reasoning and supporting arguments. A consequence is that, instead of speaking of knowledge, we more often speak of data; instead of ideas or arguments, presented are points, tables, or output/input figures.

The above-described transformations in how knowledge is understood have an impact on education: systems of testing and parameterization – to which even academics are subjected – are focused on results, on mental work's ready products and the applications thereof. Disregarded are the processes which led to those outcomes. Ultimately, it is knowledge understood precisely this way – for example, disposable, simple information – that members of the audience of political, legal, academic, and economic systems come to desire. Due to the ease with which such knowledge is gained, members of these publics feel entitled to question the existence of professional, constitutive roles, the authority of judges or professors, the legitimacy of politicians' decisions, or the competencies of teachers and physicians. Populism therefore falls on fertile soil not only in the form of an inclusive structure of symptoms, but also in an erroneous understanding of knowledge in times of growing social complexity.

4   Conclusions

Regarding the relationship between the fragmentation and inclusiveness of knowledge, alongside the ressentiments on which populism feeds, the hypothesis proffered earlier requires extensive interpretative study. That earlier premise does not rule out a range of other hypotheses with respect to populism – including those that stress economic or structural antecedents, or those associated with increased uncertainty. Essentially, economic ressentiments – a new cosmopolitan middle class (Reckwitz 2021) taking shape alongside rising disorientation amidst a populace facing new crises – can reinforce the phenomena described herein or closely related ones, especially increased uncertainty and the emergence of that social class.

Inasmuch as the hypothesis is true, it calls sharp attention to a range of dysfunctions inherent to social knowledge, among which the populistic ones have been most strongly accented. Just as important, it seems – in addition to the marginalization of individual experience – are the problems associated with information asymmetries evoked by the contemporary *modus operandi* for the processing and communication of knowledge. Finally, of no little importance is the crisis of professionalism, noticeably flourishing throughout the twentieth century. Today the roles of a judge, teacher, or psychotherapist require redefinition and adaptation to new knowledge regimens. Although the societal system seems to be increasingly reoriented toward the peripheries, it will be incapable of existence in its current form without the centers of these systems. The crux of the roles constituting those centers and the entire systems continues to be the shaping of relationships between people.

Translated by Annamaria Orla-Bukowska

References

de Condorcet, N. (1785). *Essai sur l'application de l'analyse à la probabilité des décisions rendues à la probabilité des voix*. De l'Imprimerie Royale.

Dewey, J. (1958). *Experience and nature*. Macmillan.

Easterly, W. (2015). *The tyranny of experts: Economists, dictators, and the forgotten rights of the poor*. Basic Books.

Frankenberg, G. (2020). *Autoritarismus: Verfassungstheoretische Perspektiven*. Suhrkamp.

Haddock, A., & Macpherson, F. (2011). *Disjunctivism: Perception, action, knowledge*. Oxford University Press.

Hadiz Vedi R., & Chryssogelos, A. (2017). Populism in world-politics: A comparative cross-regional perspective. *International Political Science Review*, 38(4), 399–411.

Hunter, D. (2022). *On believing: Being right and wrong in a world of possibilities*. Oxford University Press.

Kaczmarczyk, M. (2006). Radykalny funkcjonalizm Niklasa Luhmanna na tle współczesnej teorii społecznej. In N. Luhmann, *Systemy społeczne* (M. Kaczmarczyk, Trans.), Nomos.

Kaczmarczyk M. (2010). Nieposłuszeństwo obywatelskie a demokracja. *Studia Socjologiczne* 208(1), 1–20.

Kurtz T. (2011). Der Professionsansatz von Niklas Luhmann. *Soziale Systeme*, 17(1), 31–52.

Lerner, D. (1958). *The passing of traditional societies: Modernizing the Middle East*. Free Press.

Lipset, S. M. (1960). *Political man: The social bases of politics*. Doubleday.

Luhmann, N. (1995). *Social systems* (J. Bednarz & D. Becker, Trans.). Stanford University Press.

Luhmann, N. (1999). *Die Ausdifferenzierung des Rechts*. Suhrkamp.

Merton, R. K. (1973). The normative structure of science. In R. K. Merton (Ed.), *The sociology of science: Theoretical and empirical investigations* (pp. 267–278). The University of Chicago Press.

Nassehi, A. (2019). *Muster: Theorie der digitalen Gesellschaft*. C. H. Beck.

Preuss, U. K. (1984). *Politische Verantwortung und Bürgerloyalität: Von den Grenzen der Verfassung und des Gehorsams in der Demokratie*. Fischer.

Reckwitz, A. (2021). *The end of illusions: Politics, economy, and culture in late modernity*. Polity.

Revelli, M. (2017). *The new populism: Democracy stares into the abyss*. Verso.

Ruth-Lovell, S. P., & Grahn, S. (2023). Threat or corrective to democracy? The relationship between populism and different models of democracy. *European Journal of Political Research*, 62(3), 677–698.

Stephens-Davidowitz, S. (2023). *Don't trust your gut: Using data to get what you really want in life*. Dey Street Books.

Stichweh, R. (2016). *Inklusion und Exklusion: Studien zur Gesellschafttheorie*. Transcript Verlag.

Unger, M. R. (2019). *The knowledge economy*. Verso.

Waldron, J. (1999). *Law and disagreement*. Oxford University Press.

Ziman, J. (2000). *Real science: What it is and what it means*. Cambridge University Press.

CHAPTER 12

Democracy and Authoritarianism in the Twenty-First Century

Grzegorz Ekiert

> If the twentieth century was the story of slow, uneven progress toward the victory of liberal democracy over other ideologies – communism, fascism, virulent nationalism – the twenty-first century is, so far, a story of the reverse.
> ANNE APPLEBAUM, November 15, 2021

∴

1   Introduction

Contemporary research on the state of democracy in the world shows steady erosion of the quality of democratic institutions and declining respect for freedoms and civil rights. Public opinion polls register failing trust in governments, representative institutions, and political parties. Traditional political systems are falling apart, while populist and extremist parties and movements are on the rise across the globe. Autocratic leaders have tried to subvert democratic elections and employ illiberal institutional and repressive measures to stay in power. Since the early years of the twenty-first century, this growing "democratic deficit" has affected both old and new democracies, including many established Western ones (Hellmeier et al. 2020; Boese et al. 2022; Freedom House 2021, 2022).[1]

Yet, the worldwide erosion of democracy has been paralleled by another political trend that is less widely noted but equally significant and potentially more pernicious: "dictatorial drift." This drift affects both hybrid regimes and "soft" authoritarian systems that retain a degree of pluralism and some

---

1   The earlier version of this chapter was published in Polish in Collegium Civitas' *Almanach 2022*. I would like to thank Noah Desanaike for comments and research assistance.

mechanisms of constraining authority. Dictatorial drift is characterized by the emergence of autocratic leaders, an extreme concentration of executive power, the decay of rule of law, and the destruction of fundamental institutions of democracy: fair elections, separation of powers, an independent judiciary, opposition parties, free media, and independent civil society organizations. It also entails growing repressiveness and the use of force against political opposition both at home and abroad.

Do these two global political trends arise from the same causes? Are they both responses to a common set of factors? Moreover, are the intermediating mechanisms that drive the erosion of democracy the same as those behind dictatorial drift? In this chapter, I argue that democratic backsliding is mostly driven by a combination of demand- and supply-side factors, while dictatorial drift is largely engineered from above.

On the one hand, public opinion polls across the world register a growing popular demand for the defense of traditional and anti-liberal values. Additionally, there is a rising preference for populist policies that offer protection against market mechanisms and the effects of globalization, as well as a call for stricter controls on immigration. On the other hand, populist politicians are increasingly committed to proposing specific policies, constructing populist discourses, and framing issues to appeal to anti-liberal constituencies, traditional conservative political actors, and social institutions.

Dictatorial drift emerges from above by authoritarian leaders who, after legitimately winning elections, strive to concentrate executive power, marginalize political opposition and representative institutions, instrumentalize the judicial system, and manipulate electoral institutions to escape constitutional and political constraints and controls. They seek to gradually destroy independent media, civil society organizations, and formal and informal checks and balances, and they actively mobilize anti-liberal forces and incite social and political conflicts. Both the erosion of democracy and dictatorial drift are underpinned by the emergence of conservative and reactionary civil society; they mobilize and channel the demand side anti-liberal and authoritarian preferences (see Youngs 2018; Ekiert 2021; Atalay 2022: Platek 2024).

2   Democratic Backsliding

The debate about the erosion of democracy has been going on for some time now (see e.g. Diamond and Plattner 2015; Bermeo 2016; Waldner and Lust 2018; Luhrmann and Lindberg 2019). Today, however, there is a growing consensus that the political institutions in old and new democracies face seemingly unsolvable problems. In his recent evaluation of the state of democracy in the world, Diamond (2022) describes this process as "accelerating democratic recession." The uncontested hegemony of the West and liberal values that resulted from the end of the Cold War and the collapse of the Soviet bloc is under sustained assault both at home by populist and nationalist forces and from abroad by increasingly aggressive authoritarian powers.

Explaining the current predicament of democratic regimes is not easy. To some, the main culprit is contemporary capitalism, which, due to economic globalization, escaped the regulatory regimes of national states and has caused exploding inequalities and dislocations. The rise of populism and falling support for liberal political parties is seen as a direct effect of economic transformations (Piketty 2014; Rodrik 2018; Eichengreen 2018). To others, the problems of democracy are the result of accelerating technological and cultural changes that challenge traditional social arrangements and cultural systems (Norris and Inglehart 2019). Yet, for others still, the core problem is a geopolitical reordering of the world, encompassing the rise of China, the irredentism of Russia, and a perceived economic and political decline of the United States and the West more broadly.

This is often illustrated by a series of policy missteps: the war in Iraq and the subsequent struggle with Islamic terrorism, the fallout of the Arab Spring that destabilized the Middle East, and the inadequate response to the brutal war crimes perpetrated by Russian and Al-Assad regime troops in Syria – actions that made Western democracies look weak. So, too, did the failure of Western states to effectively respond to Russian military intervention in Georgia in 2008, the annexation of Crimea in 2014, and the takeover of territories in eastern Ukraine that encouraged Putin's regime to commence full-scale war in Ukraine in 2022. To this list can be added a disastrous and chaotic retreat from Afghanistan, signaling to many the end of American hegemony. The growing economic might of China as well as its authoritarian drift and escalating assertiveness were not only long ignored by the United States and Europe but were also considered unstoppable. These developments seemed to showcase the weakness and decline of Western powers even if the response to Russian aggression united the West and injected NATO with a renewed purpose.

Finally, the role of crucial events on the global and national level cannot be underestimated. The 2008 financial crisis and its consequences across the globe exposed the limitations of contemporary advanced economies, highlighted growing social inequalities, and reduced the resources available for responding to old and new social problems. The COVID-19 pandemic that disproportionally affected Western countries introduced an additional set of challenges and further exposed the weaknesses of their health and welfare systems. Mandatory vaccinations and other policies created ressentiment and anger toward the establishment. On the national level, events such as the attempted coup d'état in Turkey and the airplane accident that claimed the life of the Polish president created openings for authoritarian leaders to centralize power and attack political opposition.

All these factors contributed to the rise of populist and radical left- and right-wing parties and movements in many countries, allowing their leaders to deliberately challenge liberal values and democratic norms. Populist politicians mobilized on resentments, grievances, and growing anger toward political institutions. The electoral successes of authoritarian politicians such as Donald Trump, Jair Bolsonaro in Brazil, Recep Erdoğan in Turkey, and Narendra Modi in India, as well as many others across Latin America, Asia, and Africa, showed that determined leaders can destabilize even established and otherwise well-functioning democracies.

In other words, the last two decades have not been kind to democracy and the liberal global order constructed after the Second World War. There is nothing surprising in the fact that debates about the crisis of democracy are common in the media and across university campuses, nor that books analyzing such problems sell millions of copies. To onlookers, it seems that each approaching election is no longer a routine change of government but rather the last chance to save democracy as we have come to know it. So common are such concerns today that it is legitimate to ask whether we are perhaps exaggerating the challenges faced by democracy today. Yet, the growing evidence that democracy is in trouble cannot be ignored.

There is plenty of evidence illustrating the gradual erosion of democracy and freedom around the world. Every annual global assessment of the state of democracy now warns of a serious decline of civil liberties and quality of democratic institutions. In one of its recent reports the American think tank Freedom House (2022) concludes that

> in every region of the world, democracy is under attack by populist leaders and groups that reject pluralism and demand unchecked power to advance the particular interests of their supporters, usually at the expense of minorities and other perceived foes.

Freedom House also warned that

> Global freedom faces a dire threat. Around the world, the enemies of liberal democracy ... are accelerating their attacks. Authoritarian regimes have become more effective at co-opting or circumventing the norms

and institutions meant to support basic liberties, and at providing aid to others who wish to do the same.

Although alarm regarding the state of contemporary democratic politics is widely shared, experts from Freedom House show that the crisis has been a long time in the making. Since 2006, the number of countries that have registered a decline in freedom and civil liberties and in the quality of political institutions significantly outpaced the number of countries that have registered improvements in these dimensions (see the graph below). This trend has only strengthened in recent years. Even though we have not witnessed spectacular collapses of democratic regimes during this period, gradual democratic backsliding in numerous countries indicates that we are amid a distinct political cycle. This is what Huntington (1993) describes as a "reverse wave," which characterizes the ongoing situation where, every year, more countries move toward authoritarianism than those becoming more liberal and democratic. As Diamond (2022: 169), the world's foremost expert on democratization, notes, "for a decade, the democratic recession was sufficiently subtle, incremental, and mixed that it was reasonable to debate whether it was happening at all. But as the years have passed, the authoritarian trend has become harder to miss."

Yet, today's processes of democratic backsliding differ in a fundamental way from old assaults on democracy. According to many experts, contemporary democracies are destroyed in gradual and often imperceptible ways, whereas in the past they were victims of coup d'états, wars, and revolutions. Moreover, though many elements of democratic regime are technically left in place, they are manipulated and distorted beyond recognition. Elections are no longer considered indispensable. The way democracies die may have significant consequences for the possibilities of restoring full democratic rule after the ongoing period of democratic assault.

Figure 12.1, from the 2022 Freedom House report, shows that the global democratic recession started in 2006, albeit for some regions, backsliding began even earlier. In fact, 2005 was the last year when the general number of countries that improved their scores exceeded the number of countries that registered a decline in their score. Since then, the declining countries significantly outnumbered the countries that registered improvements. This trend slightly improved in 2022, producing thirty-five countries with declining scores and thirty-four with improving scores (Freedom House 2023).

The declining scores in the quality of democracy registered by the Freedom House are matched by other organizations producing rankings of democratic performance. In its 2022 report, Varieties of Democracy Institute (V-Dem)

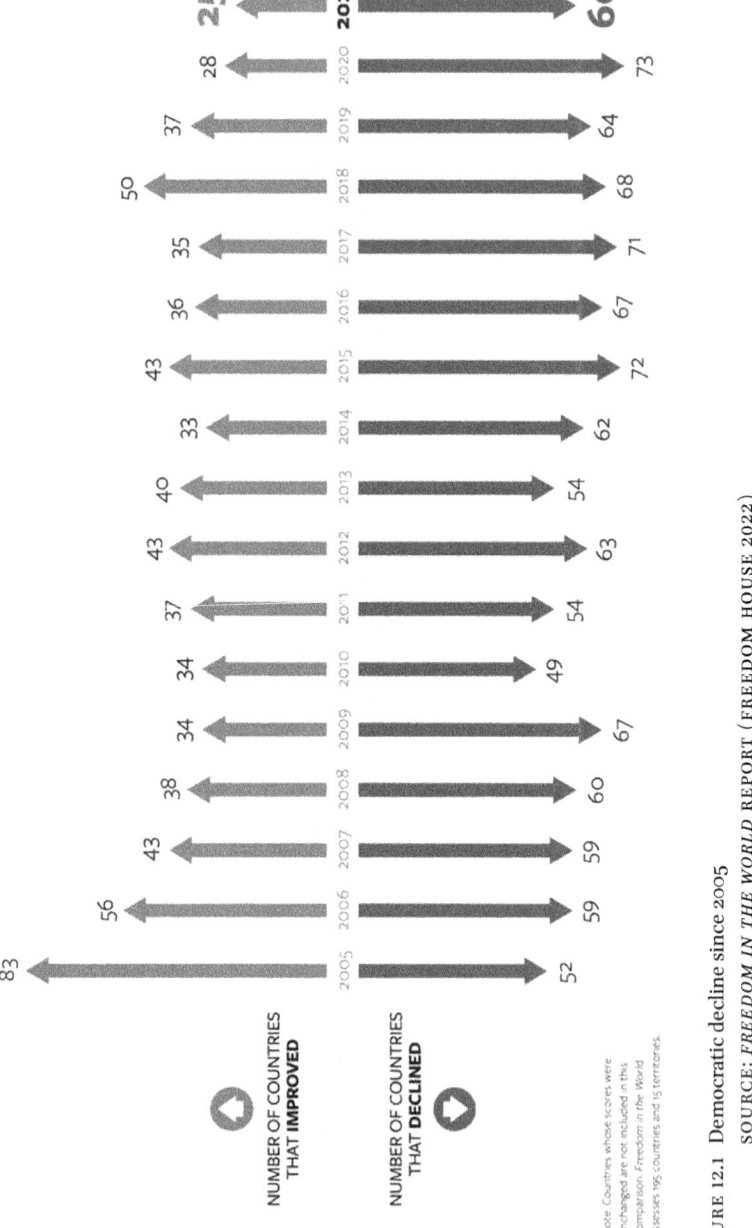

FIGURE 12.1 Democratic decline since 2005
SOURCE: *FREEDOM IN THE WORLD* REPORT (FREEDOM HOUSE 2022)

shows that not only did the number of countries shifting toward authoritarianism increase, but also several democracies experienced decline. Furthermore, the portion of the world's population living under authoritarian rule rapidly expanded. In the last ten years, this percentage increased from forty-nine to seventy (Boese et al. 2022). These trends are shown in Figure 12.2.

Researchers from the Economist Intelligence Unit reach similar conclusions about the state of democracy. Its 2021 Report Democracy Index, which rates the state of democracy across 167 countries based on five measures (electoral process and pluralism, the functioning of government, political participation, democratic political culture, and civil liberties), finds that more than a third of the world's population live under authoritarian rule, while just 6.4 percent enjoy full democracy. The "global" score fell from 5.37 in 2020 to a new low of 5.28 out of ten. This marks the greatest such decline since 2010, following the global financial crisis (*The Economist* 2022).

Central and Eastern Europe (CEE) epitomizes the global retreat from democracy. According to Freedom House (2021), "countries all over the region are turning away from democracy or find themselves trapped in cycle of setbacks and partial recoveries." In the 2021 edition of *Nations in Transit*, covering the events of 2020, a total of eighteen countries suffered declines in their democracy scores; only six countries improved, while five countries experienced no net change. This marked the seventeenth consecutive year of overall decline in the Nations in Transit (NiT) index, leaving the number of countries that are designated as democracies at its lowest point in the history of the report.

Perhaps paradoxically, the two countries that registered the biggest drop in their NiT ratings in the last decade are Hungary and Poland – the former leaders of postcommunist democratic transformation. In fact, among the fourteen postcommunist countries that were classified by the NiT as consolidated or partially consolidated democracies in 2005, only two (Estonia and Croatia) did not register any decline. All others had lower scores in 2021 than in 2005 (Figure 12.3).

All the above data and rankings show a paradox of political transformations in the region after 1989. When new and flawed democracies emerged as a result of the collapse of communist regimes, the prevailing expectation was that with time, these new regimes would become more mature, responsible, and better performing. They were expected to consolidate their new democratic institutions, expand civil rights and political liberties, strengthen the rule of law, and offer equal protection to their citizens. Instead, the highest levels of liberalization and democratic institutional performance were registered at the *beginning* of postcommunist transformations and have only declined thereafter. This applies both to countries that established democratic regimes after 1989 and

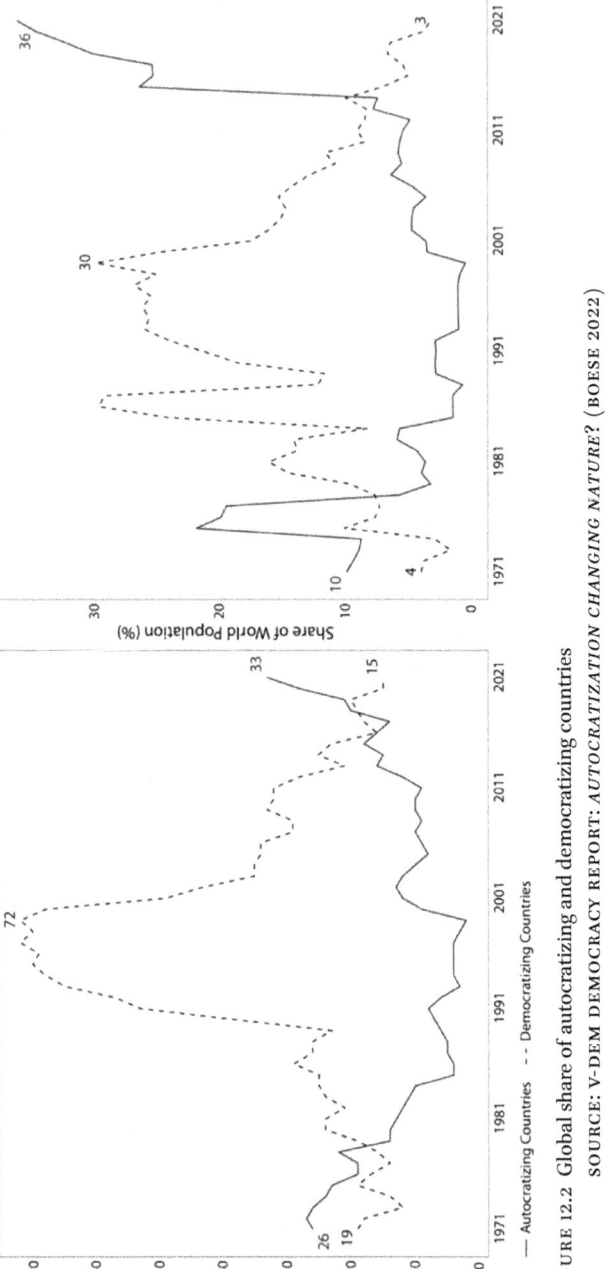

FIGURE 12.2 Global share of autocratizing and democratizing countries
SOURCE: V-DEM DEMOCRACY REPORT: *AUTOCRATIZATION CHANGING NATURE?* (BOESE 2022)

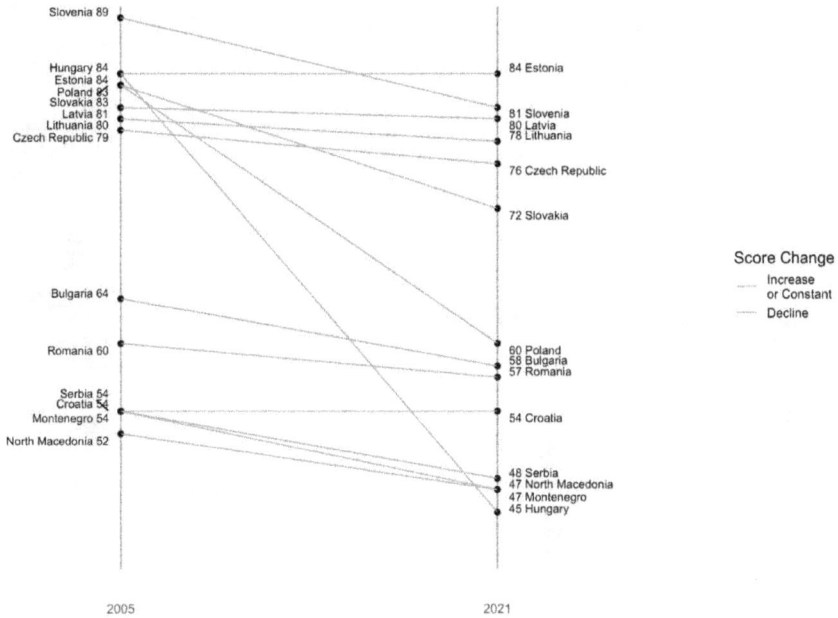

FIGURE 12.3 Consolidated and semi-consolidated democracy scores
SOURCE: *NATIONS IN TRANSIT* REPORT (FREEDOM HOUSE 2021)

to countries that never even democratized. Figure 12.4, based on the Freedom House data, illustrates well this surprising robustness of political rights and civil liberties during the initial decade of postcommunist transformation.

While it was commonly believed that EU membership was the best guarantor of the increasing quality and stability of democracy, this view needs to be revised in the light of Hungarian and Polish experiences. Currently, Hungary is the only EU member not classified as fully democratic, and Poland is quickly moving in the same direction.

The decline in the quality of democracy can be observed across several dimensions. As Levitsky and Ziblatt (2018) argue in their book, backsliding democracies show disregard for democratic rules, constitutional norms, and the rule of law; delegitimization of political opposition and liberal movements and organizations; growing tolerance for violence and hate speech directed at minorities, political opposition, and other nations; and attempts to restrict civil liberties and freedom of media. In turn, conditions that are necessary for the proper functioning of democracy – mutual toleration and restraint – are endangered. Scheppele (2018) describes this degenerative form of democracy as "autocratic legalism," where democratic institutions are used to consolidate autocratic power.

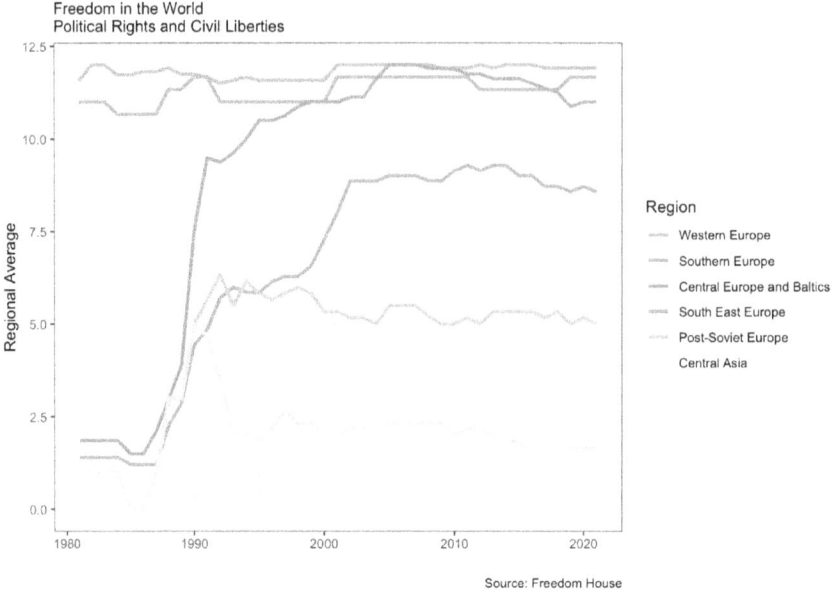

FIGURE 12.4 Regional averages in political rights and civil liberties
SOURCE: *FREEDOM IN THE WORLD* REPORT (FREEDOM HOUSE 2022)

The causes and conditions for the erosion of democracy are hotly debated and not immediately clear. First, the literature on democratic backsliding is biased in the same way as is most of the scholarship on democratization: its theoretical optics are elite-centered. The ruling elites, having won through fair elections, are seen as main culprits of democratic backsliding. They use the power of the state to gradually dismantle democracy, deliberately undermining democratic norms and institutions. Scheppele (2018: 547–548) argues that

> the autocrats who hijack constitutions seek to benefit from the superficial appearance of both democracy and legality within their states. They use their democratic mandates to launch legal reforms that remove the checks on executive power, limit the challenges to their rule, and undermine the crucial accountability institutions of a democratic state. Because these autocrats push their illiberal measures with electoral backing and use constitutional or legal methods to accomplish their aims, they can hide their autocratic designs in the pluralism of legitimate legal forms.

The democratic erosion literature is also excessively focused on institutional crafting. Authoritarians manipulate institutional designs for their advantage.

Yet, as much as setting up democratic institutions does not automatically produce democracy, undermining those institutions and replacing them with authoritarian ones does not make the electorate compliant and powerless. Instead, it is increasingly obvious that the demand side of backsliding cannot be ignored (see e.g. Sadura and Sierakowski 2023) – contrary to much of the literature, democratic decline in part occurs *because*, not in spite, of popular opinion. As Arendt (1976: 306) notes,

> it would be a still more serious mistake to forget, because of this impermanence, that the totalitarian regimes, so long as they are in power, and the totalitarian leaders, so long as they are alive, "command and rest upon mass support" up to the end. Hitler's rise to power was legal in terms of majority rule and neither he nor Stalin could have maintained the leadership of large populations, survived many interior and exterior crises, and braved the numerous dangers of relentless intra-party struggles if they had not had the confidence of the masses.

While the causes of global democratic backsliding are based on a combination of political, economic, and cultural factors and are highly context-specific, both the demand and supply side of politics are an important part of the process. In the case of postcommunist Europe, they can be summarized as follows:
- Support for anti-liberal authoritarianism varies across the region, but it is significant almost everywhere and is much higher than in the West as various public opinion polls aptly show.
- Although the main thrust in explaining backsliding is on the supply side, it is both a supply- and a demand-side phenomenon. Authoritarians are winning not only because they are ruthless and skillful manipulators, but also because they have significant public support in their countries and committed international allies abroad. Accordingly, we need to take voters' expressed preferences seriously to understand which constituencies are supporting anti-liberal and populist parties.
- Traditional values and norms are very resilient. Thus, cultural modernization takes more time than economic modernization (Norris and Inglehart 2019). Moreover, it is increasingly apparent that while traditional and illiberal values are the legitimate preferences among parts of the electorate, liberal democracy needs democrats to function properly and to survive. Even the most skillful institutional manipulation is not a substitute for normative commitments. It also needs to take seriously the "toleration paradox." Thus,

to survive, democracy needs normative commitments among electorates and must be nurtured, protected, and defended by political elites.
- Communism, despite its modernizing commitments, only preserved traditional, anti-liberal systems of norms and values that have much deeper historical roots and are grounded in the peripheral position of these countries in historical cross-European developments (see Pop-Eleches 2014).
- The initial enthusiasm for liberal democracy was misleading. It showed the confusion by, rather than normative commitment to, liberal norms and values. Democratic backsliding is, in fact, driven by hidden anti-liberal preferences that have been legitimized and mobilized by anti-liberal political actors.
- Organized religions have been the preserves of traditional values across the region before, during, and after communism. Accordingly, churches and the right-wing pillar of civil society have become the main normalizers and mobilizers of illiberal values and virulent nationalism. They make hidden anti-liberal preferences legitimate.
- The rise of nationalist/authoritarian constituencies is not a response to specific events or crises. They constitute a stable, silent "majority" that regains its voice when populist and nationalist civil society organizations and parties make such views legitimate and especially when they contest and win elections.

3   Dictatorial Drift

The collapse of communist regimes not only facilitated the emergence of new democracies but also led to the arrival of new forms of nondemocratic regimes that Levitsky and Way (2002) call "competitive authoritarianism." As they argue eighteen years later (2020: 52), "competitive authoritarianism was a post-Cold War phenomenon – a product of an international environment that was uniquely hostile to full-scale dictatorship." This new form of soft authoritarian or semi-democratic rule is characterized by "the coexistence of meaningful democratic institutions and serious incumbent abuse [that] yields electoral competition that is real but unfair." These regimes allow significant "arenas of contestation," tolerate political opposition and autonomous media and civil society organizations, and do not use overt political repression or intimidation of its critics. Guriev and Triesman (2022) similarly argue in their recent book that contemporary autocracies are "dictatorship-lite." They try "to conceal autocracy within formally democratic institutions" (Guriev and Triesman 2022: 27; see also Dobson 2012).

Levitsky and Way (2002) examine thirty-six regimes across the globe with these characteristics, including Russia, Serbia, Ukraine, Belarus, and Georgia as well as several current EU members – Bulgaria, Croatia, Romania, and Slovakia. Despite doubts about whether these regimes can be characterized by the stable equilibrium or are prone to move toward either more democratic or more authoritarian stances, the authors conclude eighteen years later that "today competitive authoritarianism remains alive and well" (Levitsky and Way 2020: 51). They note that "the persistence of competitive authoritarianism is somewhat surprising ... because the Western liberal hegemony of the 1990s, which led many full autocracies to become competitive authoritarian, has waned" (2020: 1). Moreover, they argue that "competitive politics persists because many autocrats lack the coercive and organizational capacity to consolidate hegemonic rule, and because the alternatives to multiparty elections lack legitimacy across the globe" (2020: 1). Yet, others point to the inherent instability of competitive authoritarianism. As Carothers (2018: 129) concludes, "hybrid regimes have not become a new form of stable nondemocratic rule ... of the 35 regimes identified as having been CA between 1990 and 1995, most have either democratized or been replaced by new autocracies."

While the initial shift of some Central and East European countries in a more democratic direction can be attributed to the EU (Ekiert, Kubik, and Vachudova 2007), most postcommunist countries have now firmly embraced authoritarianism. This aligns with the emerging global trend that I earlier referred to as the dictatorial drift. "Spin dictatorships" are becoming real tyrannies and very traditional highly repressive states. Although they still have not matched the record of Stalin and Hitler, the Russian war crimes in Ukraine, and China's concentration camps for its Uyghur minority, some of these regimes are becoming brutal and murderous. The view that "hard authoritarianism," as opposed to a softer form, is on the rise tends to be shared by many perceptive commentators of today's international affairs, including Anne Applebaum, Thomas Friedman, Gideon Rachman, and Larry Diamond.

In his recent book, Rachman (2022a: 11) argues that

> since 2000, the rise of the strongman leader has become a central feature of global politics. In capitals as diverse as Moscow, Beijing, Delhi, Ankara, Budapest, Warsaw, Manila, Riyadh and Brasilia, self-styled "strongmen" (and, so far, they are all men) have risen to power. ... The rise of strongman leaders across the world has fundamentally changed world politics. We are now in the midst of the most sustained global assault on liberal democratic values since the 1930s.

Friedman (2022) points to the unprecedented accumulation of unconstrained power by some current authoritarian leaders:

> If you ask me what is the most dangerous aspect of today's world, I'd say it is the fact that Putin has more unchecked power than any other Russian leader since Stalin. And Xi has more unchecked power than any other Chinese leader since Mao. But in Stalin's day, his excesses were largely confined to Russia and the borderlands he controlled. And in Mao's day, China was so isolated, his excesses touched only the Chinese people.

Similarly, Diamond (2022: 173) argues that

> although they differ significantly in political system, economic capacity, and global power, the Chinese and Russian regimes share important features and interests. Each has become dramatically more repressive in the last decade, with China moving toward a neo-totalitarian surveillance state and Russia toward more vengeful and pervasive punishment of political opposition and dissent. Each system has become increasingly dominated by a single ruler who, feeling insecure in power, tightens repression and stokes nationalism to enhance domestic control.

Russia and China are the most obvious examples of what I call the "dictatorial drift." But the evidence from the postcommunist world tends to support the view that this is a more general trend and that hybrid regimes and soft authoritarian regimes that emerged post-communism have become more authoritarian over time. As seen in Figure 12.5, only four out of fifteen regimes classified as hybrid, semi-, or fully consolidated authoritarian by Freedom House in 2005 did not shift to a more authoritarian stance. A common thread among these four countries is their shared existential geopolitical threat (from Russia and Serbia). They need Western support to balance their precarious geopolitical situation and consequently are more responsive to Western leverage.

Moreover, many countries shifting toward authoritarian have ended up with extreme forms of authoritarian rule. As indicated by Freedom House's NiT index, six of the eight consolidated authoritarian regimes in the post-Soviet region now have the lowest possible National Democratic Governance ratings (Figure 12.6).

These new emerging dictatorships share many characteristics. As Applebaum (2021) notes,

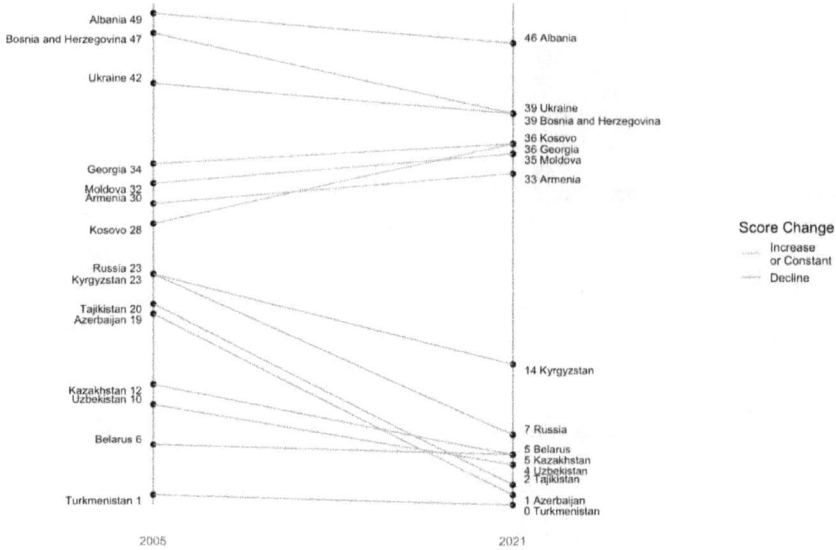

FIGURE 12.5 Hybrid to fully authoritarian democracy scores
SOURCE: *NATIONS IN TRANSIT* REPORT (FREEDOM HOUSE 2021)

nowadays, autocracies are run not by one bad guy, but by sophisticated networks composed of kleptocratic financial structures, security services (military, police, paramilitary groups, surveillance), and professional propagandists. The members of these networks are connected not only within a given country, but among many countries. The corrupt, state-controlled companies in one dictatorship do business with corrupt, state-controlled companies in another. The police in one country can arm, equip, and train the police in another. The propagandists share resources – the troll farms that promote one dictator's propaganda can also be used to promote the propaganda of another – and themes, pounding home *the same messages about the weakness of democracy* and the evil of America.

Applebaum refers to the aspect of dictatorial drift that is especially striking, namely the growing collaboration among authoritarian regimes as "Autocracy Inc.," emphasizing intertwined and often nontransparent political and economic cooperation. This cooperation is further reflected by the formation of formal regional alliances led by authoritarian states that could provide alternatives to liberal regional institutions (see Libman and Obydenkova 2018). According to Rachman (2022b), "in 2022, Putin and Xi are determined to make the world safe for autocracy. ... They share a determination to create a new

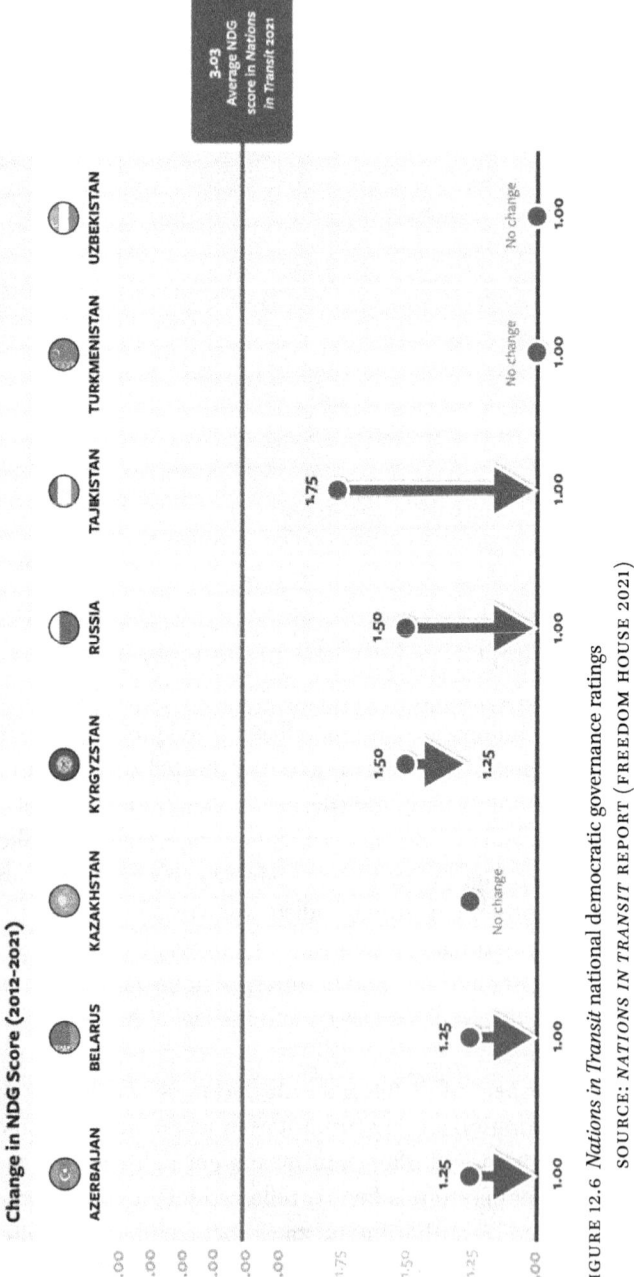

FIGURE 12.6 *Nations in Transit* national democratic governance ratings
SOURCE: *NATIONS IN TRANSIT* REPORT (FREEDOM HOUSE 2021)

world order that will better accommodate the interests of Russia and China – as defined by their current leaders." Relatedly, Diamond (2022: 172) notes that

> China leads four of the fifteen specialized UN agencies and, in cooperation with Russia and other authoritarian regimes, is working energetically to degrade human rights norms and democratic civil society participation within existing global institutions, such as the UN and its Human Rights Council, while seeking to craft new global rules to make the world safe for autocracy, kleptocracy, and digital repression.

The dictatorial drift and increasing cooperation between authoritarian regimes seeking to challenge Western liberal hegemony creates a new, much more dangerous world. The recent unprovoked aggression by Russia on her neighbor with the tacit approval of China is the most striking example of what may happen if dictatorial ambitions and unconstrained leaders are not kept in check by the global community of liberal democracies. Diamond (2022: 176) is right – and, indeed prescient, as he wrote before the Russian invasion of Ukraine – that

> the dictatorships in Russia and China could destroy world peace before they destroy themselves. As they face the deep contradictions of their stultifying models, the authoritarian rulers of Russia and China will find their legitimacy waning. If they do not embrace political reform – a prospect that fills them with dread, given the fate of Gorbachev – they will have to rely increasingly on the exercise of raw power at home and abroad to preserve their rule. This is likely to propel them on a fascistic path, in which relentless repression of internal pluralism becomes inseparably bound up with ultranationalism, expansionism, and intense ideological hostility to all liberal and democratic values and rivals.

4 Conclusions

What causes dictatorial drift? Are the underlying conditions for democratic backsliding and dictatorial drift the same? What mechanisms drive both backsliding and the drift? Regarding democratic backsliding, I pointed out that this pattern results from both demand- and supply-side factors. On the demand side, the initially hidden preferences of conservative and authoritarian electorates are being legitimized and mobilized by competing politicians, parties, churches, conservative movements, and right-wing civil society organizations.

On the supply side, new discourses of grievance, new distorted framings of history, state-sponsored culture wars, and populist economic and social policies fortify the control of anti-liberal and nationalist leaders. Once they secure power through democratic elections, autocrats often begin a gradual – or sometimes hasty – dismantling of democratic institutions.

Dictatorial drift occurs through a gradual process that László Rajk, the infamous Stalinist Interior Minister of Hungary, described as "salami tactics." This strategy involves destroying liberal political institutions and taking over opposition parties, independent media, and civil society organizations, one thin slice at a time. The result is the destruction of alternative sources of power and of checks and balances, individual freedoms, and civil rights. In short, dictatorial drift is driven from above by authoritarian leaders who can escape controls and who, once in power, gradually destroy independent institutions together with checks and balances and actively mobilize anti-liberal forces.

Still, consolidating dictatorship is not easy. To establish a stable dictatorship, rulers must actively mobilize anti-liberal groups, cultivate relationships with anti-liberal organizations, provoke conflicts, and polarize the electorate. They must also buy support through populist policies, clientelism, and corrupt practice, as well as intimidate and repress those who refuse to be bought. Moreover, they mobilize their supporters through skillfully manipulating their fears and concerns and of the norms and values that appeal to them. These rulers constantly search for internal and external enemies to integrate and mobilize their supporters. Using relentless propaganda from state-controlled media, they manipulate the public and hide their own misdeeds and failures. As a result, they establish a system free of constraints on executive power and political guardrails that otherwise exist in democracies and soft authoritarian systems.

Such unchecked power results in leaders who no longer face restraint. This is evident in how Putin was able to start a brutal war of aggression in the middle of Europe and how Xi could destroy all independent institutions, breaking the agreement that guaranteed the autonomy of Hong Kong (see Maizland 2022). One could easily imagine that he may decide to invade Taiwan or provoke military conflicts with neighboring countries to control the East China Sea.

There is agreement among those studying democratic backsliding and dictatorial drift that the weakening of Western liberal hegemony underlies such processes. Levitsky and Way (2010) attribute the success of post-Cold War democratic transformations to Western "linkage and leverage." Western linkage describes the intensity of the connections and the cross-border relationships between a country and the West, while leverage describes the level of vulnerability to Western pressure, including economic sanctions. One can argue that with the weakening of the West's economic position and the perception that democracy as a political system is in crisis, both linkage and leverage are much weaker today than they were at the end of the Cold War. According to Mounk (2022), "with democracy in crisis around the globe, its enemies no longer feel the need to hide their authoritarian ambitions."

The weakening position of the West and the emergence of the "dictator international" – global networks of support among autocracies – has allowed both the creation of new forms of authoritarian rule as described by Applebaum (2021) and the emergence of strongman leaders, as described by Gidon Rachman. In contrast to competitive authoritarianism, this combination of domestic and international factors has a much better chance of producing a stable equilibrium. The authoritarian equilibrium rests on three pillars: economic security, lies, and fear (Gerschewski 2013). Today, economic cooperation among dictatorships provides them with a greater degree of security and the capacity to survive economic sanctions. Control of the media and communications as well as collaboration among propaganda systems allows lies to pervade public space unchallenged.

Finally, military and internal security cooperation provides the necessary level of fear to prevent domestic challenges to dictatorial rule. None of these factors emerged overnight but rather are the result of long processes of political learning, as dictatorial states experiment with different strategies and solutions that are then copied by other autocrats in their global network. There are countless examples of such learning: in Poland, Kaczyński's claim to follow Hungarian strategies in Warsaw; Russia adopting China's strategies to control Internet communication; Russian security police training their Belarusian counterparts; and Central Asian countries employing Russian strategies of controlling and repressing civil society organizations, among many others.

To counter the rise of ruthless dictatorships and the human catastrophes and abuses of power they produce, the liberal West needs to get its act together. The EU must defend the rule of law, liberal norms and values, and fair democratic practices among its members. It must also play a more assertive role in global politics commensurate with its economic power. NATO, too, needs to better deter military threats from Russia and remain open to European countries seeking protection from external threats. Liberal democracies need to counter the military ambitions of China and prevent the takeover of international organizations by authoritarian powers and their supporters. They should also be prepared to pay the price for protecting liberal values and principles and must realize that hypocrisy is a losing strategy in the long run. As the 2022 Freedom House report notes, "the global order is nearing a tipping point, and if democracy's defenders do not work together to help guarantee freedom for all people, the authoritarian model will prevail" (2022: 1). How exactly this can be done is, of course, another story.

References

Applebaum, A. (2021, November 15). The bad guys are wining. *The Atlantic*.
Arendt, H. (1976). *The origins of totalitarianism*. Harcourt, Brace & Company.
Atalay, Z. (2022). The mutual constitution of illiberal civil society and neoauthoritarianism: Evidence from Turkey. *Current Sociology*, 70(3), 338–357.
Bermeo, N. (2016). On democratic backsliding. *Journal of Democracy*, 27(1), 5–20.
Boese, V. A. (2022). *Autocratization changing nature? Democracy report 2022*. Varieties of Democracy Institute.
Boese, V. A., Lundstedt, M., Morrison, K., Sato, Y., & Lindberg, S. I. (2022) State of the world 2021: Autocratizing changing its nature? *Democratization* 29(6), 983–1013.
Carothers, C. (2018). The surprising instability of competitive authoritarianism. *Journal of Democracy*, 29(4), 129–135.
Diamond, L. (2022). Democracy's arc from resurgent to imperiled. *Journal of Democracy*, 33(1), 163–179.
Diamond, L., & Plattner, M. F. (Eds.). (2015). *Democracy in decline?* Johns Hopkins University Press.
Dobson, W. (2012). *The dictator's learning curve: Inside the global battle for democracy*. Doubleday.
Eichengreen, B. (2018). *The populist temptation*. Oxford University Press.
Ekiert, G. (2021). Civil society as a threat to democracy. In N. Stoltzfus & C. Osmar (Eds.), *The power of populism and people* (pp. 53–71). Bloomsbury Academic.
Ekiert, G., Kubik, J., & Vachudova, M. (2007). Democracy in postcommunist world: An unending quest. *East European Politics and Societies*, 21(1), 1–24.
Freedom House. (2021). *Nations in transit 2021: The antidemocratic turn*.
Freedom House. (2022). *Freedom in the world 2022: The global expansion of authoritarian rule*.
Freedom House. (2023). *Freedom in the world 2023: Marking 50 years in the struggle for democracy*.
Friedman, T. L. (2022, March 22). Xi, Putin and Trump: The strongmen follies. *New York Times*.
Gerschewski, J. (2013). The three pillars of stability: Legitimacy, repression and cooptation in authoritarian regimes. *Democratization*, 20(1), 13–38.
Guriev, S., & Triesman, D. (2022). *Spin dictators: The changing face of tyranny in the 21st century*. Princeton University Press.

Hellmeier, S., Cole, S., Grahn, S., Kolvani, P., Lachapelle, J., Lührmann, A., Maerz, S. F., Pillai, S., & Lindberg, S. I. (2020). State of the world 2020: Autocratization turns viral. *Democratization, 28*(6), 1053–1074.

Huntington, S. (1993). *The third wave: Democratization in the late 20th century*. University of Oklahoma Press.

Levitsky, S., & Way, L. (2002). Elections without democracy: The rise of competitive authoritarianism. *Journal of Democracy, 13*(2), 51–65.

Levitsky, S., & Way, L. (2010). *Competitive authoritarianism: Hybrid regimes after the Cold War*. Cambridge University Press.

Levitsky, S., & Way, L. (2020). The new competitive authoritarianism. *Journal of Democracy, 31*(1), 51–65.

Levitsky, S., & Ziblatt, D. (2018). *How democracies die*. Broadway Books.

Libman, A., & Obydenkova, A. (2018). Understanding authoritarian regionalism. *Journal of Democracy, 29*(4), 151–165.

Lührmann, A., & Lindberg, S. I. (2019). A third wave of autocratization is here: What is new about it? *Democratization, 26*(7), 1095–1113.

Maizland, L. (2022, May 19). *Hong Kong's freedoms: What China promised and how it's cracking down*. Council on Foreign Relations. https://www.cfr.org/backgrounder/hong-kong-freedoms-democracy-protests-china-crackdown.

Mounk, Y. (2022, February 24). Dictators aren't pretending anymore. *The Atlantic*.

Norris, P., & Inglehart, R. (2019). *Cultural backlash: Trump, Brexit and authoritarian populism*. Cambridge University Press.

Piketty, T. (2014). *Capital in the twenty-first century*. Harvard University Press.

Platek, D. (2024). Towards pillarization? Coalitions of Polish protest in 2020. *East European Politics, 40*(1), 129–153.

Pop-Eleches, G. (2014). Communist development and postcommunist democratic deficit. In S. Kotkin & M. Beissinger (Eds.), *Historical legacies of communism in Russia and Eastern Europe* (pp. 28–51). Cambridge University Press.

Rachman, G. (2022a). *The age of strongman: How the cult of the leader threatens democracy around the world*. Bodley Head.

Rachman, G. (2022b, January 23). Russia and China's plans for a new world order. *Financial Times*.

Rodrik, D. (2018). Populism and the economics of globalization. *Journal of International Business Policy 1*(1), 12–33.

Sadura, P., & Sierakowski, S. (2023). *Społeczeństwo populistów*. Wydawnictwo Krytyki Politycznej.

Scheppele, K. (2018). Autocratic legalism. *University of Chicago Law Review, 85*, 545–576.

The Economist. (2022). A new low for global democracy. February 9.

Waldner, D., & Lust, E. (2018). Unwelcome change: Coming to terms with democratic backsliding. *Annual Review of Political Science*, *21*, 93–113.

Youngs, R. (Ed.). (2018). *The mobilization of conservative civil society*. Carnegie Endowment for International Peace.

CHAPTER 13

On the Influence of Sociology on Society and on the Sociologist

Krzysztof T. Konecki

1   Introduction: on the Debunking Motive

In this chapter I wish to offer several reflections on the social significance and impact of sociology on society, a phenomenon often called the "social function of sociology."[1]

At the core of sociology lies the debunking motive, and I am strongly attached to this idea. Exposing the motives of actions and presuppositions of social actors can be fascinating, revealing, and surprising (Berger 2007; Frieske 2012; Słaboń 1991; Mills 2007). Personal problems may be rooted in broader structures or imposed cultural norms (Mills 2007). Moreover, while it certainly is intellectually interesting to showcase to the broader audience certain phenomena that do not fully exist in the public sphere and media communication, as well as to expose their *modus operandi*, it also has an emancipatory value. What lies behind the *smokescreen* of the language of justification and rationalization is often the determinant of our actions (Berger 2007; Berger and Luckmann 1983). A sociologist with a sociological imagination, that is, one who is able to "understand the larger historical scene in terms of its meaning for the inner life and the external career of a variety of individuals" (Mills 2000: 5), can uncover the "false consciousness" of individuals with regard to their position in the social structure.

The debunking is done by a sociologist distrustful of language, institutions, the media, and the actions of various social groups and individuals in certain social positions. It is carried out by a sociologist who *knows* how to expose the interests and political or ideological goals of institutions and social groups. A sociologist who *knows much* is shrouded in a certain mystery. However, they use a method that obscures things even when those are revealed. This method usually becomes a veil hiding the person – a researcher operating in a particular

---

1   This chapter is a significantly expanded version of responses to a sociological survey announced by the organizers of the 18th Polish Sociological Congress – "Society of the Future: Recompositions," held in Warsaw in 2022.

situation. The assumption of mistrust is hidden behind a method that is supposed to reveal things which go beyond the conscious intentions, that is, beyond the openly expressed definitions of the circumstances. Paradoxically, then, the method used conceals certain aspects. From its description, one learns very little about the demiurge of the research situation itself: the sociologist and their placement in the lifeworld. Even if a sociologist presents their preferences, as does Mills (2007: 73) in his famous book, they remain purely theoretical and methodological. And even if these are values, there is still more behind them.

The researcher – usually a solitary mind – feels comfortable when locked in the wardrobe of methodology (see Bachelard 1976, 2002), where, arranged in the linear order, hang research methods and techniques, instructions on how to maintain research distance, and the need to objectify data and subject it to intersubjective examination. Squeezed side by side, the clothes put on the hangers are the methodological curtains that allow the researcher to hide. Usually, the researcher themself is located even further: behind the wardrobe, wedged between the wall and the back of the cabinet. They are suffocating but safe as they cannot breathe in the freedom of new associations. The wardrobe is full and nothing new can be added there anymore, and the researcher is not even allowed to do so. Instead, they can only add more distrust to their views, and that makes them content. In addition, they may discover that they are happy to pursue their career. This is, however, mainly the "happiness of the system" and not their own, genuinely experienced happiness.

2   Will the Sociologist Ever Come Out from behind the Wardrobe?

I believe that sociology should also reveal the truth about the author – the researcher and the debunker. Moreover, it ought to disclose the sociologist's presuppositions, their positioning in life and the research process, and their moral right to expose and place themself next to, above, or critically in relation to others. These two aspects are related. Thus, the debunking motive is also a motive of self-debunking. This takes courage because it involves intense sensations, namely lived experiences, which would have to be revealed in order to be credible. After all, we are constantly balancing between the world of science and the world of everyday life. If we are consistent in our critical and debunking role, then we cannot put ourselves aside and justify ourselves by the need for objectivity and non-interference in the studied phenomenon or social groups. We should also explain the assumptions underlying this method, that is, the lack of trust in what is officially presented, the lack of trust in what others say, our desire to objectify the research, the methodological reference to the natural sciences, the infinite horizon of verification, and our personal need for constant verification of our research results and analyses. Having exposed the above assumptions and explained them in relation to our position as a researcher–analyst, situating our embodied knowledge (Merleau-Ponty 2005), perhaps we can see where this locates us in the society's moral order. Coming out from behind the wardrobe can be healing and make our pale, even cadaverous, sociological face blush again.

This involves one more issue that reveals our attitude toward society. The sociologists' lack of trust in popular opinions and common knowledge may also have another side, namely the lack of trust in sociological research in society, or perhaps the lack of trust in science:

> It may be argued that science, as the enemy of opinion, often fights against it, correcting its errors. However, the success of this task is only possible if science itself has sufficient authority, which only opinion can offer. When the people have no confidence in science, then no scientific evidence will have an impact on their minds. And even today, if science was to go against some very strong current of public opinion, it would risk losing trust.
>
> DURKHEIM 2010: 182

This lack of trust was especially noticeable in the postpandemic period: even natural science research was unable to help prevent or accurately diagnose the dangers of the pandemic. Scientists' opinions were contradictory – which is only natural in science – but in a threatening situation this could be perceived as the science's vulnerability to the dangers of the global natural–social–economic–technological environment.

The objectivity associated with research and analytical procedures, often declared in sociology, is an accepted convention. This agreement has social implications though. First, it creates a "me–they" division between the researcher and the researched. Second, this convention has specific practical applications. The method itself does not work; instead, it is applied, and its application is already a *social practice*. Some methodologists claim that it needs to be accurately described and sociologically situated, for example, in social relations in the research process itself. While the mere description of research practices and their location is certainly helpful in discovering what the sociologist really wants to convey from within and what comes from the method, it is insufficient. One can sense more here: something understated, *something living and feeling*, hidden behind the veil of scientific language–jargon.

To discover that additional layer, one needs an analysis of this *shadow* that shifts behind the practices, and the shadow is the living and feeling human being. It is not, after all, a *methodical homunculus* in the form of a sociologist imagined and constructed in textbooks, a sociologist who is *translucent down to the bone marrow*. The skeleton is the method, but inside it there is the marrow which deserves a more detailed description. The red bone marrow is responsible for blood production. It contains hematopoietic stem cells which make life possible because this is where platelets as well as red and white blood cells are produced. However, a look at the images of bones that contain marrow reveals blackouts, flashes, and streaks of colors. Furthermore, one can infer from those also the genes inherited, traumas, and injuries, including visible fracture marks. Self-debunking would thus involve a description of these obscure and colored spots, and their incorporation into the research perspective itself. Research is more than just a method; it has its subject too – a person squeezed behind the cabinet who is very much alive even though they pretend to be dead.

In sociology, there has long existed a research trend that attaches great importance to the description and analysis of the social actor's point of view, which includes qualitative sociology (Konecki 2017). We are then interested in definitions of the situation, motives or a vocabulary of motives, the humanistic coefficient, and similar aspects (Znaniecki 1988). However, even if we describe the point of view of a social actor other than the researcher themself, the entire ideology associated with the humanistic approach to research – "describe the actor's point of view" – is incomplete without taking into account the point of view held by the actor–sociologist, that is, mainly their immersion in the world of practical activities, their embodied practices, and their social involvement, and without revealing their frequent lack of confidence in themself as a researcher.

This is exactly what Polish sociology is missing: a description of the world from the points of view of the social actor–sociologist–researcher and their location in the lifeworld when studying a given phenomenon. There is strong resistance in the community to this type of research. The doubts that arise are related to alleged lack of objectivity, subjectivity of research, lack of intersubjectivity in research, and difficulty in assessing the reliability of the obtained data and the conclusions. One should note that all these arguments are related to particular research optics, which can be referred to as "error methodology" (Kacperczyk 2014, 2020). In this approach, one looks for an error, and in research, falsification is the goal. Consequently, science is concerned with reducing doubt rather than making positive claims. The researcher brings this kind of methodological baggage with them, guarding their wardrobe like a keeper of the seals. For them, falsifying a result means a satisfactory result; pointing out or eliminating an error equals a positive scientific achievement and signifies progress which has an infinite horizon. Improvement and refinement never end, even though the human's temporal horizon in the lifeworld is finite in nature – and the researcher knows this when pursuing their scientific career.

An undisclosed side of this procedure is *the emotional side*, and the researcher rejoices in the power of their own criticism – the power to refute theses they classify as false. These theses appear to them as ideologies, justifications, rationalizations, or rhetorical tricks, and in scientific discourse the researcher also refutes the conclusions of an adversary who has different views or research results. This forms their professional, highly regarded research methods built not only on the assumptions of distrust and a critical approach to everything that is visible to the naked eye in society, but also on distrust of their own second-degree descriptions (Schütz 2011, 2008; Manterys 2008). The result is the sociologist's image as an inquisitive, meticulous researcher and analyst. *This joy* is not usually revealed openly, as it comes with an aftertaste of *schadenfreude*, but it does appear – in scientific discussions, at conferences, workshops, seminars, and symposia, and also in articles and scientific reviews. These motives are not expressed openly, but they are always present in the social world of sociology – one I most often refer to in this chapter. Frequently, the more critical a researcher is, the more admiration they enjoy, and the more scared others are of being criticized by them. The motto of greatness here is: *The less trusting and the more critical you are, the more professional you are.* I wish to add that the criticism in question is often coupled with denying any legitimacy to one's adversary; it is often all-out criticism.

However, upon looking closer at the motives for this type of action, one notices the *because motives* in the background. The likely line of reasoning in such case may be verbalized as follows: "I criticize because I was raised that way; skepticism and criticism affected me in the past – why should I spare others? After all, this is the right way to do science. My great masters built their greatness on challenging other views, theses, and theories, so I will try that too." Naturally, one does not expose these motives; they operate somewhere in secret. However, such reasoning appears when one starts writing from a first-person perspective about one's actual position in the process of research, analysis, and scientific discussion. Still, it is immediately pushed out of consciousness because the researcher believes they have to be presuppositionally pure. The assumptions existing in their lifeworld cannot come into play in the world of science, where only the method counts. The researcher thinks that there are lines which they cannot cross (Konecki 2021a). Crossing boundaries introduces chaos: the different orders of various worlds mix, and one's identity as a researcher becomes blurred.

3 The Dehumanization of Social Sciences

The dehumanization of social sciences is a trend consistently developed in science, itself a religion of modernity. Dehumanization often applies to qualitative research, even one regarded as following the path of humanism. It is obvious to me as I am immersed in this process myself. The huge number of methodological texts published that try to prove the legitimacy of qualitative research in relation to quantitative research is often indicative of the drive to become more similar to objectivizing social research. The idea of natural science is always in the background as a point of reference, and sometimes even blindness (Husserl 1983; see also Husserl 1999). Researchers continue to hide behind the method. Some, like me, become methodologists to fit into the tradition of relevance and reliability, and to avoid showing the true face of a sociologist who feels emotions such as empathy, sympathy, anger, and even envy at various points in the scientific creative process. Envy is actually a taboo in the scientific community (Żywczok 2020). It is supposedly offensive, embarrassing, and unworthy of a scholar who should be pure in their intentions and when verifying the theses of other sociologists. The scholar should even assist their opponents if they wish to reach the same truth that the former is investigating. Much effort is put into self-presentation here to ensure that the emotion of envy is not shown outwardly. The criticism is styled as purely scientific, and there is no room for personal emotions.

Denial and criticism of the *raison d'etre* of those who think and research differently can stem from fear and envy alike. Other people's successes are difficult to accept, but the critical method, searching for errors and breaking down definitions of concepts to show their inaccuracy and inconsistency, can work here and offset these achievements. Consequently, the author of these analyses gains prestige and glory in the community of those hidden behind the wardrobe.

This trend to *methodologize sociology* and to hide the true intentions inherent in the "art of distrust" pushes researchers away from themselves. It alienates them from their essence: a living and feeling human being with a body, albeit a human being at work, in supposedly purely practical and rationally planned endeavors. Sociologists study social reality either by stepping outside of it or by pretending to be outside, beside, or above society. If this is the case, they inhabit two roles and two dimensions alternately because science is the realm of the sacred and daily life is the realm of the profane, and they cannot overlap. Still, this reflection remains just an assumption.

To reach the actors' – and one's own – point of view requires methodological justifications and an explanation of the issues of generalization, sample, and one's exclusion from the research situation. Usually, this is how the inferiority complex of qualitative sociologists with a humanist option manifests itself. It is evident in the paragraphs, methodological chapters, and appendices of their works in relation, if only implicitly, to this *true*, statistical sociology – even though we all know that the very concepts we use in sociology have a generalizing value, not just the statistically validated conclusions. General concepts derived from observations of social reality are tested by their analytical applications (Simmel 2009; Zerubavel 1980, 1991, 1995, 2020).

However, generalization can also originate from first-person descriptions. Individual cases may serve as a picture and expression of broader, more general relationships and social phenomena. When a researcher immersed in a particular environment describes their observations, sensory experiences, and emotions, those are not a product of their mind's fantasies. Instead, they are a product of the environment surrounding the researcher in question. Their own experience of the world occurs here and now, or there and then, always in the situation into which they are ultimately cast. This is because the researcher can decide to be in a certain place, but then they cannot always control their immersion and actions. Even though their decisions are important, they are still co-conditioned by the situation, and objectified by entering into relationships with others and through this co-conditioning. While in a particular situation, the researcher can describe it from their point of view. However, this point of view is no longer merely individual but has a socialized value, both in terms of practices and body sensations as well as emotions. Situations, although subjectively unique, tend to reproduce themselves, revealing – and allowing the reader to understand – the frequently shared feelings and structures of situations and phenomena that they experience. Here, one enters a deeper level of experiencing reality. This is oftentimes an unconscious level, and therefore it requires reflection and contemplation. Hence, it would be necessary to open this wardrobe – so tightly sealed against external influences (Konecki 2022: 155–157) – and look through the now dusty clothes.

4   Theorizing and Debunking

In order to be practiced, sociology needs theory. Theory is an indispensable basis both in research and in diagnoses and interpretations of social phenomena. The theoretical approach seems to be an immanent quality of sociological reasoning. However, theorizing in sociology tends to have a *disembodied character*:

> We may now sum up some of the features of the *epoché* peculiar to the scientific attitude. In this *epoché* there is "bracketed" (suspended): (1) the subjectivity of the thinker as a man among fellow-men, including his bodily existence as a psycho-physical human being within the world; (2) the system of orientation by which the world of everyday life is grouped in zones within actual, restorable, attainable reach; (3) the fundamental anxiety and the system of pragmatic relevances originating therein.
> SCHÜTZ 1962: 249

According to Schütz, existential anxiety also disappears with putting our everyday life's entanglement in *parentheses*. This is paradoxical because theorizing stems from existential anxiety, from that unknown that is constantly on the horizon of the ever-conscious subject's future (fundamental anxiety).

A theoretical attitude is impractical as the sociologist becomes an uninvolved observer. The sociologist's body and actions are usually outside their field of interest. If their body is alienated though, how can they observe and describe the reality around them in an empathetic and socially sensitive way? Thus, they describe the world while not being intentionally in it, even though they are thrown into it and their research or analysis is a *being-in-the-world* (Merleau-Ponty 2005; Maciejczak 2001). This is precisely the burden of sociology – this *theoretical detachment from reality*, already inherent in the origins of sociological thinking, both in ancient and modern philosophers as well as full-fledged sociologists from the nineteenth century onwards, when sociology entered the academic world of science.

There is actually a certain similarity between a theorizing sociologist and a philosopher with a theoretical attitude: "Therefore, to the theoretical attitude of the philosopher, belongs also that he is constantly and pre-emptively determined to always devote his future life, in the sense of universal life, to the tasks of theory, to pile theoretical cognitions upon theoretical cognitions *in infinitum*" (Husserl 1983: 333). However, there is an element of life practice here, as their theory is immersed in their decisions, which come from and are rooted in everyday life. Their daily life becomes an endless search for truth because the one who theorizes is a real person. The theorist's daily life is paradoxical as their practical decision is an impractical action. Added to this type of action is an ideology of pursuing the truth at all costs, without any personal benefit in mind. It is frequently compounded by the rationalization of one's activities in the form of self-imputed exclusion and stigmatization. This raises the theorist's prestige, naturally in line with the convention of self-presentation.

Consequently, the theoretician has to forget about their body in order to completely blend into abstract ideas using their mind, which defines concepts and breaks them down into parts. They no longer directly reference the material world, and therefore remembering the body could hinder this purely abstract and logical disentangling, or operating in categories, in the world of ideas. It is the forgetting of one's body that is extremely significant here. Abstraction is *a symbol* of being rooted in a culture that does not give a chance for embodied sensations – one that does not accommodate a humanistic and ideational approach to interpreting nature and merging with nature, which is, after all, a part of humanity. Moreover, in relation to the topic analyzed in this paper, it is a form of embodying and situating the scientist in the natural and material world. The natural world is always our world, and there would be no nature in our perceptions if there were no humans, with their categories, but also their senses that allow them to observe and experience nature in their embodied existence. All *new* ideas come from the bodily sensations; the emergence process begins there, followed by capturing ideas into words associated with other words which often come from diverse theoretical traditions – and finally, an abstraction emerges.

While it must be stressed that certain approaches to constructing concepts are based on inductive research, the constructed theory is usually a compilation and summary of ideas invented by others in the past. It is necessary to familiarize oneself with them, which means reading and reflecting on the many works of our great predecessors. The generated theory is also a critique of these ideas: deceased thinkers no longer have bodies, just as ideas are mostly detached from the lifeworld in which they were produced. Thus, the analyst–theorist positions themself on the same plane as abstract ideas, which nevertheless appear in a materialized form as books or research papers. Those acquire meaning not only through their date of publication and republication, but also through the dates of their reception here and now, in a given existential situation. A theorist's book is a cultural fact and event; furthermore, it is socially and emotionally relational, which is rarely taken into account in the theorizing process (Żywczok 2020: 217–18).

Looking at this phenomenon from the perspective of the phenomenology of reading, one sees that reading is a reception associated with the emergence of our own experiences – often related to our sensory responses and the lifeworld – and with generating interpretations flowing out of one's self and *fantasizing*, which often happens unconsciously but can also be a useful thought experiment. Fantasizing often appears as necessary for understanding the text: the reader disengages from it for a moment in order to contemplate it. The textual boundary between the reader, the narrative content, and the narrator, including an implicit one, disappears. As one reads, one becomes the narrator and perceives the world according to one's own perceptual categories. The mood that appears in the text is then the reader's mood, for example, a mood of detachment or empathy and compassion, the will to act, or simply the desire to understand and reflect. The work being read comes alive because the reader is alive. Reading is a journey to the new antipodes of one's horizons of thinking and feeling, but it can also be a trap that locks one into the conceptual cage of the sociologist–theorist's perception of the world.

5   Creativity

By relying on tradition and constantly referring to the same ideas and theories, one may be doomed to imitate. On the one hand, referring to theories that already exist is a sign of being well-read and subscribing to tradition, which can be and is viewed positively in the academia. On the other hand, tradition and inherited language, whether more or less precise, is a major constraint to creative intelligence. One cannot go beyond language in one's statement about the world and oneself. However, one can look for the kind of linguistic powers that are not included in the existing tradition. Poetry and poetic imagination provide such opportunities (Gurgul 2022; Bachelard 1998). This does not mean that researchers should write poetry instead of doing science. Rather, they should at least take advantage of the new opportunities to associate facts and realize what can happen but is not yet confirmed by facts.

Looking ahead, relying on dreams and imaginative transformation of objects, nature, identity, relationships, and soul can help in generating new theoretical theses and ideas for research experiments. Listening to what flows from the inner self may be subjective in nature at the moment of recording one's intuitions in consciousness, but in fact what flows from the subconscious is universal in character. This is because there is a connection with the collective unconscious which is expressed with the aid of intersubjective language. Perhaps this language is not yet precise and appears illogical or even poetic, and perhaps human expression is simply pure poetry, which does not mean that it should be omitted during the creative process.

The world of ideas and theories is revealed in an infinite horizon of past analyses and critiques, correcting misinterpretations, and current critical references as well as future ones which cannot be accurately predicted in terms of emerging new orientations, categories, and interpretive paradigms. This infinite horizon of the theoretical world affects the theorist's attitude – their caution in expressing opinions and theses. Thus, they prefer to rely on proposing ideas, by formulating certain hypotheses that have their explicit or implicit confirmation, in sentences and phrases previously written down by others. It is difficult to make a new claim, relying on intuition or gut feeling, because they are rooted in corporeality, and this domain has been excluded from the work of the theorist's mind.

6 The Game of Theorizing: the Fun of Self-Debunking

The theorist is a person of game – a player. In other words, *they play the chess of ideas* and definitely enjoy the process. The pieces in this game are ideas: knights symbolize insecure ideas jumping from one meaning to another; bishops embody the main analytical categories; rooks stand for old and widely accepted categories that defend the queen; finally, the queen is a preliminary theory which cannot be challenged and which in turn defends the king – the ultimate core of the theory. The main idea needs support – a supporting category – but when it turns out to be a woman, no male theorist will admit that his ideas are gendered; otherwise, he would already be approaching the embodiment of his ideas and his theorizing. There is no room for weakness here; theory is usually a masculinized game. The joy of play is the happiness of a winning man.

What is happening here? To be precise, *I am theorizing* about theorists and doing the theorizing as an activity. I am fully immersed in this activity by thinking and writing. However, I would also like to make an effort of self-debunking, of revealing my assumptions that led me to undertake this task. Some of them have already been disclosed. Following C. Wright Mills (2007), I place myself and my thinking in the social structure and in the historical process of which I am an active component but do not really choose the place and time to participate in it.

First, I think this consideration is guided by the *conviction* that my situation as an individual immersed in the academic world causes me to relate what I have written to the world around me. I relate it to a lifeworld that I find difficult to accept due to its rejection of the category of embodying one's scientific activity and situating it in a specific social and historical context – a context in which quantifiability and practicality of applications are the main criteria for evaluating scientific reasoning. I feel strongly the impact of what surrounds me in the academic lifeworld: the bureaucratic politics of science, the bureaucratization of the methods and minds of researchers (Mills 2007: 295–297), ignoring the scientific achievements of humanistically oriented researchers, ignoring innovative social scientists, and envy, which incites the feelings of anxiety and danger – indications of faulty reasoning. All of this causes mental distress. I am in the process of a major acceleration in the economic, technological, and social spheres (Rosa 2020). Even though I try, I cannot keep up. This leads to downright existential anxiety, both in the realm of individual and social relations. Perhaps it is a figment of my imagination though? I check it by documenting the facts. It turns out that my imagination is working, but only in exaggerating the facts. I have evidence of my immersion in the acceleration process and the widespread anxiety that occurs as a reaction to this phenomenon. This all happens in my geographic and political cage of the Western world (Giddens 1990, 1991). There are also dreams of a better world, but they are quickly pushed back by negative internal monologues. The "me" does not allow the dreams and desires of my "I" to fully come out (Mead 1934). I hear similar opinions among my colleagues in the academia, so the dialogue eventually becomes intersubjective. I would still have to confirm this in a research study. Thus, I return to verification methodology, where there is an endless yearning for certainty.

Second, I am convinced that the academic world rejects first-person, contemplative perspectives that take into account emotions and corporeality – elements which could show the *positioning* of the researchers, especially theorists, about whom we usually know little except where they work and what they do. We need to situate them in the lifeworld and in the biographical timeline. My intuition and experience tell me that it is these *biographical, historical, institutional, and relational* factors that are of tremendous importance in the theorizing process, but this is often hidden. Pushing these motives into the subconscious does not have to be intentional; the social control that leads to self-censorship can be imperceptible, natural, and embodied. I notice it in myself when I use self-censorship in my writings. The underlying thought of *what they will say* – "they" denotes reviewers, audience, students, and colleagues from the academia – constantly accompanies me: it resides in my body–mind, and I do not have to be actively aware of it.

Researchers who conduct analyses of particular social problems are in a similar situation. It is no coincidence that they undertake those issues: their personal biographies make them observe life from a specific point of view and place in society. One does not know the connections between the construction of a research concept and the research itself, between the research practice happening here and now and a biography rooted in the lifeworld. Within it, the researcher may be heavily involved in the activities they are studying. Even if we are not willing to investigate this, we should at least contemplate the very phenomenon of the researcher's or theorist's immersion in a given study. If there is no personal biographical connection there, perhaps the researcher/theorist simply yields to current trends of subject and methodological interest. Indeed, conformity emerges at the center of the trend. However, it may also be a matter of exciting the public with an "exotic" topic, making people interested in oneself, and focusing attention on oneself through an extravagant object of study or theoretical analysis.

I am not opposed to theorizing. On the contrary, I believe that a sociologist cannot do without theory. My objection against theoretical and empirical studies – procedurally regulated, performed according to logical and methodical instructions – stems from the fundamental assumption, leading to a disagreement with the fictitious thought–institutional system. The assumption in question suggests that objective inquiry in the humanities or in humanistically oriented sociology is possible only in the sense postulated so far by the methodology that mimics natural sciences, which states that the subject can objectify knowledge using the only available objective methodology and that subjective intuitions can only be a starting point for making judgments. Even in historically oriented critical sociology (Rosa 2020: 77–78), *existential ahistoricism* is evident, for the inclusion of the historical dimension in the construction of phenomenal and theoretical categories does not show the theorist's involvement with the lifeworld, even when they believe they are using phenomenological inspirations. In such case, however, it remains unknown how personal biographical involvements have affected the construction of the theory, and whether there are projections or suppressions at play – a concept highly regarded in the communities of sociology and critical philosophy:

> This is why I am convinced that the current academic discourse, at least as far as the humanities and social sciences are concerned, too rarely follows the logic of better argument and critical review of validity claims. After all, how can we talk about collective deliberation, when we are dealing with an uncontrolled and constantly encouraged drive to publish, confer and participate in research grants, the success of which is not due to the strength of the arguments, but rather to an extensive network of well-established academic contacts?
>
> ROSA 2020: 84

The question that arises is: how does the author writing the words above situate himself in this process of acceleration and overpublication? Again, this remains unknown, although he appears to stand by and observe, and seemingly does not belong to the crowd of authors rushing to publish more and more articles and books.

7 Limitations and Possibilities

Adopting the assumptions of this naturalistic methodology, even minimally, is not only cognitively limiting but also destructive toward creative minds that rely on hunches and intuitions, which can bring new ideas to the analyzed phenomena. The role of premonition and intuition in philosophical research was pointed out by Husserl:

> But all this is not meant to be a speculative interpretation of our history, but the expression of a vivid premonition that grows within a thought liberated from all superstition. This premonition gives us an intentional common thread that allows us to see particularly important connections in European history; tracing these connections will turn our premonition into certainty. Premonition is the emotional signpost of all discoveries.
> HUSSERL 1983: 323

Adopting these assumptions can also be the driving force in terms of social practices, and a sociologist should see this. This usually involves excluding those who have different assumptions and ideas about the practice of sociology from the academic community. I am referring to the aggressive rejection of, for example, first-person perspectives, which mirrors the rejection of qualitative sociology in the past. I also mean the critical and ironic approach to, among other things, studies of animal–human relationships as well as gender and transgender studies, or the nonacceptance of contemplative research inspired by non-Western cultural traditions. This does not always mean full exclusion; sometimes it manifests as marginalization, in which researchers with great sensitivity and capacity for insight into themselves and their positioning live and work on the fringes of the academia. At times, they are even stigmatized and labeled as misfits, which allows them to exist and work, but with the appropriate label of a *marginal person*. Such labeling of otherness may be an expression of tolerance, but it does not equal an acceptance of full-fledged participation in the academic world. There is an emerging phenomenon of ignoring and failing to notice these dissenters in the world of academic communication. This means, for example, no response to publications, lack of references and jobs, or no invitations to prestigious scientific committees, in addition to lack of promotions in the academic hierarchy. The latter, however, seems to be irrelevant to these types of researchers and theorists themselves. Importantly, their critics are unwilling to engage in a genuine dialogue, put themselves in the shoes of researchers who think differently, or see the world from their perspective. They shun all empathy because it does not belong in the world of bureaucratized scientific minds, dominated by procedures, methods, and techniques. Empathy can be perceived as a weakness and an obstacle to objective evaluation of researchers' achievements. However, if critics do not exercise empathy – and seems to be no chance they will do so in the near future – they will also fail to see their own positioning and the embodiment of their scientific activity, especially in the theoretical work, where disembodiment is visible and noticeable as a phenomenon of *the absent body* (Leder 1990).

This phenomenon of being locked in one's own methodological, theoretical, and ideological bubble can also affect the opposite side. Researchers focused on emphasizing gender, age (ageism, *dziaderyzm*),[2] and ethnic differences in their criticism do not open their minds and bodies to otherness – to the distinctive vision of the world that many people adopt in their admittedly hidden assumptions. Failure to let other theories play a part, pressuring people to be "with us or against us," does not lead to resonance (Rosa 2020), which is the basis of honest intellectual discussion. Critical sensitivity can result in closing off of one's mental world rather than expanding its horizons. Emotional reactions and bodily responses to other people's views can serve as evidence of this – a phenomenon which everyone is able to check for themselves.

8 Conclusions

If sociology is to regain society's trust and have influence on public opinion as well as transform individual concerns into public issues, and if sociologists are to regain trust in themselves, the debunking motive has to be applied consistently and thoroughly. A sociologist should not stand beside society and, from the position of a demiurge creating unique knowledge, lift the veils created by society that obscure it. Being a product of this society themselves, they should show how their mind and heart, that is, bodily sensations and emotions, bind them to it, push them back, or bring them closer to achieving self-awareness;

---

2 In Polish, *dziaders* is a pejorative term for "a person who treats young people in a disrespectful and condescending manner and often has archaic views on social issues, especially the role of women" (*Wielki Słownik Języka Polskiego*, n.d., retrieved December 7, 2023). Thus, *dziaderyzm* would be a very particular subset of ageism. Translator's note.

the latter includes being knowledgeable about their own person, immersed in the lifeworld at a given historical moment. The academia is their world, so they ought to perceive it as "my world." The grades achieved – in the form of ministerial points, grants, or academic degrees – as well as publications or their lack, awards, invitations to lectures and plenary sessions at conferences, dismissals, and reprimands apply to particular participants in this world. All those occur at a specific historical and biographical moment; there is no academic world *per se*. When a theorist or researcher fully demonstrates their positioning in the process of theorizing or empirical research, respectively, they may come closer to what humanistic sociology wishes to and can achieve.

For their inquiries to have social resonance, a researcher must open up not only to their interaction partners, but also to the most important partner – themself. When a sociologist starts a dialogue with themself, they should not hide it, making it appear as if an external voice is speaking through them, rather than admitting to the often-contradictory thoughts and sensations that form part of intellectual work. Many of reactions are pre-reflective; for instance, fear is often expressed unconsciously in one's opinions on others. The *schadenfreude* in the competitors' failures and mistakes often appears spontaneously and unreflectively. These are habits of body and mind shaped by the history and culture of the academia, as well as by the contemporary era of late modernity which manifests itself in merciless competition and rivalry in the academic world. These habits indicate certain divisions and shut out other ones. A researcher's positioning and body is not simply a signifier in the social space; it constitutes a living and responsive object/subject which should be within the scope of their interest.

For this, one needs the sociological imagination that Mills writes about; however, I wish to supplement Mills's concept here. My sociological imagination would look as follows: I believe that historical conditions and the influence of broader social structures on the biography of an individual is an extremely important factor in sociological analyses. This is the sociological imagination of the highest order – but nevertheless, not one of deep insight. *In-depth sociological imagination* would be related to the analysis of the place occupied by the sociologist, a subject using sociological imagination as defined by Mills (2007). It concerns positioning the research subject not only in the social structure, but also in a specific existential situation. A sociologist's life is perhaps determined by the historical type of the social structure in which they find themself, and even if history is made behind their back (Mills 2007), their intentions and individual choices are relevant to their fate, identity, and well-being. They can oppose the political and academic dictatorship or ignore it and remain indifferent. Here the sociologist must help themself; their choices are both moral and political at the same time, and their existential fears and anxieties are their concern, something they can turn into a public problem. If they fail to protest against dictatorships and attempts to curb freedom, they are influencing reality by being indifferent because inaction also has an impact on the lifeworld.

This applies also to methodological choices to avoid monopolistic tendencies in methodology – the "bureaucratization of reason" and scientific discussion. The choice of methodology – both method and practice – which is considered the only legitimate methodology in the social sciences can resemble doctrinal thinking of monopoly nature: "The idea of such a monopoly in the sphere of social ideas is one of the authoritarian notions which lie under the view of 'The Method' of the science-makers as administrators of reason, and which is so thinly disguised in the 'sacred values' of grand theorists" (Mills 2000: 190). "This role [of reason] requires only that the social scientist get on with the work of social science and that he avoids furthering the bureaucratization of reason and of discourse" (Mills 2000: 192). Thus, it would be necessary to see how the sociologist's mind works, what assumptions they hold, what they want to achieve, what their values are, whether scientism – that is, the bureaucratic style of research – obscures certain social problems, and whether their place in the social structure allows them to see only certain social problems and not others. Geography and location in the global space – but also the immediate one – also matters here. Sociology is dominated by the values of the Western world as it exists in late modernity.

Furthermore, a sociologist's knowledge is usually embodied – we are not a disembodied intellect, even though we often present as such in our public appearances (Mills 2007: 298), and so it is necessary to approach the body as a knowing and feeling subject. This would not equal solipsism because it is not only the mind that participates in this type of cognition, but also the body, the flesh to which we are condemned. Through this *flesh*, we are hurled into the world (Merleau-Ponty 2005), in which the body is also socialized, and we face this world through movement, namely through our actions in the everyday world.

Such an open explication of oneself and one's positioning vis-à-vis others can trigger a resonance (Rosa 2020) that would be a prelude to an authentic dialogue and an encounter with others in a space that is not just purely academic, but also embodied and human. In such space, empathy and compassion of the sensitive citizen–sociologist who participates in everyday life could exist as an alternative to the cold and calculating mindset of the academic–scientist.

Translated by Anna Weksej

References

Bachelard, G. (1976). Poetyka przestrzeni: szuflada, kufry i szafy. *Pamiętnik Literacki: czasopismo kwartalne poświęcone historii i krytyce literatury polskiej, 67*(1), 233–243.
Bachelard, G. (1998). *Poetyka marzenia*. Słowo/obraz terytoria.
Bachelard, G. (2002). *Kształtowanie się umysłu naukowego*. Słowo/obraz terytoria.
Berger, P. L. (2007). *Zaproszenie do socjologii*. PWN.
Berger, P., & Luckmann, T. (1983). *Społeczne tworzenie rzeczywistości*. Państwowy Instytut Wydawniczy.
Durkheim, E. (2010). *Elementarne formy życia religijnego. System totemiczny w Australii*. PWN.
Frieske, K. (2012). Socjologia demaskatorska. *Normy, Dewiacje i Kontrola Społeczna, 13*, 36–52.
Giddens, A. (1990). *The consequences of modernity*. Polity Press.
Giddens, A. (1991). *Modernity and self-identity: Self and society in the late modern age*. Polity Press.
Gurgul, P. (2022). *Filozoficzne ujęcia wyobraźni poetyckiej*. Słowo/obraz terytoria.
Husserl, E. (1983). Kryzys kultury europejskiej i filozofia. *Archiwum Historii Filozofii i Myśli Społecznej, 29*, 315–353.
Husserl, E. (1999). *Kryzys nauk europejskich i fenomenologia transcendentalna* (S. Walczewska, Trans.). Wydawnictwo Rolewski.
Dziaders. (n.d.). In *Wielki Słownik Języka Polskiego*. Retrieved December 7, 2023, from https://wsjp.pl/haslo/podglad/104377/dziaders.
Kacperczyk, A. (2014). Autoetnografia: technika, metoda, nowy paradygmat? O metodologicznym statusie autoetnografii. *Przegląd Socjologii Jakościowej, 10*(3), 32–74. http://qualitativesociologyreview.org/PL/Volume27/PSJ_10_3_Kacperczyk.pdf.
Kacperczyk, A. (2020). Autoetnograficzna inicjacja. In M. Kafar & A. Kacperczyk (Eds.), *Autoetnograficzne "zbliżenia" i "oddalenia." O autoetnografii w Polsce* (pp. 43–78). Wydawnictwo Uniwersytetu Łódzkiego.
Konecki, K. T. (2017). Qualitative sociology In K. O. Korgen (Ed.), *The Cambridge handbook of sociology: Vol. 1. Core areas in sociology and the development of the discipline* (pp. 143–152). Cambridge University Press.
Konecki, K. T. (2021). Distinctions and something between: An inspection of Eviatar Zerubavel's concept driven sociology. *The Qualitative Report, 26*(4), 1150–1156. https://doi.org/10.46743/2160-3715/2021.4840.
Konecki, K. T. (2021a). *Przekraczanie granic, zamykanie granic. Perspektywa pierwszoosobowa w badaniach socjologicznych*. Wydawnictwo IFiS PAN.
Konecki, K. T. (2022). *The meaning of contemplation for social qualitative research: Applications and examples*. Routledge.
Leder, D. (1990). *The absent body*. The University of Chicago Press.

Mead, G. H. (1934). *Mind, Self, and Society from the Standpoint of a Social Behaviorist*, edited by Charles W. Morris. University of Chicago Press.

Maciejczak, Marek. (2001). *Świat według ciała w fenomenologii percepcji M. Merleau-Ponty'ego*. IFiS PAN.

Manterys, A. (2008). Działanie i sprawczość w socjologii Schütza. In A. Schütz, *O wielości światów. Szkice z socjologii fenomenologicznej* (pp. VII–XVIII). Nomos.

Merleau-Ponty, M. (2005). *Phenomenology of perception*. Routledge.

Mills, C. W. (2000). *The sociological imagination*. Oxford University Press.

Mills, C. W. (2007). *Wyobraźnia socjologiczna*. PWN.

Rosa, H. (2020). *Przyspieszenie, wyobcowanie, rezonans. Projekt krytycznej teorii późnonowoczesnej czasowości*. Europejskie Centrum Solidarności.

Słaboń, A. (1991). O demaskatorskiej funkcji socjologii. *Cracow Review of Economics and Management, 353*, 37–52.

Schütz, A. (1962). *Collected papers I: The problem of social reality*. Martinus Nijhoff Publishers.

Schütz, A. (2008). *O wielości światów*. Nomos.

Schütz, A. (2011). *Collected papers V: Phenomenology and the social sciences*. Springer.

Simmel, G. (2009). *Sociology: Inquiries into the Construction of Social Forms*. Brill.

Zerubavel, E. (1980). If Simmel were a fieldworker: On formal sociological theory and analytical field research. *Symbolic Interaction, 3*(2), 25–34.

Zerubavel, E. (1991). *The fine line: Making distinctions in everyday life*. The University of Chicago Press.

Zerubavel, E. (1995). The rigid, the fuzzy, and the flexible: Notes on the mental sculpting of academic identity. *Social Research, 62*(4), 1093–1106.

Zerubavel, E. (2020). *Generally speaking: An invitation to concept driven sociology*. Oxford University Press.

Znaniecki, F. (1988). *Wstęp do socjologii*. PWN.

Żywczok, A. (2020). *Zazdrość i działalność naukowa. Studium z zakresu naukoznawstwa pedagogicznego*. Wydawnictwo Uniwersytetu Śląskiego.

Index

Abel, Theodore   53, 59
Abramovich, Roman   100
Adamski, Władysław   47, 59
Adorno, Theodor   48, 53, 59
Africa   72, 74, 75, 76, 77, 79
Alexander, Jeffrey   46, 58, 59
algorithms   113, 114
alienation   4, 17, 18, 30
alienation of knowledge   17, 18
Amazon   193, 194, 198
Antal, Atilla   197, 198
Anthropocene   8, 185, 186, 187, 188, 189, 191, 192, 192n4, 194, 195, 196, 197n6, 198, 199, 200
anti-ruralism   38
Applebaum, Anne   229, 230, 231, 235, 236
Arendt, Hannah   75, 84, 227, 236
Ariese, Csilla E.   78, 84
aristocracy   92, 93
artificial intelligence   114, 116
Ashar, Meera   78, 84
Asia   72, 73, 76, 79
associative mode   19, 20, 22, 26, 27
Atalay, Zeynep   218, 236
Austria-Hungary   67
Austrian Empire   93
authoritarian systems   217, 234
authoritarianism   9, 221, 223, 227, 228, 229, 235, 236, 237
autocratic   218, 225, 226
axiological order   180

Bakuła, Barbara   74, 75, 84
Balibar, Etienne   50, 60
Balkan countries   68
Balkans   68, 69, 89
Balogun, Bolaji   81, 84
Baltic states   68, 72, 73
Barbier, Edward B.   200
Barkavi, Tarak   73, 84
Bateman, Ian   200
Bauman, Zygmunt   173, 180
Beck, Ulrich   55, 62, 173, 181
Belarus   72, 73
Belarusians   74, 75

Bell, Daniel   38, 49
Bendix, Reinhard   39, 40, 60
Berger, Peter   37, 239, 256
Bermeo, Nancy   218, 236
Betlii, Olena   73, 84
Bhabha, Homi K.   66
Bill, Stanley   65, 83, 84
Bińczyk, Ewa   191, 192n4, 199
biographical narrative interviews   156, 158
Black Lives Matter   65
Boatcă, Manuela   2, 10, 66, 88, 107
Bobinac, Martin   68, 84
Bodenstedt, Andreas   38, 60
body   244, 245, 246, 247, 250, 253, 254, 255, 256
Boese, Vanessa A.   217, 223, 236
Bolshevik Revolution   92, 95, 96, 105
Bolsheviks   74
Borawski, Piotr   74, 84
Borkowska, Grażyna   75, 84
Böröcz, József   103, 106
Bourdieu, Pierre   57, 60, 92
bourgeoisie   92, 93, 94, 95, 96, 97, 101, 103, 104, 105, 106
Bralczyk, Jerzy   42, 60
Braudel, Fernand   37
Bruun, Hans Henrich   182
Buchanan, Ian   191, 199
Bucholc, Marta   81, 84
Buchowski, Michał   70, 84
Bukowiecki, Łukasz   78, 84
Bulgaria   68
Burawoy, Michael   52, 60
Burke, Edmund   40, 60
Burski, Jacek   151
Buruma, Ian   71, 85

Carey, Henry F.   71, 72, 85
Carothers, Christopher   229, 236
Castells, Manuel   55, 175, 181
Cavanagh, Claire   2, 10, 67, 85
CEE   1, 2, 3, 5, 10
Central and Eastern Europe   1
Césaire, Aime   75, 85
Chakrabarty, Dipesh   66, 189, 190, 199

changes in values   175
Chari, Sharad   76, 85
Chryssogelos, Angelos   201, 215
Chwe, Michael S.Y.   29, 33
Clair, Judith   153, 170
climate change   186, 196
Cobel-Tokarska, Marta   73, 79, 82, 85
Cohen, Allison K.   167, 169
Cold War   66, 76, 77, 85
Collins, Randall   53
colonization   2, 3, 4, 6, 10
colonizing   1, 3
common   17, 22, 24, 25, 26, 29, 33
common knowledge   17, 25, 26, 29, 33
common social knowledge   24, 29
communication   201, 203, 204, 205, 208, 212, 214, 215
communities of meaning   180
community mode   19, 20, 22, 27
Comte, August   15, 16, 21, 22, 33, 34
Condorcet de, Nicolas   201, 215
Congress Kingdom of Poland   91, 94
Connell, Raewyn   59, 60
contemplative perspectives   250
Costa, Sergio   2, 10
country of immigration   133, 134, 135
COVID-19   7, 151, 152, 153, 154, 156, 157, 161, 161n5, 162n6, 165, 167, 169, 170, 171
creativity   248
Credit Suisse Research Institute   100
crisis   1, 2, 3, 4, 6, 7, 8, 9, 10
crisis solidarity   153
Croft, Charlotte   171
Cromwell, Jonathan R.   169
Csáky, Moritz   68, 85
Csepeli, Gyorgy   85
cultural patterns   176
culture   172, 173, 175, 177, 179, 180, 181
cyber-physical system   113
Czech Republic   98, 99, 100, 103
Czechia   68
Czemiel, Grzegorz   181

Dąbrowa Basin   91
datafication   128
de Moor, R.A.   173, 181
debunking motive   239, 240, 253
Decolonization   5
decolonizing   2
dehumanization of social sciences   244

Delanty, Gerard   151, 169
Democracy   9
democratic backsliding   218, 221, 226, 227, 233, 234, 236, 238
Dewey, John   201, 215
Dhondt, Steven   171
Diamond, Larry   218, 219, 221, 229, 230, 233, 236
dictatorial drift   217, 218, 229, 230, 231, 233, 234
digital economy   116, 121
digitalization   128
Diner, Dan   50, 61
Disruption   17, 21, 26, 27, 30, 31, 32
Dobson, William   228, 236
Domecka, Markieta   171
Drozdowski, Rafał   152, 155, 169
Du Bois, William E.B.   75, 85
Dubiński, Aleksander   74, 84
Dunn, Elisabeth   4, 11
durkheim, Emil   241
Dworkin, Ronald   195, 199

Easterly, William   9, 11, 202, 215
effervescence collective   32
Eichengreen, Barry   219, 236
Ekiert, George   217, 218, 229, 236
Elias, Norbert   15, 18, 19, 20, 22, 24, 28, 34
Ellis, Erle C.   186, 187, 199
emancipation   18, 25
emergent creativity   167
emotions   244, 245, 250, 253
Enlightenment   68, 69, 89, 193, 194
epistemic patriotism   59
Eppinger, Monica   73, 85
Epstein, Seth   198, 199
erosion of democracy   217, 218, 220, 226
essential work   151, 167
Ester, Peter   173, 181
Etkind, Alexander   67, 85
eurocentrism   87
European Union   69, 98, 99, 103
everyday uncertainty   176, 177, 179
expert knowledge   201, 202
expropriation   18

family reunification   134, 135
Fanon, Frantz   66, 83
Feichtinger, Johannes   68, 85
Felstead, Alan   151, 169

Finch, Tracy   154, 169
First World War   76, 92, 95, 101
first-person perspective   243
Fiut, Aleksandra   74, 85
Flanagan, Scott C.   174, 175, 181
Fleck, Ludwik   54
focus group interview   156, 158
Fomina, Joanna   81, 85
Forbes   100
Foucault, Michel   37, 53
Fourth Industrial Revolution   114, 119, 120, 122, 123, 124, 125, 126, 130, 132
Frankenberg, Gunter   202, 215
French, Duncan   187n3, 199
friendliness   141, 147
frontline workers   155, 157, 158, 164, 167
frugal innovation   155, 167
Fukuyama, Francis   43, 44, 61
future essentialism   122
future generations   196, 197

Gadamer, Hans Georg   53
Galicia   68, 86
Gallie, Duncan   155, 169
Gandhi, Leela   66, 83
Gardawski, Juliusz   168, 169
Gemeinschaft   19, 20, 23n4, 32, 35
Gerasimov, Ilya   73, 85
Germany   67, 69, 85, 86, 92, 100
Gernsheim, Elisabeth   173, 181
Gerschewski, Johannes   235, 236
Gesellschaft   19, 20
Gibbs, Graham   157, 169
Giddens, Anthony   55, 62, 172n1, 173, 181
Gill, Valentine   87
Glinski, Mikołaj   85
Goldthorpe, John   55, 61
Gosk, Hanna   75, 85
Grabski, Władysław   96
Grahn, Sandra   202, 216, 237
Great Britain   67
Greece   100
Grocholski, Zdzisław   96
Guriev, Sergei   228, 236
Gutierrez, Rodrigues   10

Habermas, Jurgen   38, 61
Habsburg   68, 84, 85, 86
Haddock, Adrian   211, 215
Hadiz, Vedi R.   201, 215

Halman, Loek   173, 181
Hampden-Turner, Charles   42, 61
Hart, herbert L.   198, 199
Hartmann, Nicolai   20
Harvey, David   98, 101, 102, 103
Hayek, Friedrich von   40, 61
Heelas, Paul   181
Heidegger, Martin   4, 11
Hellmeier, Sebastian   217, 237
Hensel, Joanna   94
Herero   75
Hitler, Adolf   76
Hladík, Radim   85
Hochschild, Arlie   175, 181
Hofstede, Geer   176, 176n2, 177, 181
Holocaust   75, 87, 88, 90
Holocene   185, 185n2, 186, 187
hostility   141, 148
Hrynevych, Liudmilla   73, 89
Huigen, Siegfried   69, 83, 86, 89
Hull, Isabel   76, 85
Hungary   98, 99, 101, 102, 103
Hunter, David   212, 215
Huntington, Samuel   54
Husserl, Edmund   244, 246, 252, 256

identity   172, 172n1, 175, 178, 181
Igo, Sarah   29, 34
illiberal values   227, 228
Illner, Peer   153, 168, 169
Illouz, Eva   173, 175, 181
image of the world   173
immigration   133, 134, 137, 138, 146, 147, 148
Improvisation   171
improvised innovation   152
individualization   22
Industry 4.0   6, 113, 114, 115, 116, 117, 119, 120, 121, 122, 123, 124, 125, 126, 127, 128, 129, 130, 131, 132
Inglehart, Ronald   173, 174, 175, 181, 219, 227, 237
institutional order   174, 175, 177, 180
institutional work   154, 169
integration   136, 137, 141, 143, 147
intelligent factory   114
intelligentsia   92, 93, 94, 95, 96, 97, 98, 101, 102, 103, 105, 106
intermarriage   135
International Monetary Fund, IMF   69, 95
interpretive   21, 26

Jansens, Marleke 171
Jaruga, Barbara 179
Jasanoff, Sheila 6, 11
Jasiecki, Krzysztof 99, 100
Jasińska-Kania, Aleksandra 173, 181
Jews 74, 75

Kacperczyk, Anna 242, 256
Kałczewiak, Mariusz 68, 74, 86
Kalinovsky, Artemy M. 77, 87
Kalisz 133, 138, 139, 140, 141, 145, 147
Kalmar, Ivan 81, 85
Kalnačs, Benedikts 72, 85
Kaps, Klemens 68, 86
Kaufmann, Jean Claude 54, 61
Keim, Wiebke 69, 86
Khodorkovsky, Mikhail 100
Kim, Sang-Hyun 6, 11
Kiossev, Alexander 67, 70, 86
Knorr-Cetina, Karin 6, 11
knowledge 3, 4, 6, 8, 9, 11
Kola, Adam 71, 77, 86
Kolarz, Walter 72, 86
Kołodziejczyk, Dorota 69, 83, 86, 89
Kolvani, Palina 237
Koneczny, Feliks 45, 54, 61
Kopp, Kristin 69, 86
Korablyova, Valeriya 73, 86
Korek, Janusz 72, 86, 88
Korolov, Genadii 73, 86
Kościańska, Agnieszka 81, 86
Kotzé, Louis J. 187n3, 199
Kowalik, Tadeusz 102
Kowalski, Michał 74, 86
Kozek, Wiesława 152, 155, 169
Kozłowska, Magdalena 68, 74, 86
Krajewski, Marek 169
Kubacka, Małgorzata 169
Kubik, Jan 66, 86
Kuhn, Thomas 54
Kula, Witold 94
Kušić, Katarina 69, 79, 81, 86
Kuvlesky, William and Coop, James 38, 61

labour market 140
labour migration 135
Laing, Ronald D. 172n1, 181
Lakatos, Imre 57, 62

landed gentry 92, 93, 95, 96, 104
language 7
Lash, Scott 181
Latour, Bruno 10, 11, 24, 32, 35, 53, 62
law 8, 9, 189, 193, 194, 195, 196, 197, 197n6, 198, 199
Lawrence, Thomas B. 154, 169
Lazarus, Neil 82, 83, 86
Lebensraum 75
Leca, Bernard 169
Leder, Andrzej 177, 181
Lee, Aie Rie 174, 175, 181
Leher, Erica 87
Leopold, David 30, 31, 35
Lerner, Daniel 201, 216
Leszczynski, Adam 87
level of collective life 19
Levitsky, Steven 225, 228, 229, 234, 237
liberal values 218, 219, 220, 235
Libman, Alexander 231, 237
Lim, Jie-Hyun 82, 87
Lindberg, Staffan I. 218, 236, 237
lingua franca 145
linguistic 133, 137, 142, 144, 145
linguistic beliefs and practices 7
Lipset, Seymour M. 201, 216
Łódź 91, 94
Lotman, Juri 45, 46, 62
Lottholz, Philipp 69, 79, 81, 86
Lower, Wendy 76, 87
Luckmann, Thomas 37
Łuczewski, Michał 82, 87
Luczys, Piotr 169
Luhmann, Niklas 179, 181, 203, 205, 215, 216
Lührmann, Anna 237
Łukaszyk, Ewa 80, 87
Lukes, Steven 53, 62
Lundstedt, Martin 236
Lust, Ellen 218, 238
Luxemburg, Rosa 91

Macpherson, Fiona 211, 215
Majkowska, Grażyna 42, 60
majority language 138, 142, 147
Mälksoo, Maria 73, 87
Mannheim, Karl 40, 62
Manolova, Polina 69, 79, 81, 86
Margalit, Avishai 71, 85

Mark, James   76, 77, 87
Marody, Mira   172, 173, 174, 181
Marung, Steffi   77, 87
May, Carl   154, 169
Mayblin, Lucy   74, 87
Mazurek, Małgorzata   77, 87
McCallum, Jamie M.   151, 152, 155, 169
McGivern, Gerry   171
McKinsey   113, 114, 119, 123, 124, 125, 132
McLaren, Glenn   20, 31, 35
McLennan, Gregor   67, 83, 87
meaning   172, 174, 175, 180
memory   5
Merleau-Ponty, Maurice   241, 246, 255, 257
Merton, Robert K.   155, 169, 207, 216
Mezzadri, Alessandra   156, 169
Mianowski Foundation   94
microaggressions   142
micro-innovation   152, 155
Middle East   77
Mignolo, Walter   78, 87
migration   6, 7
migration experience   147
migration process   134
migration transition   133, 137, 138, 147, 149
Milburn, Thomas   153, 170
Mills, Charles W.   239, 240, 249, 254, 255, 257
mind   240, 245, 246, 247, 249, 250, 253, 254, 255
Mitteleuropa   69
modern   15, 16, 17, 18, 19, 20, 21, 22, 24, 25, 27, 32, 35, 36
modern culture   173, 174
modern society   1, 4, 15, 16, 17, 20, 22, 32
modern values   20
modernity   5, 10, 11, 172, 175, 179, 181
modernization   1, 3, 4, 5, 8, 10, 15, 16, 17, 18, 20, 21, 23, 32, 173, 174, 175
modernizing   1
Moldova   72
monolingual language ideology   137, 141
Moore, David C.   65, 84, 87
Morozov, Vadim   67, 70, 73, 87
Morris, Paul   181
Morrison, Kelly   236
Mrozowicki, Adam   151, 153*n*3, 157, 170
Mulgan, Geoff   151, 170
Müller, Martin   2, 11

multicultural policies   136
multicultural policy   136, 142
multiculturalism   7, 133, 134, 135, 136, 149
Multilingualism   7, 133, 137, 147
Myant, Martin   99

Najam, Adil   195, 199
Nakoneczny, Tomasz   74, 87
Nama   75
Nassehi, Armin   211, 212, 216
nation state   15, 18
NATO   69
Nazism   66
Nelson, Robert   67, 69, 87
Neuger, Leonard   69, 88
Ngwenya, Dumisani M.   193, 199
Nölke, Andreas   99, 155, 167, 170
normalization   154, 157, 168, 169
normalization process theory   154, 169
Norris, Pipa   174, 175, 181, 219, 227, 237

Oakeshott, Michael   40, 62
Obydenkova, Anastasia   231, 237
ontological insecurity   172
ontology   185, 191, 194, 199
Orbán, Viktor   103
Orientalizing society   49
Örkény, Antal   70, 85
Ost, David   4, 11, 47, 48, 62
Ottoman Empire   67, 68, 73, 74

Parsons, Talcott   53
Parvulescu, Anca   66, 88
patchwork capitalism   168
Pawlicka, Aleksandra   178, 182
Pearson, Christine M.   153, 170
Petryk, Michał   86
Piacentini, Laura   2, 11
Piatkowski, Marcin   95
picture of reality   175
Piekut, Aneta   87
Piketty, Thomas   98, 219, 237
Piła   133, 138, 140, 141, 144, 145, 147
Platek, Daniel   218, 237
platformization   128
Plattner, Marc F.   218, 236
Płock   133, 138, 141, 145, 147
pluralistic ignorance   29

Poetry   248
Polish Cities of Immigration and Emigration, project   138
Polish Eastern Borderlands   74
Polish Economic Elite   5
Polish People's Republic   102, 104
Polish-Lithuanian Commonwealth   65, 73
Polonocentrism   82
Pop-Eleches, Grigore   228, 237
populism   9, 219, 236, 237
Portes, Alejandro   154, 170
positivist   16, 17, 21, 22, 30
postcolonial   2, 3, 5
Pot, Frank   171
Preuss, Ulrich K.   209, 216
professional roles   204
Prussia   93
Prutschand, Ursula   68, 85
public policies   19, 23, 25, 26, 32
Puchalski, Piotr   74, 88
Pulignano, Valeria   171
Putin, Vladimir   73
Putnam, Robert   43, 63

quality of life   140
quasi-nature   16, 27

Rachman, Gideon   229, 231, 235, 237
Raciborski, Rafał   71, 72, 85
Radzińska, Jowita   153, 170
Rampley, Matthew   74, 79, 88
rational bureaucracy   15
receiving country identity   134
Reckwitz, Andreas   214, 216
Red Army   104
relational innovation   157, 165, 166, 168
reprivatization   104, 105
responsibility   189, 190, 196
Revelli, Marco   202, 216
Rexhepi, Piro   68, 88
Riabczuk, Mykoła   68, 88
rights of nature   197, 198
Ritter, Mark   181
Rodrik, Dani   219, 237
Rok, Bolesław   151, 154, 170, 171
Rolf, Malte   71, 88
Rorty, Richard   53
Rosa, Hartmut   250, 251, 253, 255, 257
Rostow, Walt   38

Rothberg, Michael   66, 75, 88
Ruane, Joseph   73, 89
Russia   66, 67, 68, 70, 71, 72, 73, 77, 79, 81, 82, 84, 85, 86, 87, 89, 91, 92, 93, 95, 96, 98, 100, 105
Russian   133, 135, 139, 141, 142, 144, 145, 146, 147
Ruthenians   74
Ruth-Lovell, Saskia P.   202, 216

Sadura, Przemysław   178, 227, 237
Said, Edward   66, 68, 73, 82, 88
Sarr, Felwine   78, 88
Sato, Yuko   236
Savoy, Benedicte   78, 88
Scheppele, Kim   85, 225, 226, 237
Schuler, Randall S.   170
Schumpeter, Joseph   153, 154, 170
Schütz, Alfred   243, 246, 257
Schütze, Fritz   156, 170
Schwab, Klaus   118
Schweitzer, Albert   192, 192n5, 193, 199, 200
science   202, 206, 207, 208, 213, 216
scientific knowledge   18, 23, 24, 25, 29
Scruton, Roger   42, 63
Second Polish Republic   93, 95, 96
Second World War   92, 96, 100, 101
self-colonizing   32
separation of nature   191, 192
settlement   134, 135, 138
Shklar, Judith   53, 63
Sieg, Katrin   78, 88
Sienkiewicz, Henryk   94
Sierakowski, Sławomir   178, 227, 237
Simmel, Georg   19, 31, 36
Singer, Peter   189, 200
Skorczewski, Dariusz   88
Slade, Gavin   2, 11
Slavist   65
Śledziewska, Katarzyna   151, 170
Slobodian, Quinn   76, 87
Sloterdijk, Peter   4, 11, 21, 22, 36
Slovakia   98, 99
Snochowska-Gonzalez, Claudia   75, 88
social changes   1, 5
Social innovation   170, 171
social knowledge   202, 211, 215
social life   6
social sciences   2, 4, 6, 10

INDEX

social system   20, 27, 211
socio-demographic diversification   135
socio-demographic diversity   140
sociological imagination   239, 254, 257
sociology   1, 2, 4, 8, 10, 11
sociotechnical imaginaries   115
Sociotechnical Imaginary   6
Soviet bloc   105
Soviet Union   66, 67, 68, 70, 71, 72, 76, 77, 95, 96, 101, 103, 104, 105
Sowa, Jan   67, 70, 75, 88
Spivak, Gayatri Chakravorty   66
Stalinist period   92
state   15, 18, 20, 22, 26, 27
Ştefănescu, Bogdan   88
Stein, Arlene   175, 182
Stephens-Davidowitz, Seth   213, 216
Sterner, Thomas   187, 200
Stichweh, Rudolf   204, 216
Strumińska-Kutra, Marta   151, 154, 170, 171
Suddaby, Roy   169
Superdiversity   150
Surman, Jan   68, 86
Surynt, Izabela   69, 88
Surzhik   139
Sweden   100
Święchowicz, Małgorzata   179, 182
symbolic violence   129
Sznaider, Natan   75, 88
Szelényi, Ivan   97
Sztompka, Piotr   42, 48, 52, 55, 62, 63

Taiyab, Nadaa   195, 199
technological innovation   159, 168
theorizing   245, 249
Third Reich   76
Third World   76, 77, 87
Thomas, Julia A.   189, 191, 200
Thompson, Ewa   71, 82, 83, 87, 88, 89
Thorner, Daniel   38
threat   188, 192
Tittenbrun, Jacek   102, 103
Tlostanova, Madina   70, 71, 72, 77, 78, 89
Todorova, Mariia   69, 89
Törnquist-Plewa, Barbara   73, 89
Totterdill, Peter   153, 154, 155, 171
Touraine, Alain   173, 174, 182
Toynbee, Arnold   54
traditional   19, 20, 21, 23, 24, 32

traditional society   20, 21, 32
transformation   2, 3, 4, 5, 6, 10
transformation losers   46
Treaty of Riga 1921   92, 95, 96, 104
Triesman, Daniel   228, 236
Trompenaars, Alfons   42, 61
Trump, Donald   174, 181
Turkowski, Andrzej   97

Uffelman, Dirk   70, 82, 83, 89
Ukraine   65, 67, 72, 73, 82, 84, 85, 86, 87, 88, 89, 96, 98
Ukrainian language   144, 149
Ukrainian speakers   139
Ukrainians   7, 74, 75
Uncertainty   8, 172, 173, 176, 177, 178, 179, 180, 203, 214, 215
uncertainty avoidance   176, 177
Unger, Roberto M.   206, 216
United States   102
urban chauvinism   38
urban sociabilities   141, 148

Vachudova, Milada   229, 236
values   174, 175, 176, 180
Velychenko, Stephen   73, 89
Verdery, Katherine   76, 85
Vermeerbergen, Lander   155, 171
vision of reality   172
Vliegenthart, Arjan   99

Waldner, David   218, 238
Waldron, Jeremy   201, 216
Wallerstein, Immanuel   38, 50, 60, 63
Warsaw   91, 94
Watman, Kenneth C.   170
Wawelberg, Hipolit   94
Wawrzyniak, Joanna   65, 78, 84, 87
Way, Lucan   228, 229, 234, 237
Weber, Max   16, 17, 26, 27, 28, 35, 36, 52, 53, 63, 172, 182
Wedel, Janine R.   4, 11
Welzel, Christian   174, 181
West   66, 68, 69, 70, 71, 73, 74, 75, 81, 82, 85, 86, 219, 227, 234, 235
Western Europe   68, 79
Westra, Laura   196, 200
Whimster, Sam   182
Wiedner, Rene   152, 153, 155, 167, 171

Winkin, Yves   53, 63
Wise, Andrew K.   11
Włoch, Renata   151, 170
Wolff, Larry   2, 11, 69, 89
workplace crisis   153
workplace innovation   7, 151, 152, 153, 153n3, 155, 167
World Bank, WB   69, 95
World Economic Forum   115, 118
Wróblewska, Magdalena   78, 84

Yoshino, Etsuo   54, 64

Young, Robert   66
Youngs, Richard   218, 238
Yurchuk, Yuliya   73, 89

Zajączkowska, Barbara   179
Zarycki, Tomasz   67, 72, 73, 74, 75, 80, 81, 89
Zelinsky, Wilbur   133, 150
Zerubavel, Eviatar   245, 256, 257
Ziblatt, Daniel   225, 237
Ziman, John   208, 216
Zimmerer, Jürgen   75, 76, 89, 90
Zinovyev, Aleksander   46, 47, 64

www.ingramcontent.com/pod-product-compliance
Lightning Source LLC
Chambersburg PA
CBHW070615030426
42337CB00020B/3805